Praise for *Write More, Publish More, Stress Less!*

"**This book covers it all** using a variety of innovative approaches that will appeal greatly to a wide range of readers. There are over 50 tables, charts, drawings, side-bars, and self-assessment exercises that will capture your attention. In addition, the appendices have logs and study-sheets you can fill out as you go along, helping you stay on schedule in your writing. You can dive in almost anywhere and come away with something useful to you at that very moment! Who knew that, even after being an emeritus professor for 10 years, I would both want and need to read this book."
—*Richard Reis*, editor, Tomorrow's Professor eNewsletter

"Stevens delivers *again*! Following the pattern established in her previous books on rubrics and journal keeping, this text is extremely useful, immensely practical, and carefully grounded in sound scholarship. From the topics covered—such as how to foster creativity in academic writing or how to structure writing groups—to the numerous templates provided—for introducing an argument or for analyzing the structure of a text—**Stevens's book is a treasure trove, which stands to become a classic in the academic writing genre**. A 'must-try' toolkit!"—*Patricia Goodson*, *Presidential Professor for Teaching Excellence, Department of Health and Kinesiology, Texas A&M University*

"Dannelle D. Stevens has spent her career studying academic writing. In this help-ful book, she shares five key principles and scores of practical strategies to guide your writing. Everyone from new graduate students to experienced professors will find valuable insights and inspiration in this book. **I plan to keep a copy near my desk as I strive to write more and stress less.**"—**Peter Felten**, Assistant Provost for Teaching and Learning, Director of the Center for Engaged Learning, and Professor of History, Elon University

"**In this practical, sympathetic guide for beleaguered academics** who aspire to 'write more, publish more, [and] stress less,' Dannelle D. Stevens offers 5 overarching principles; 12 information-packed chapters; 8 useful appendices; and more than 50 illustrative charts, figures, and templates. Whether your goal is to build a sustain-able writing routine, to develop a nuanced critical voice, or to explore creative ele-ments in your scholarship, **this book will help you publish and flourish.**"—*Helen Sword*, *Professor and Director, Centre for Learning and Research in Higher Education, The University of Auckland, New Zealand*

"Stevens starts her book not by laying out a set of best practices for writing but by asking readers to think about who they are as writers. Then she moves into examin-ing the components of good writing, stressing particularly the need for a clear focus and purpose. **In skillful and helpful prose, she draws on her own experience of**

writing for different kinds of scholarly outlets: peer reviewed journals, conference papers, and books."—*Stephen D. Brookfield, John Ireland Endowed Chair, University of St. Thomas*

"**HOORAY**! Dannelle D. Stevens's new book is now available, and it is a book not only about writing and getting published but also how to do so with less stress. The stress level in academic writing has increased to a point where too many people give up or must pay a price in their health, relationships, and other work. **Dannelle offers practical strategies and advice that demystifies processes**. She conveys trustworthiness; people will read and then integrate her ideas into practice."—*Meggin McIntosh, The PhD of Productivity, https://meggin.com*

"As a first-generation faculty with no professional writing preparation, I've always felt like an impostor. Who would read anything I would write; how could I have anything of value to say? Bearing in mind the five key principles, the practical guidance that will benefit any writer, and the call for self-reflection, writing this book review has helped crystallize my own thinking about writing—an opportunity to turn criticality into self-reflection and improvement. **I wish I had this volume before**."—*Terrel L. Rhodes, Vice President, Office of Quality, Curriculum and Assessment, Executive Director of VALUE, Association of American Colleges & Universities*

"Veteran academic author and writing coach, Dannelle D. Stevens has created **a comprehensive and practical guide that I can't wait to share with authors**. What makes this book different from the rest is the way Stevens helps readers understand academic writing as its own genre. Particularly helpful are exercises she outlines to help researchers understand the often unstated expectations about the structure and style of successful articles in their own fields."—*Amy Benson Brown, Writing Coach, Academic Coaching & Writing*

"Most researchers will tell you that they chose their career to do research, not to write about it, and writing makes them feel uncomfortable. Dannelle D. Stevens expertly emphasises the development of positive attitudes that defuse that discomfort. So, **this book can benefit all young researchers as part of their apprenticeship and those many established researchers who still feel uncomfortable when they face the inevitable task of having to tell the world what they have discovered**."—*David Lindsay, former Researcher and Teacher, Animal Biology and Behaviour, University of Western Australia; and author of* Scientific Writing = Thinking in Words

"Reading Stevens's book is like meeting with the kindest and most practical writing mentor you can imagine. Her tips and strategies are actionable and realistic, and her knowledge of the ins and outs of academic writing is unparalleled. Stevens has been in the trenches and is generously sharing all she has learned to make our writing lives better. **I highly recommend *Write More, Publish More, Stress Less* for academic writers at all levels**."—*Katie Linder, Research Director, Ecampus, Oregon State University*

"Dannelle D. Stevens **breaks down the highly personal act of writing into manageable elements that are both cognitive and practical**. This book is a good tool for early career writers and scholars to understand the practice of writing as well the professional norms around the publishing cycle."—*Vasti Torres, Professor, Center for the Study of Higher and Postsecondary Education; and Associated Faculty, Latino Studies, University of Michigan*

WRITE MORE, PUBLISH MORE, STRESS LESS!

WRITE MORE, PUBLISH MORE, STRESS LESS!

Five Key Principles for a Creative and Sustainable Scholarly Practice

Dannelle D. Stevens

Foreword by

Stephen Brookfield

STERLING, VIRGINIA

Published by Stylus Publishing, LLC.
22883 Quicksilver Drive
Sterling, Virginia 20166-2019

Library of Congress Cataloging-in-Publication Data
Names: Stevens, Dannelle D., author.
Title: Write more, publish more, stress less! : five key principles for a creative and sustainable scholarly practice / Dannelle D. Stevens.
Description: Sterling, Virginia : Stylus Publishing, 2019. |
Includes bibliographical references and index.
Identifiers: LCCN 2018022993 (print) | LCCN 2018038984 (ebook) |
  ISBN 9781620365182 (uPDF) | ISBN 9781620365199 (ePub, mobi) |
  ISBN 9781620365168 (cloth :alk. paper) | ISBN 9781620365175 (pbk. : alk. paper) |
  ISBN 9781620365182 (library networkable e-edition) |
  ISBN 9781620365199 (consumer e-edition)
Subjects: LCSH: Authorship. | Academic writing. | Scholarly publishing. |
College teachers as authors.
Classification: LCC PN146 (ebook) | LCC PN146 .S745 2019 (print) |
  DDC 808.02--dc23
LC record available at https://lccn.loc.gov/2018022993

13-digit ISBN: 978-1-62036-516-8 (cloth)
13-digit ISBN: 978-1-62036-517-5 (paperback)
13-digit ISBN: 978-1-62036-518-2 (library networkable e-edition)
13-digit ISBN: 978-1-62036-519-9 (consumer e-edition)

Bulk Purchases
Quantity discounts are available for use in workshops and for staff development.
Call 1-800-232-0223

First Edition, 2019

First of all, I dedicate this book to my faculty colleagues who add their unique and positive contributions to healing this planet through the written word.
Second, I dedicate this book to my daughter and granddaughter who have always been at my side.

CONTENTS

BOXES, EXERCISES, SIDEBARS, FIGURES, AND TABLES

Boxes

Exercises

Sidebars

Figures

Tables

I remember well the first time the idea of writing a book crossed my mind. I had been fired from a job as an adult education lecturer/organizer and had found employment in a series of temporary positions in three different countries. I realized that if I wanted my life to have some sort of stability I needed to have a book to my name. A book would bring me scholarly credibility and allow me to fool people into thinking I actually knew something.

The problem was that, to me, books were written by real intellectuals, people with something to say. How could my opinions be worth anything? I had a strong sense of impostorship; feeling that if I did send a proposal to a publisher it would be sent back with an "Are you kidding?" response. I asked myself, "What right do I have to publish something?" I didn't feel I had anything new or original to say

What got me out of this funk was thinking about my time as a student. I had read so many books and articles that covered a piece of intellectual territory and, even though many took the same sort of perspective, some were far more helpful than others. What defined this sense of helpfulness for me? Readability. Books that were well organized, strove for clear writing, used plenty of examples to illustrate complex concepts, and didn't engage much in the intellectual posturing represented by an overuse of academic jargon were the ones I found helpful. This reminded me that you don't have to say anything original or profound to get published. You just have to say what is already known but in a clearer or better way than others out there.

Then I thought about the worst textbook I had been required to plow through in graduate school. "Turgid" and "demoralizing" were some of the kinder words I could use to describe how it felt to prop my eyes open as I forced myself to read each page of mind-numbing irrelevance. Not the slightest flicker of enthusiasm was ignited in me by reading this text. It was dreadfulness exemplified. However, one of the things that most helped me move past my sense of impostorship was telling myself regularly that even I couldn't produce something as bad as this abomination that had been forced on me.

If I had had access to Dannelle D. Stevens's book, I would have been able to get to a point of submitting my work for publication far more quickly than was the case. Just the self-talk guidelines in Figure 1.1 would have made a big difference! (Of course I would add "Remember all the crap you had to read in grad school? You can't produce anything worse than that, and that got into print!"). Stevens starts her book not by laying out a set of best practices for writing but by asking readers to think about who they are as writers. Then she moves into examining the components of good writing, stressing particularly the need for a clear focus and purpose. In skillful and helpful prose, she draws on her own experience of writing for different kinds of scholarly outlets such as peer-reviewed journals, conference papers, and books.

Stephen Brookfield
John Ireland Endowed Chair
University of St. Thomas
Minneapolis-St. Paul

A preface is a greeting offering the reader a quick overview of the origin and landscape of the text. This book did not begin a few years ago, but many years ago when I entered a university as a newly minted doctoral student. I realized that traveling along the path to success in the academy required a set of skills and dispositions that I was not taught; that is, how to write and publish. I thought I was alone. My subsequent research has proven otherwise. Over the years, my work with faculty has reinforced the notion that faculty have no formal training in academic writing no matter what discipline they embrace. Many faculty members are not aware of the components of a steady and sustainable writing practice. The purpose of this book is to demystify the academic writing process and illuminate the components of a productive writing practice that reduces stress and fosters confidence. My vision is to encourage you to contribute your powerful voice and distinct views to the conversation.

This book begins with the five key principles. A key assumption that flows through these principles is that academic writing is much, much more than composing the text; that is only one half of the practice. The other half is getting acquainted with the psychological, social, and emotional context in which you write. How do you see yourself as a writer? What strategies do you use to schedule time to write? What support groups do you have to help you overcome blocks and fears? How do you keep up momentum and interest in your writing projects? How do you bring voice into your work? The five key principles are designed to address questions like these. Principle one (chapter 1) presents several ways for you to know yourself as a writer. Principle two (chapter 2), know the genre of academic writing, offers a variety of ways to analyze academic writing. Principle three (chapter 3) encourages you to be strategic, that is, intentional in allotting time and writing goals to build a real and sustainable writing practice. Principle four (chapter 4), be social, describes how to work with others in a variety of writing groups. Principle five (chapter 5), be creative and reflective, presents a set of exercises that help you reflect and bring voice into your academic writing.

After the foundation of the five key principles, this book turns to applying those principles in a variety of venues, including keeping a journal in your professional life (chapter 6), writing book reviews (chapter 7), writing conference proposals (chapter 8), writing journal articles (chapter 9), writing books (chapter 10), and responding to feedback from editors in the revise-and-resubmit process (chapter 11). This book concludes with a chapter on setting up a writing program on your own campus (chapter 12).

My work on academic writing includes conference proposals, journal articles, workshops, writing retreats, writing programs, and writing coaching at local, national, and international settings. During these engagements I was able to field-test this book's unique templates, exercises, guides, and figures with faculty across all the disciplines. In particular, as the Portland State University's (PSU) faculty-in-residence for academic writing, I have developed and facilitated a well-established program for our faculty academic writing community. You will find quotations, sidebars, and samples of PSU faculty work throughout the book. Along with the many others I have worked with, the conversations and engagement with my PSU colleagues have contributed in countless ways to the durability and usefulness of the ideas in this book.

Academic writing is a conversation, a give-and-take of ideas, research, and experiences. I can hear the voices and recall the written words from so many others who have encouraged, enlightened, and challenged me. I wish to acknowledge my PSU colleagues: Katy Barber, John Bershaw, Matt Carlson, Micki Caskey, Liu-Qui Yang, Espie De La Vega, Oscar Fernandez, Martha McCormack, Christina Gildersleeve-Neumann, Vicki Reitenaur, Candyce Reynolds, Lynn Santelmann, Christina Sun, Janelle Voegele, Ellen West, and Hyeyoung Woo. I acknowledge the continuous support and encouragement from Maureen Foerster from the Textbook and Academic Authoring Association. In addition, the feedback from Amy Benson Brown from the Academic Coaching and Writing Association was invaluable. Meggin McIntosh has inspired me to keep on going. I sincerely thank the PSU administration for supporting the Jumpstart Writing Program. Finally, my hat goes off to John von Knorring, my editor from Stylus Publishing, who has believed in me and encouraged me all along the way to create this book for all faculty who struggle as writers.

CHAPTER 1

Know Yourself as a Writer

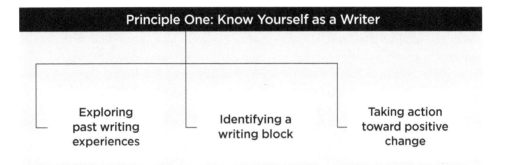

Scene: I started high school in a new suburban California school built around aging oak trees. As a member of the second graduating class and proud of creating the history for our school, I was enthusiastic about the school, my classes, and the future. My friends and family often asked me, "What will be your college major?" I kept thinking about what subject was my strength. English was a possibility. Then, again, I vividly recall this scene from my freshman English class:

Miss Cullen: "A few days ago, I asked you all to write an essay about a toy or object from childhood that meant something to you. Dannelle, would you please read your essay about your little red wagon?"

Dannelle: "Sure . . ."

Miss Cullen: "Thank you. I hoped others could see what a good job you did."

A bit embarrassed, I looked down at my A and thought, "I will never major in English."

You might think an A would encourage me to consider a college major in the subject. However, my only thought was, "Whatever I put into that essay was a miracle. I could never major in English. I do not know how to consistently perform miracles."

Following those early high school years, I was expected to write, of course. I majored in the social sciences and wrote my fair share of essays and research papers. The feedback I got was minimal, vague, often contradictory, as well as confusing. Undeterred, I plugged on. On the way to where I am now as a full professor, I majored in educational psychology and fulfilled the expectations to conduct research and write and publish frequently enough to be promoted. I always had a vague sense that my own research articles were examples of describing a problem in the world and showing how my research sought to explain or address the problem. That was where I started writing. I knew little else. I have written many journal articles and five books and have received several large grants. It is ironic that, even though the adage "publish or perish" is alive and well in academe, I never received any formal training in academic writing. As Cameron, Nairn, and Higgins (2009) and Dankoski and colleagues (2012) note, I am not alone.

Because of the publishing expectations for new professors, I realized I had just better get on with it: Write and hope for the best. Then, I had a revelation: Why not study academic writing? After all, I knew how to study something. I just needed to study academic writing like I studied anything else. I needed to make a place in my library for academic writing books. I needed to reflect on my successes and challenges and find strategies that gave me more confidence. My writing practice changed and became more about reflection, awareness, and intentional practice rather than just facing the blank page and hoping for the best. I savored the challenge of figuring out how to write consistently as well as how to communicate with as few words as possible. The more I learned about writing, the more I began to get encouraged that I could write and share my ideas, perspectives, and insights with others. I knew I had many skills as a scholar. Yet, to write and publish more, I realized I needed to use my analytical and reflective skills to build a sustainable academic writing practice. Over time, it seeped into my consciousness that academic writing requires a complex skill set infused with insight, the ability to take risks, and curiosity, and, best of all, by studying it, I could consistently perform my own kind of miracles.

As I was beginning to know more about my own writing practice, I started to share my work with others in different disciplines and in different venues. I learned that, no matter our discipline, to advance in our careers it is essential that we write and publish our work in peer-reviewed journals. While this may not be the case for all colleges and universities, it is certainly true for many. In fact, the current campus climate demands faculty members not only write but also jump in and publish more than they used to (Dickson-Swift et al., 2009; Harman, 2005). On the path to promotion, the dean and faculty committees review our files and, as one colleague said, "Many deans and committees don't read, but they can surely count." Therefore, given this pressure, I realized that I have to figure out how to put the writing and publishing part of my career at the top of my to-do list to ensure that I do not perish.

To not perish, we obviously must have command of our disciplinary knowledge. Yet, disciplinary knowledge is not enough. Academic writing includes more: a host of dispositions, such as persistence and patience, and behaviors, such as organizational skills and time management practices, which can be called on to help us maintain momentum when faced with a plethora of competing demands. As Antoniou and Moriarty (2008) observe,

> Writing, of whatever genre, involves all aspects of the self: intellectual, physical, emotional and spiritual. Thus, our approach to teaching writing is holistic. We advocate stepping back from the mechanics of writing and inviting writers to examine questions such as: Who am I? What are my values? What are my passions? What is my own experience of the creative process? What does writing mean for me? And only after that: What do I have to say and how do I want to say it? (p. 159)

Antoniou and Moriarty (2008) suggest that we start with knowing more about our feelings that affect our identities as writers.

In the work I have done over the last 15 years with academic writers in the United States and international settings, I have learned that both novices and experienced writers across all disciplines grapple with meeting writing challenges. Some feel embarrassed that they have not figured out how to do this "obvious endeavor" that their colleagues seem to take for granted. Others feel frustrated and discouraged when articles are rejected. Some experience stronger feelings such as fear, anxiety, and self-doubt, so that even starting a manuscript is difficult. Needless to say, writing seems to call up many emotions that can, at times, be self-defeating (Devlin & Radloff, 2014; Lee & Boud, 2003). The trick is to not let these negative emotions chip away at our confidence, lower our productivity, and deaden our desire to write. One way to tackle these emotions is to become better acquainted with ourselves as writers.

By exploring more about ourselves as writers, thinkers, and creators we open the door to writing more and publishing more. Therefore, our work is more widely distributed and can play a part in influencing the world around us. As writers, we leave our own unique tracks on the path for future generations to contemplate and to improve the human endeavors on this small planet.

In this chapter, I offer several exercises designed to help you learn more about the writer in you. In the first section, the writing prompts lead you to explore your history as a writer. In the second section, you complete a self-assessment on writing blocks. At the conclusion of the chapter, you can select some other strategies to heighten awareness of your current practice and boost your confidence. Not all the suggested strategies may appeal to you. Just pick and choose those that make sense. The overall purpose in this first chapter is for you to know more about your feelings and experiences associated with writing so that they don't undermine your writing practice. In the end, this is the path to publishing more and stressing less so that you, too, can become a student of writing.

Principle one: Knowing more about yourself as a writer leads to greater insight; awareness; and positive, sustainable changes in your academic writing practice.

Exploring Past Writing Experiences

To begin the journey of knowing more about yourself as a writer, you need to get a firm grip on the wheel of your experience as a writer. You are already a writer. You write all the time. Think about student and peer recommendations; syllabi; assignment descriptions; committee reports; annual reports; reviews of journal articles; committee work; feedback to students; and, let us not forget, e-mails. While these kinds of writings are different from the skills and habits you need to mobilize to write book reviews, conference proposals, journal articles, and books, you are still writing every day. Don't ever forget that you are a writer. As such, you have many feelings about and experiences with writing.

Writing is a habit that, like any habit, has been developed over time. To change a less productive academic writing habit to a more satisfying and productive one takes time and attention. As Lee and Boud (2003) acknowledge, "[A]ny writing change strategy needs to be mindful of how fears can be managed and desires developed productively" (p. 190). Your feelings may have very little to do with what you are writing about but may have a whole lot to do with how you approach your writing tasks. Through exploring the experiences and feelings you have about writing, you are building a solid base on which to develop a sustainable writing practice.

Take a few moments now and respond to prompts 1 and 2 in Exercise 1.1, "Exploring your feelings, thoughts, and experiences with writing." By reflecting on your experiences in your writing history, you are learning about the feelings and thoughts that can affect your writing today.

EXERCISE 1.1
Exploring your feelings, thoughts, and experiences with writing

---

The writing prompts in this exercise are designed to help you get to know yourself as a writer. This is nonjudgmental, exploratory work where you are seeking to discover and examine both the conscious and unconscious feelings you have about writing.

Directions: If you keep a journal, you can write your responses in your journal. If you prefer to keep a file on your computer about yourself as a writer, do so instead. Otherwise use a blank sheet of paper. Set a timer for 10 minutes for each prompt. Let your ideas and feelings tumble onto the page. Remember, no one will see this. Do not worry about spelling or grammar. Just write. This is your time to let all of these feelings flow onto the page. Write down everything that comes to mind as you answer the question, even if it seems random and may not make sense now. Remember, there are no right or wrong answers. Put your pen to the page, or your fingers to the keyboard, and don't stop writing until the timer goes off. Some people use their smartphone for a timer. Others use a kitchen timer. Others just look at the clock. Again, for each prompt, let the ideas bubble up in your consciousness and don't edit them. Just keep writing for 10 minutes to surface all the feelings and experiences you have had.

(Continues)

EXERCISE 1.1 (*Continued*)

PROMPT #1: Think back to a time when things seemed to work well for you in your writing. This does not have to be academic writing, just any writing.

What were some of the good experiences you had with writing?
What were you doing then?
How did you respond to those experiences?
How did you feel?

PROMPT #2: Let us get more specific now. Think back about writing in your schooling and in your university work when it was challenging and discouraging.

What experiences did you have that were challenging and discouraging?
What were the feelings associated with those experiences?
How did you respond to those experiences?
What do you feel now as you think about what happened?

PROMPT #3: Meta-reflection is a reflection on the written reflections in prompts 1 and 2. Read your responses to both prompts. Take a few minutes to think about what you have written.

As you read these two prompts, what do you notice about your writing experiences?
Are there any similarities/differences in the feelings?
What do you think about this writing process of getting words on the page and not editing?

After completing these prompts, some faculty realized that, while one or several incidents in their writing lives were encouraging and hopeful, there were other experiences that were discouraging and caused them to doubt their abilities as writers. What can you learn from writing about your experiences with writing?

For prompt 2 you wrote about any discouraging experiences you have had with writing. Some of you may not have written about these experiences before, especially in such detail. Psychologically, these subjective experiences can influence your behaviors, attitudes, and feelings toward writing today in unconscious ways. By writing about them, you are making them more conscious, concrete, and less subjective. You are objectifying them so that you can identify their origins, and see if they make sense for you today. My story at the beginning of this chapter about my experience writing an essay on my little red wagon has stuck in my brain for many years. Before graduate school, I truly believed that the only people who really knew how to write and not struggle with writing were English majors. Of course, this is extremely naïve and does not demonstrate the truth that all writing is rewriting and rewriting.

You may have also observed the power of self-talk. What we say to ourselves influences our feelings and behaviors. By exposing and reflecting on your writing experiences, you can strengthen the power of positive messages while shrinking the power of negative messages. Exploring negative self-talk associated with your writing experiences and converting this to positive self-talk may seem a bit artificial at first. Yet, it is a step toward increasing confidence and reducing stress.

Some faculty members think of themselves as their own writing coach. You know how coaches work. When athletes practice, their coach encourages them. "You can do it!" "Hang in there!" Similarly, as your own writing coach, you can imagine reframing any self-defeating talk to more positive self-talk. Instead of saying "I don't really know how to write," you can say, "I am a writer." "I can do this." "Just one step at a time!" Figure 1.1 is a list of positive self-talk phrases. Some faculty members select a phrase that is meaningful to them and post it in their offices or on their computers. As writers, positive self-talk builds confidence and increases the motivation to write (Englert, Raphael, Anderson, Anthony, & Stevens, 1991; Neck & Manz, 1996). Positive self-talk gradually reframes the writer's approach to writing.

Exploring your experiences with writing is not the only strategy to build a more sustainable writing practice. The next section offers you a way to get to know yourself as a writer through completing a self-assessment on your writing blocks. The goal is to delve more deeply into those specific times when you feel there are blocks that impede progress in your writing and, then, recall what you say to yourself in those instances. Some people refer to these experiences as "writing blocks"; others refer to them as "roadblocks" (King, 2013).

Identifying a Writing Block

A writing block is a set of behaviors, feelings, and/or beliefs that results in the writer being unable to write. Almost everyone experiences a block at some time or another. Blocks range from mild and brief to debilitating and extensive. A writer can have a combination of blocks or one block that stands out from the others. Writing blocks can be associated with the current demands of life, such as a new committee assignment or preparation for a new course that gobbles up the time needed to write. Blocks can also be linked to the feelings you have about a particular manuscript you

Figure 1.1 Positive self-talk about writing

> I am a writer.
> I know how to write. I have published a lot in the past.
> Today I can write 250 words on my manuscript.
> I am a unique person with a different perspective. I want to write about that.
> Seat time. Seat time. Write and see what bubbles up.
> Just write through to the end of the section. Then, go back and edit. I can do that!
> I am smart.
> I know how to do this.
> I don't know how to do this and I will dive in and see how it goes.
> As I keep on writing, I find I know more than I thought I did about this topic.
> Set the timer for 20 minutes, keep focused, and see how many words I can produce.
> I am stuck now. I just need to try a different strategy to get myself engaged again.
> There is nothing wrong with me. I have written before, and I can write now.
> I have something to say that is unique and important that is based on my experience.
> I have something important to say that is unique and that is based on my experience.

are working on. Sometimes a block is temporary. Other times the block extends over time and is a deeply held but unexamined belief about writing.

Whereas the prompts in Figure 1.1 focused on past experiences about writing, this section provides a self-assessment to help you identify the particular blocks besetting you now. Knowing which block dominates your writing can guide you to appropriate activities to chip away at the block and get you writing again. Both Boice (1990) and Rose (1981) designed surveys to self-assess underlying patterns with writing blocks. They found that the most common blocks academic writers encounter are as follows:

Perfectionism—a belief
Rules—a belief
Procrastination—a behavior
Writing anxiety—a feeling
Impatience—a feeling

Based on their work, I designed the writing block experiences self-assessment (WBESA) that measures which one or more blocks seem to represent your current writing practice (see Table 1.1).

TABLE 1.1
Writing block experiences self-assessment (WBESA)
Respond to each statement with a number that corresponds to *what you do or how you feel.*
1 = Almost never (0–10% of the time)   **2** = Occasionally (25%)   **3** = Sometimes (50%)
4 = Often (75%)   **5** = Almost always (90–100%)

Column 1		Column 2	
1. Even though I wait until the last minute, I manage to get papers done under pressure.	1 2 3 4 5	6. When I sit down to write, I feel nervous as I start to write.	1 2 3 4 5
2. There is so little time. I wish I had not agreed to write this paper.	1 2 3 4 5	7. I am not as good a writer as my peers.	1 2 3 4 5
3. I like to wait until I am in the mood to write after all the other things that need to be done.	1 2 3 4 5	8. Even as I begin writing, I feel tired and exhausted.	1 2 3 4 5
4. Because I am so busy, I generally put off writing until just before the deadline if there is one.	1 2 3 4 5	9. I know it is better not to discuss my writing challenges with others.	1 2 3 4 5
5. Once I am set up to write, I spend a lot of time wondering where to start.	1 2 3 4 5	10. My writing problems are unique to me. It seems that others do not suffer as I do when I write.	1 2 3 4 5
Total Column 1		**Total Column 2**	

(Continues)

TABLE 1.1 (*Continued*)

Column 3		Column 4	
11. I need to work faster as a writer. I have so much to do and so little time.	1 2 3 4 5	16. If I make an error in my first draft, I find it is important to stop and correct errors right away.	1 2 3 4 5
12. I don't seem to be a very efficient writer because writing does not come to me easily.	1 2 3 4 5	17. Before I send out a piece for review, I keep thinking, "What if I have overlooked a key reference? How could I send this out in this form?"	1 2 3 4 5
13. I really am too busy to share my writing with others for feedback.	1 2 3 4 5	18. No matter how long I have worked on a paper I like to keep revising and perfecting, even after I suspect the paper is "good enough."	1 2 3 4 5
14. I often submit papers without much, if any, feedback from others just to get them off my to-do list.	1 2 3 4 5	19. I worry that others will think less of me if they see an example of my unedited writing.	1 2 3 4 5
15. My writing style is to work for long periods in an intense and hurried fashion.	1 2 3 4 5	20. I tend to include too much information in my manuscript because I don't want to miss anything.	1 2 3 4 5
Total Column 3		**Total Column 4**	

Column 5		**Score:** *Add total in a column; divide by 5.*	*Total*	*Average*
21. I learned a set of rules for writing and others would be successful if they followed these rules as well.	1 2 3 4 5	Column 1: Procrastination	_____ ÷ 5	
22. Over the years I have found that it is best to write alone and not depend on others.	1 2 3 4 5	Column 2: Writing anxiety	_____ ÷ 5	
23. I write only when I have a clear idea of exactly what I want to say.	1 2 3 4 5	Column 3: Impatience	_____ ÷ 5	
24. I have always followed my own set of rules for writing that works for me and should work for others.	1 2 3 4 5	Column 4: Perfectionism	_____ ÷ 5	
25. Writing is really only for those people who have something to say; otherwise, it is better if people don't write.	1 2 3 4 5	Column 5: Rules	_____ ÷ 5	
Total Column 5				

Adapted from Boice (1990) and Rose (1981).

After responding to each item on the WBESA, you can summarize your scores by adding up each column and inserting the totals in the scoring box in the lower right of the WBESA. Compute the average by dividing each column total by five, the number of items in that column. Look down the scores in the scoring box. Circle the highest score. Put a box around the lowest score.

Your highest score that you circled is the block that seems to be your greatest challenge. The lowest score that you boxed is the writing block that you don't have to worry about. If two scores are close to each other on the high end, it means those two blocks are reinforcing each other.

Taking Action Toward Positive Change

The self-assessment offers you a way to become aware of your writing block(s). This is the first step in chipping away and reducing the block to the size of a pebble. Just like becoming aware of your writing experiences in the first section of the chapter, awareness is the first step toward making any long-lasting change in your writing practice. After awareness, the next step is action. In this section, I define each block and describe its positive and negative characteristics. Table 1.2 summarizes each writing block with a definition and suggests activities to overcome some of the inhibiting aspects of the block.

Perfectionism

Perfectionism is a set of beliefs that the writer holds about the quality of her work. During the writing process, the perfectionist more than likely belabors the quality of a single sentence for an extended period of time at the cost of attending to the whole manuscript. The perfectionist believes that the manuscript has to meet very high standards that others share, and these others will judge the work accordingly. It is certainly good to have high standards; however, the question is, "What is high enough?" Being a perfectionist can cause the writer to not submit the work or not share it with others for feedback. Therefore, perfectionism in the extreme can inhibit productivity. The perfectionist may fear that she does not have enough of the most recent references or that the argument is not persuasive. The perfectionist may say, "If you send it out, you will be embarrassed. Wait." However, perfectionism can actually serve the writer. The manuscript that is "perfect" may result in fewer reviewer comments, and, therefore, may be published sooner.

What can you do if you have a high score on perfectionism? If your perfectionist score is high, think about your responses to the writing prompts earlier: Did you write about internal criticism? Or critical voices from the past? These voices can feed into your perfectionism and undermine your confidence in generating text more freely. Perfectionism can get in the way, particularly in the beginning of a writing project, when you need to be more inventive, more playful, and less stressed

TABLE 1.2

Strategies designed to overcome writing blocks

Writing block	Characteristics	Strategies for overcoming the block
Perfectionism—*belief*	• Attention to detail • Often unable to submit manuscripts because they are never perfect enough • High standards for writing • Editing while writing that can curtail the free flow of ideas	• Send the manuscript out before you feel it is ready and look forward to the feedback. • Change your framework: Realize and appreciate that all writing is rewriting. Share your work in progress with others (chapter 4). • Create due dates in your calendar, stick to them, and create plans that set out specific steps to completion (chapter 3). • Write with a person who does not seem to be a perfectionist. • Produce text first. Edit later (chapter 5).
Rules—*belief*	• Rigid adherence to a set of strict rules for writing	• Observe the effect of your rules on your productivity. Do they work? • Write out the "rules" you have for writing. • Join a writing group to see how others manage their writing (chapter 4).
Procrastination—*behavior*	• Always doing things at the last minute, close to the deadline • Unable to prioritize writing to proceed in a planned and timely manner	• *ACT:* Write 5 days a week for 20 to 30 minutes. Not necessarily longer. • Track your progress by counting, listing, and tracking (chapter 3). • Give yourself rewards, even small rewards, for progress (chapter 3). • Be accountable to a writing group that meets weekly (chapter 4).
Writing anxiety—*feeling*	• General anxiety when approaching writing so that little or no writing is completed • Nervousness	• Create a "feel-good" file to remind yourself of the successes you have had in writing in the past. Read it when feeling anxious. • Free-write for 5 to 10 minutes before starting to write to alleviate your anxieties about writing (chapter 5). • Make your daily writing tasks short, small, and doable. Record what you have accomplished (chapter 3).
Impatience—*feeling*	• Not concerned about things being perfect • Concerned about getting writing off the "to-do" list • Always feeling that you are never caught up	• List small doable tasks for each day, starting with an action verb, such as "read," "write," or "organize" (chapter 3). • Use a timer to push yourself through tasks that seem tedious, such as checking the format of references (chapter 3).

in producing text. Yet, at the end of a manuscript when you need to make sure all your references match the in-text citations, a perfectionist tendency is helpful.

Before realizing what an extreme perfectionist he was, Greg, a faculty member, would work on one paragraph for hours. Then, he took the WBESA and realized he had a very high score in perfectionism. In telling me this story, he laughed and said,

> I can see the problem with my perfectionism. I just don't write enough. I belabor each word, each sentence, and each paragraph. I decided how to keep my perfectionist happy. When I feel the need to make things perfect and not just generate ideas and make connections, I turn from freely generating text in the manuscript to editing my reference list to meet all the American Psychological Association (APA) standards. Reviewers often comment how pleased they were to find a reference list that needed no corrections. In fact, it was perfect.

One way to manage perfectionism and not let it become maladaptive is to practice writing strategies that encourage you to write with no judgment or editing. Exercises in this book, such as the free-write and the focused free-write (Exercises 5.1 and 5.2) or the Post-it concept map (Exercise 5.7), describe how to write before your ideas are fully formed. When you use these strategies, you may feel uncomfortable at first because it is not your typical approach to writing. Yet, as you read what you have written you may realize that it is just fine to start writing even before you feel ready. In fact, often in these timed, free-flowing writing exercises, you make connections that you have not thought of before. Your manuscript benefits from these fresh insights.

Another way to tame your perfectionist tendencies is to share your "less than perfect" writing with other readers; you can guide their feedback by focusing their attention on certain aspects of the text about which you are concerned. Box 4.1 suggests a variety of different approaches when you ask others to provide feedback. Table 1.2 suggests others.

Rules

The next writing block, rules, leads to a set of beliefs that the writer has about how writing should proceed. Rules "involve rigid ways of dealing with writing" (Boice, 1990, p. 153). A high score in rules indicates that the writer believes there is a set way to approach writing that all writers need to use to be successful. A concomitant judgment with the rules block is that if others do not seem to follow the rules then they should not be writing. The rules might be, "You cannot write without knowing all the literature," "You always need to make sure you read all your references before you start writing," or "You must always have an outline before you start writing." Taking each one of these alone may make sense, but putting them in a rigid framework, where the writer believes that these rules are the only ones that work, can cause the writer to not want to write without meeting the standards of the rule.

As with most writing blocks, there is a maladaptive as well as an adaptive side. The maladaptive side of rules is that the writer has a rigid adherence to the way things must be done. More than likely, the person with the extreme rules writing block was taught that writing has a set of universal rules that all writers must follow. Sometimes, this rigidity makes it difficult to collaborate with peers who might not share the same rules. The writer may be unable to adapt her rules to a new circumstance and will be inhibited in the production and submission of manuscripts (Boice, 1990). Rules limit the common understanding that writing is inherently rewriting. Yet, rules can be adaptive for the writer because she is confident that there are some standards in writing that, when followed, will ensure success. Because she has an outline, the manuscript will be organized and easily understood.

What can you do if you have a high score on rules? Take small steps to approach writing in a different way. Reflect on the effect of these steps on the quality of your writing. Similar to the perfectionist, you can challenge the rules writing block belief by practicing writing strategies, such as freewriting and focused freewriting (Exercises 5.1 and 5.2). These exercises loosen up your strict notions of how to write, especially in generating text in the beginning of a project, and can affirm that rules are not the only way to produce quality work. Another way is to join a writing group where each person in the group discusses her own writing processes. A writing group acquaints you with the different ways that others write. When a faculty member in Computer Science, Charles, took the WBESA questionnaire, he realized that he definitely had some rules about how to approach writing. "I always start with an outline and I make my students do that, too." Then, after receiving a very high score on the rules section of the WBESA, he thought that he might revisit that belief. To learn more about how others approached writing, he asked his students and colleagues if they used outlines. From their responses he realized they had other approaches that worked. At that point, he decided to not require his students to have an outline before they wrote their papers. Table 1.2 suggests other ways to address the maladaptive side of the belief that there are certain rules that each writer must follow.

Procrastination

Procrastination is a behavior of delaying action on something that needs to be done. If you think about it, it is not like procrastinators don't do anything. The procrastinator makes time for the things that are important, urgent, and often associated with hard deadlines that cannot be renegotiated. The procrastinator may grade papers, write committee reports, and submit conference proposals. All of these have strict deadlines. Unfortunately, too often for the procrastinator, the other important and urgent things bump one very important thing, such as steady progress on academic writing, to the bottom of the to-do list and she procrastinates about her academic writing.

With the pressure of deadlines, the positive side of procrastination is that many procrastinators may ultimately get manuscripts out the door, even if it is at the last minute. Procrastination seems to work. Especially if the writer has strong perfectionist tendencies along with procrastination, being forced to meet the deadline can actually save self-esteem. This is how the procrastination/perfectionism writing block works. If the submission met the deadline and was accepted, the procrastinator/perfectionist may feel lucky, even though it was not his or her best work, and, therefore, his or her self-esteem is not damaged. If the submission met the deadline and was not accepted, the procrastinator/perfectionist might say, "Well, actually I knew it was not my best work." Thus, self-esteem remains unaffected.

When procrastination is at a maladaptive level, not much writing gets done at all. The writer procrastinates and ends up having too many writing projects. He or she cannot decide what to do and when to do it. In addition, even though procrastination may produce a level of excitement during the completion and submission of manuscripts, it is very stressful. In the end, the writing product may be hurried and truly not the writer's best work because writing is always rewriting and revising, and then rewriting again.

What can you do if you have a high score on procrastination? Overcoming procrastination tendencies requires being reflective and proactive. Reflecting on what you need to do, and then making decisions on how to get things done, begins to overcome procrastination habits. Invoking some time management or, as I call them, *time-allocation strategies* (chapter 3) moves you toward project completion. Taking writing tasks and cutting them up into small, daily, doable tasks helps avoid the last-minute rush (chapter 3). Reflecting on and rewarding completion of these small steps reinforces how to accomplish tasks in a less hurried manner. Table 1.2 offers other ideas of how to tackle procrastination.

Writing Anxiety

Writing anxiety is a feeling that is characterized by generalized nervousness about writing. The writer who has a generalized feeling of anxiety about writing feels isolated and alone. He or she believes that no one else experiences these debilitating feelings. Even as he or she tries to write, he or she feels exhausted and tired before he or she even starts. A maladaptive case of writing anxiety eats away at the writer's confidence. In the extreme, the writer cannot even sit at a desk to start writing. The source of extreme writing anxiety is hard to identify. Was it a past experience with writing that created this anxiety? Or does the writer lack self-esteem in general and this flows over into writing? Because extreme writing anxiety is so complex, it may be wise for the writer to meet with a counselor to get at the root causes.

What can you do if you have a high score on writing anxiety? Being a bit anxious as a writer is normal. After all, you may say, "I am the sole source of this text. The text would not get written the way it is written without my doing it. I am exposed to criticism and ridicule." Minor writing anxieties can be managed and overcome through attention and action. Some faculty members have found that if they write for five minutes each day about how they feel about writing before they start on their academic writing, their anxiety lessens. As Palumbo (2016) blogged, "[S]truggling with these doubts and fears [about writing] doesn't say anything about you as a writer. Other than that you ARE a writer" (para. 7). Again, the extreme case is where anxiety can totally cripple your writing so that no writing gets done. Table 1.2 also has more suggestions.

Impatience

Impatience is a feeling of urgency that things need to get done as soon as possible. The writer with impatience as a writing block may feel rushed to write all the time and feel pressured to send his or her writing out for review. The writer who is impatient with the process may not be burdened with procrastination or perfectionism, but with an urgency to clear his or her to-do list. Thus, perfectionism falls to the side, and procrastination is not necessarily evident. There are so many other things to be done, and since he or she cannot do this one thing perfectly, he or she will just send it out in the imperfect stage.

Like the other blocks, impatience has a maladaptive as well as an adaptive side. Due to the submission of a hurried product, the maladaptive side is that work may be rejected. Unless the writer is resilient, the reviews from a hurried product may be devastating. One faculty member tells me that she writes with a person who has perfectionist tendencies to counter some of her impatience to submit manuscripts, no matter what! The plus side of impatience is that work gets submitted. The impatient writer may submit many projects in a short period of time, maybe even more than his or her peers. The other positive side of impatience is that the work does get reviewed.

What can you do if you have a high score on impatience? Because you tend to focus on the outcome, a submitted paper, try to take the time to analyze all the steps it takes to accomplish a task. After allocating writing time for the week, you can assign small doable tasks to each day. At the end of the week, review what you have accomplished and reward yourself for your patience. Because reviewer feedback can be lengthy, you can create a plan to respond that organizes their comments and that encourages you to systematically and patiently respond (chapter 11). Table 1.2 offers some additional suggestions.

Conclusion

This chapter elaborates on the first principle of creative and sustainable scholarly writing, that is, knowing yourself as a writer. As Holligan, Wilson, and Hume (2011) note, there is a need for "a deeper understanding of the complex social and emotional factors that impact academic well-being" (p. 713). Writing about your feelings, beliefs, and experiences leads you toward a greater awareness of how your history as a writer influences your present attitudes, feelings, and behaviors. Responding to the items in the WBESA helps you to identify some of your specific writing challenges. Knowing more about yourself as a writer has a powerful effect on what you write, how you write, and when you write. As the writer in you grows more conscious, observant, and confident, you may find that you write and publish more. Because writing and publishing are so central to our academic life, having a greater understanding of ourselves as writers means we will spend less time fretting about writing. Therefore, a residual but not-to-be-ignored benefit is that by increasing your awareness of yourself as a writer, you are building your capacity to engage in other activities that support your academic well-being. For example, you may have more time for self-care such as exercise, meditation, and spending time with your family.

CHAPTER 2

Understand the Genre
of Academic Writing

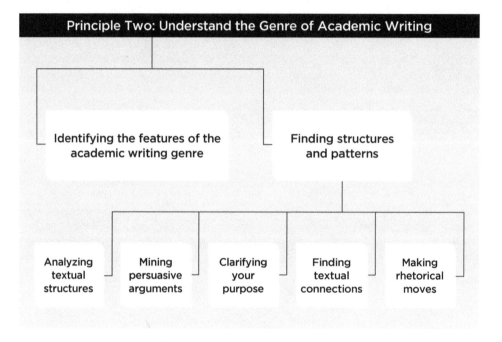

Scene I: Having finished his dissertation, Hiro lands a treasured tenure-line position. Fall term starts and he opens his word-processing program, and there it is, the dreaded blank page. "I gathered the research data in my dissertation. But, how do I begin to write this article?"

Scene II: Elena sees an e-mail from the *Journal of Urban Planning and Development* to which she submitted a paper six months ago. "Ah," she says as she realizes she has a reprieve, not a rejection . . . just a revise-and-resubmit (R & R) request. In looking at the review, she wonders how much work it will take to respond to the reviewer comment, "You have not shown me that your work contributes to the field."

These two scenes illustrate typical and stressful events in academic writing: not knowing where to start and not knowing exactly how to respond to reviewers. Both can be addressed more readily by gaining knowledge about the craft of academic writing. In this chapter, I change the focus from inward, knowing yourself as a writer (chapter 1), to outward, knowing more about academic writing itself. As we have established, you are already an academic writer. Most of you have written at least a thesis, and others, a dissertation. Most of you have written for publication. All the same, you may still feel stuck as you embark on a new writing project. Or, you may feel that you don't understand what the reviewer or publishers are asking of you.

Knowing more about the typical structures, patterns, and expectations of works that are classified as "academic writing" can help you along the path to increased confidence and success with publication. Once you get a feel for the typical patterns, I hope you will find this stimulates your thinking and opens you to powerful and persuasive options that ease your approach to writing. You have been trained to focus on gleaning new insights and adding depth to your knowledge through reading the scholarship of others. By the end of this chapter, my hope is that you will find yourself reading your disciplinary scholarship not just for the content, but also for the rhetorical patterns and underlying text structures. You will be also reading like a writer, with the curiosity and enthusiasm that comes with looking at something familiar in a new way. My overall purpose is to describe the not-so-obvious rhetorical moves that underlie the craft of academic writing as a genre.

This chapter is divided into two sections. The first foundational section expands on the idea that academic writing is a genre that has its own unique features. The second presents five strategies that are designed to illustrate the typical text structures and patterns found in academic writing.

> **Principle two: Understanding that academic writing is a genre orients the writer to identify patterns and structures that facilitate expression and foster communication.**

Identifying the Features of the Academic Writing Genre

You want your work to be read. Readers keep on reading when your work is engaging at several levels. One level is the content of what you are saying, that is, your disciplinary expertise and your unique contribution. Another level is the underlying structure. When you use familiar structures and patterns found in academic writing, readers (and reviewers) continue reading because they don't have to struggle with how this work fits in with what they typically expect. As an extreme example, if you presented your research results in the form of a long poem, a clever and creative presentation, to be sure, I surmise that many might not get past the first stanza. The poem format wouldn't fit readers' expectations. Similarly, driving in traffic works best, of course, if you follow the conventions of staying in the lane, signaling, and obeying the signs and lights. The trip is predictable and less stressful.

Using structures, conventions, and other recognized patterns as you write allows the reader to focus more on the content and less on the structure and format of the work. Information-processing theorists argue that the brain can process and remember only a certain amount of information in a short period of time and then, when processed, the information moves on to working memory (Sweller, 1988). What you are paying attention to, then, maximizes your limited "cognitive load." You cannot pay attention to everything at once. As readers, you tend to focus on what grabs your attention. When you use the typical and familiar signposts of the disciplinary genre in your writing, the reader can focus on the content of your message rather than being distracted by an incorrect APA citation or the potential confusion when a reader expects a purpose statement and there is none.

At the very basic level, academic writing is, of course, a genre within the nonfiction writing category. Academic writing has certain characteristics that distinguish it from e-mails, reports, recommendation letters, curriculum guides, and assessment documents. It includes journal articles, conference proposals, books, book chapters, book reviews, commentaries, grants, and essays. Academic writing is reviewed, shared, and published among people involved in the higher education community. Unlike government reports and curriculum guides, academic writing seeks not only to inform readers about a specific topic but also, more importantly, to persuade readers that the work contributes to the field.

Genre is a class or category. In the genre of academic writing, publications often share a particular form, content, and technique. As a writer, when I write with the awareness of reader expectations in the academic writing genre, I will spend less time inventing the structures and patterns and more time on the content. Academic writing, of course, subsumes many subgenres specific to different disciplines. Yet, even across disciplines, there are common structural signposts, such as the typical use of an abstract as a beginning summary of a journal article or frequently used phrases (e.g., "The purpose of the book is to . . .") that provide the rhetorical glue that quickly orients the reader to the manuscript.

The elements of a genre don't have to be rigidly applied but should present useful and predictable patterns for communicating within our discourse communities. For example, all academic disciplines have publication conventions. Within disciplines there are specific guidelines: APA style for the social sciences, Modern Language Association (MLA) and *The Chicago Manual of Style* for the humanities, Council of Science Editors (CSE) for biology and other sciences, American Chemical Society (ACS) for chemistry, and American Medical Association (AMA) for medicine. Knowing, first, that guidelines exist; second, that they differ by discipline; and, third, that your submission needs to follow the correct guidelines saves you and your reviewers time and indicates that you are a well-informed member of that discourse community.

Beyond the guidelines, when you know more about the genre of academic writing expected by journals and scholarly and professional presses, you can write more readily, more confidently, and more efficiently because you will be able to match your manuscript to the language and expectations of a particular scholarly community. Manuscript reviewers and readers will notice that you are speaking in their "language." In the next section, my goal is to suggest some strategies for revealing the not-so-obvious text structures in the genre of academic writing.

Finding Structures and Patterns

This section of the chapter is designed to help you navigate academic writing by addressing the following questions:

> What are the essential text structural expectations in academic writing?
> How do I become more aware of these sometimes not-so-obvious expectations?

Over the years in my work with faculty as a workshop presenter, writing program organizer, and writing coach, I have tested out many different strategies designed to acquaint faculty members and graduate students with the signposts of academic writing. With unanimity, faculty colleagues have confirmed the value of the following five strategies in heightening their awareness of the academic writing genre and in improving their productivity as well as confidence:

> Strategy I: Analyzing textual structures: Text structure analysis (TSA) templates
> Strategy II: "Mining" persuasive arguments: Argument templates
> Strategy III: Clarifying your purpose: Purpose statement template
> Strategy IV: Finding textual connections: Title-argument-gap-purpose patterns
> Strategy V: Making rhetorical moves: Common academic writing phrase templates

Strategy I: Analyzing Textual Structures: Text Structure Analysis (TSA) Templates

TSA templates can be used for different types of manuscripts. I have developed specific TSA templates for book reviews (chapter 7), journal articles (chapter 9), and edited books (chapter 10). The appendices include blank copies of these templates. In addition, the Stylus website (https://styluspub2.presswarehouse.com/landing/WM-PM-SL) contains downloadable forms.

To show you how the TSA template works, I will describe the use of the TSA template for journal articles. Your first decision in publishing your work is determining where you will submit it. With 28,100 active scholarly peer-reviewed journals and 2.5 million new scientific papers published in a year (Boon, 2016), deciding where you publish your manuscript can be a daunting task. It is, indeed, but there are several ways to make it manageable (see chapter 9 for strategies). Once you have narrowed down your potential publication outlets to three or four, you can complete a TSA template for each journal. By filling out a TSA template for each journal in which you wish to publish, you can compare and contrast the key structural features and patterns across the journals to find an appropriate match for submission. Some faculty have found that completing the TSA template before they start writing helps them think about which journal is best for submission. In addition, faculty have used the TSA template as a guide for structuring their manuscript, such as, how many paragraphs to devote to the introduction or how many references are typical for this journal. Others find that completing the TSA template later in manuscript development helps them edit more wisely.

Early in my career, before I developed the TSA template, I would scan several journals to see which one was best for my manuscript submission. This seemed to be a logical first step: Review what is already published. My reviews consisted of a brief scan of the table of contents to see if my work fit into the scope of the journal (or, with a book, to check out the publisher's website or book exhibit at national conferences to see if the publisher was active in my topic area). During my review, I also tried to get a sense of the journal's or publisher's intended audience. From this quick exercise, I got a "feel" for the topics, audiences, layout, content, and length of journal articles.

To see if my work was the right fit for a specific journal or publisher, I also checked the author guidelines on the journal's or book publisher's website. To find the guidelines on the website, it took some digging to find the correct link. The guidelines were variously called "author guidelines," "for contributors," "resources," "submit," "for authors," or just a direct statement, such as the one Stylus uses for books, "submitting a proposal."

While scanning the journal quickly and following the author guidelines are very important steps in shaping your submission, completing a TSA template will provide deeper insight into text structures and patterns that thread through the published work. Whereas author guidelines deal with the basic content requirements for submission, the TSA template illuminates some of the common patterns and implicit expectations about text structures. Table 2.1 is a comparison of the focus and content of author guidelines and a TSA template. Author guidelines, on one hand, focus on the scope of the work that the publisher accepts along with a brief explanation of how the manuscript should be formatted. Author guidelines also tell you specific and essential considerations, such as the word limit, the reference- style expectations (APA, MLA, Chicago, etc.), and the table and figure formats. Ignore these and more than likely the editor will just reject the article or book proposal outright, even before it is sent off to the reviewers.

In contrast to the author guidelines, the TSA template provides a detailed analysis of at least 10 textual features across three sample works. Filling in the TSA template goes beyond the mere cursory scan I used early in my career. When you complete a TSA template, you will have gathered comparable textual features across three different works. The content of the works used for the TSA template is not very important because you are looking at the structure of the work. What materials should you gather for different types of academic writing to complete a TSA template?

- For book reviews, find three current book reviews from the journal to which you will submit your review.
- For journal articles, pick three articles from a current year from one journal in which you wish to publish.
- For books, select three relatively current books from one publisher.

By not only listing the features but also summarizing and comparing the commonalities across three works in the TSA template, you become very familiar with the expectations of the editors or book publishers. Then, you can structure your submission to match those expectations.

As an example of how the TSA template works, consider one of the first textual elements you write down on the TSA template, the title of each of the three works. If you are using the TSA template for journal articles, you can compare the three titles and

TABLE 2.1

Comparison of key elements in publishers' author guidelines and TSA template

	Author guidelines in general	*TSA template*
Where do I find author guidelines and the TSA template?	Find author guidelines on publisher's website.	Find the TSA template in the examples provided in this book. Specific examples are in chapter 2 and appendix A.
What is the purpose?	To describe journal scope, expectations, and formatting for authors prior to submission	To illuminate text structures, formats, patterns, and detailed expectations of a particular journal by analyzing several recent journal articles or published books
What are the specific differences between author guidelines and the TSA?	Includes statement about journal's broad scope, formatting expectations, and submission expectations • Describe scope of journal or publisher • Include expectations, such as only submitting work to one journal, or inclusion of one to two chapters for book proposals State format expectations: • Inclusion of abstract • Length of manuscript • Tables and figures • Type of style guide (APA, etc.) • Format of references	Focuses your attention on the text structures and patterns used across three recently published works, such as the following: • The level of formality of the title • The number and type of headings • The number of paragraphs devoted to each section (introduction, methods, etc.) • The number and type of references

put the results in the last column of the template. Ask yourself, do the journal editors and reviewers want a title that is friendly, less formal, and engaging, such as this one published in *College Teaching*: "'I'm in a Professional School! Why Are You Making Me Do This?' A Cross-Disciplinary Study of the Use of Creative Classroom Projects on Student Learning" (Reynolds, Stevens, & West, 2013)? Or, are the editors seeking a more formal, less casual title such as this one published in *Educational Psychology*: "The Effects of Feedback on Achievement, Interest and Self-Evaluation: The Role of Feedback's Perceived Usefulness" (Harks, Rakoczy, Hattie, Besser, & Klieme, 2014)? By looking at the titles across three works, you can begin to discern the acceptable patterns and write the kind of title that matches the level of formality and tone of that publication. You can be more confident that your title will open the door for serious review.

Another benefit of comparing the three articles from one journal on the template is that it reveals how high the bar is for publishing in that particular journal. It may not be quite as high as you thought. The TSA template allows you to take a "balcony view" of the common rhetorical patterns across the works and assess the amount of effort it may take to complete a section of the manuscript. After filling in the TSA template, faculty members have said to me, "This journal seems to require only 4 to 6 paragraphs in the introduction, background, and literature review sections. I can do that" or "Oh, I only need 15 to 20 references, not the 50 I had for my last article." Faculty members have commented that they would never submit anything in the future without completing the TSA template. Many have noted that it has helped them calibrate their effort; increase their confidence; and, concomitantly, reduce stress.

Completing the TSA template involves three basic steps:

Step 1: Prepare
Step 2: Analyze
Step 3: Identify patterns

Step 1: Preparing for Completing a TSA Template

In the preparation step, collect three recent sample works. The initial criterion for selection is to find works from the same journal or the same publisher.

The first person who will receive your submission is the editor. For journals, editors are your first hurdle because they make the decision about whether your manuscript is sent out for review. If they judge your work as worthwhile and suitable for that journal, they will send the manuscript to two to three other faculty for review. If acquisitions editors for book publishers decide your project has potential for their list, they will get back to you to discuss your outline. If that conversation goes well, they will send your book proposal to qualified faculty peers for review. The results of the book proposal review may, in turn, require you to make further modifications. Further, in the book proposal review process, once the book passes the review of peers, the editors will pass your proposal on to the publications board, who also have the power to approve or disapprove your project (chapter 10 has many more details on this process). Note that when acquisitions editors change, editorial policy may change, and the emphasis of the journal or book acquisition program may shift. This leads us to the second criterion for selecting the works for the TSA template: The more recent the work, the better. Editors change, policies change, and you want your final manuscript to reflect any of these editorial changes.

The next criterion is finding works to compare on the TSA template that are in your discipline or area of expertise. Faculty members often ask me if the three works that they select should closely match their topic. While helpful, it is not necessary to find works that do so. You should, however, select works from a journal or publisher that publishes in your area of interest. If you are writing a journal article about human geography, articles from a journal that focus on physical geography probably won't be helpful. For books that you select for this analysis, look for books that share a similar theoretical perspective on the topic that you want to write about.

Step 2: Analyzing the Texts

After you have collected your three sample works, you are ready to analyze the text and fill in the TSA template.

Table 2.2 is a completed TSA template for three articles from the journal *College Teaching*. You may note that the TSA template is only one page. I made the cells very small to encourage faculty to take brief notes. This formatting serves as a reminder that you are just skimming for the essential textual features. As one faculty member remarked, "I like the small cells to write in. Otherwise, I would spend too much time on it." Remember, completing a TSA template is not about content. It is about finding structures and common patterns across the three works. You do not have to read much of the article to fill in the cells on the TSA template.

In any TSA template, there are five columns. The first column describes a text structure feature. The next three columns contain your notes from the analysis of the three different works, one in each column. The final column on the right is where you summarize any patterns that you notice across the three works. In Table 2.2, after I wrote down the titles of the three journal articles and looked at their commonalities, I noticed that all three titles started with gerunds: "designing," "creating," and "teaching." This is a common text structure for this journal that I will keep in mind when I create the title for my submission. In fact, the title of my recent coauthored article to *College Teaching* is "Fostering Master's Students' Metacognition and Self-Regulation Practices for Research Writing" (Santelmann, Stevens, & Martin, 2018). We used the pattern found in the TSA to start the title with a gerund. Who knows if that really made a difference, but the article was published in 2018.

During step 2 of completing the TSA template, you are scanning, counting, and listing certain textual features such as the number of paragraphs devoted to different sections and the number and type of references. Look at the sample TSA (Table 2.2) once again to see the range of textual features noted. A little bit of advice here for completing a TSA for journal articles: I usually find it is easier and faster to flip through the pages with a hard copy of the article. Others manage quite well with viewing the article on their computer.

Step 3: Identify Patterns Across the Texts

Finally, after filling in the three columns from your three sample works, the most important step in the TSA process is to look for patterns across all three of the works. Once you have the patterns, use them to develop the structure of your own manuscript. For example, in the completed TSA template in Table 2.2, in the last column the patterns across the textual features in each article are summarized. Several patterns persist across all three articles that I would keep in mind as I write and shape my article for submission to *College Teaching*: The abstract is no longer than 200 words, the references include both journal articles and books, there is no direct purpose statement, and there are no research questions. I know more about what I can include and not include in my submission. The task became much more doable!

As you can see, completing the TSA makes you better prepared to approach writing. In the appendices I have provided blank TSA templates for journal articles (A), book reviews (C), and edited books (D). Appendix B gives a detailed analysis of how to complete a TSA template for a journal article.

TABLE 2.2
Example of a completed TSA for three journal articles from *College Teaching*

Compare the articles for the following textual structures. Look for patterns in journal articles across one journal.
Title of journal: *College Teaching*
Date of review: November 18, 2015

Textual structure and descriptors: author, year	Article #1 Kumar & . . . , 2013	Article #2 Piergiovanni, 2014	Article #3 Peterson & . . . , 2015	Patterns across articles
1. Brief 10-word gist of article, not sentences	Problem-based learning, composition, college, rubric, self-assess	Critical thinking, education students, writing, first-year class	Creative writing, history, two types of assignments	Writing, teaching methods, student-centered
2. Title: Friendly, formal, long, colon, tone, inviting, academic	"Designing a problem-based learning intermediate composition course"	"Creating a critical thinker"	"Teaching historical analysis through creative writing assignments"	All have action word in title. All have either assignment or student outcome description.
3. Abstract–length, content	One hundred fifty-six words; describing teaching activities and student work	One hundred eight words; evaluate critical thinking activity, compare pre-writing with final paper	Eighty-eight words; contains purpose of study, teaching methods, author reflections, qualitative	One hundred to two hundred words; describe teaching and results
4. Purpose of research: Where is it stated? What is it?	No direct statement	No direct statement	To offer theoretical frame; to give specific models of assignments	No direct statement such as "The purpose of the study is . . ."
5. Research questions, evident, clear	No	No	No	Research questions are not expected.
6. Headings in article—number, level	Five headings, all same level	Eleven headings: 4 level 1; 7 level 2	Six headings same level	Five to 6 level 1; subheads Okay

7. Paragraphs devoted to introduction, literature review, method, results, discussion, references	Intro/Literature: 9; Teaching methods: 6; Methods: Included in teaching methods; Results: Implementation, 8; Discussion: 4; Conclusion: 2; References: 1 page	Intro/Literature: 12; Teaching methods: 5; Results: 16; Conclusion: 4; References: Half page	Intro: 1; Literature: 4, including theory; Teaching methods: 11; Methods: 4; Results: 4; Conclusion: 2; References: 1 page	Short introduction; details on teaching methods; results vary; conclusion short; references short
8. Number of figures/tables	None	7 tables; 1 figure	None	Okay to have tables/figures
9. Methods: Type (survey, etc.), participants	Included in teaching methods: Problem-based learning assignment	Photo journal analysis plus reflection; writing	Analysis of student writing projects	Qualitative methods
10. Overall tone of article (first person, third person)	Uses "I" and "we"	Uses "I" and "we"	Uses "I" and "we"	Uses "I" and "we"
11. References: Number, type (journals [J], book [B], book chapters [BC], report [R], conference presentation [CP], other [O]. Articles from this journal?	Total = 24: J = 15; B = 6; BC = 0; CP = 1; O = 2; Articles from *College Teaching* = 0	Total = 15: J =13; B = 1; BC = 1; Articles from *College Teaching* = 2	Total = 30: J = 15; B = 11; Web = 3; O = 1; Articles from *College Teaching* = 1	Number: 15 to 30 in all; journal articles the majority; very few references from *College Teaching*
12. Other noteworthy items	Not formal research article with methods and data presentation	The author had students make a paper quilt from their photos.	Uses list of anonymous student work in references	No reference to theoretical foundations; more interested in teaching methods

Recalling the scene from the beginning of the chapter, Hiro now has something he can do even before he puts words on the page. After identifying an appropriate journal for his work, he can complete a TSA template. By looking at the patterns across the three articles, he has many clues about the basic textual features that can frame his writing approach: for example, the titles are formal, the abstract has less than 200 words, and the introduction and background section have no more than eight paragraphs. Hiro can avoid all of the debilitating feelings that come with staring at the dreaded blank page. By beginning with a TSA, he can outline the essential features of his final manuscript and calibrate his effort and time to match the expectations for each of those structural elements that are important to this journal. When he finally submits his article, the editor may notice that the article looks and feels similar to others in the journal. By doing the TSA template, Hiro is on the path to having a publication that matches the specific structures and patterns from a particular journal.

Strategy II: "Mining" Persuasive Arguments: Argument Templates

Strategy II focuses on the secret sauce of a journal article. It is not the methods or the results. The key ingredient is the argument. The argument adds that extra spice that engages the reader at the beginning of the manuscript. In the chapter opening, Elena, in scene II, could use this section to answer the reviewer comment about the need to show how her work contributes to the literature.

Some people may think of argument as a rather loud disagreement, punctuated with high emotional drama. An academic argument, on the other hand, consists of a set of written statements that place the work in context of the work of others with whom the author may or may not agree. An academic argument includes citations to other published works that bear on the work presented in the manuscript. Because the citations reinforce or contrast with your purpose, the goal of the argument is to persuade the reviewer and the reader that your work will make a significant contribution. One very good reason to deepen your understanding of argument is that, as Belcher (2009b) asserts, the main reason journal articles are rejected is the lack of an argument. Of course, avoiding rejection of your manuscript is a very compelling reason to pay attention to building a strong argument.

A persuasive argument assures the reader that you, the author, have done the following:

1. Read the recent literature on this topic
2. Demonstrated how the literature review is related to the topic
3. Shown how the work contributes to or contrasts with what has been done in the past
4. Established that the work makes a significant and unique contribution

When reviewers critique your work with questions such as "Have you included work by. . . ?" or "How does your work add to the field?" and "Why is this work significant?" they are pointing out a problem with the scope and depth of the argument.

That is, you have not paid attention to the ideas of other writers and researchers who are already engaged in this academic conversation about your topic. Questions about scope mean you have not included enough of the current work on the topic, and ones about depth mean that you may have included the literature but have not read it carefully. In all, by writing a clear, compelling, and persuasive argument based on previous work, you have joined the "academic conversation." Let us look at an example of an argument in a research article.

The following is the opening paragraph of an article by Gopee and Deane (2013) in the journal *Nurse Education Today.* Some arguments can be short, like this one; others are much longer. Gopee and Deane demonstrate how straightforward an argument can be:

> There is a wealth of literature on writing development for university students (e.g.[,] Murray, 2009), textbooks on writing strategies (e.g.[,] Cottrell, 2008), and online resources designed specifically for university students (e.g.[,] Purdue Writing Lab, 2012); and there are various models for writing development such as one-to-one writing tutorials (Borg [&] Deane, 2011), group sessions, short courses, and writing groups (Rickard et al., 2009; Jackson, 2009), as well as self-study resources. However, surprisingly little attention has been paid to what students have to say about the support that they need to improve their academic writing. (p. 1624)

Note that there are six references in this one short paragraph. The oldest is 2009, while the article itself was published in 2013 and probably submitted in 2011 or 2012. For the sciences and the social sciences in particular, it is important to cite recent work so that you don't miss any current thinking on the topic. To begin to write a better argument, I turn to the fine work of several rhetoricians and linguists.

In the book *They Say/I Say: The Moves That Matter in Academic Writing*, Graff and Birkenstein (2010), rhetoricians, have abstracted a variety of templates that are embedded in academic writing. The templates are sentence-starters. For example, in the chapter on "the art of metacommentary," one template presented was as follows: "Ultimately, then, my goal is to demonstrate that . . ." (p. 132). This sentence-starter, or a similar one, is another version of a purpose statement commonly found in academic writing. In your final work, of course, you may find yourself editing out the exact words from the sentence-starters. However, these assist you in identifying key phrases that "lubricate" your writing.

I have frequently used the templates in Figure 2.1 in workshops with faculty. In their early stages of argument construction, faculty comment on how useful these are. Argument template I frames an argument around a controversial issue. Argument template II focuses on an area where there is general agreement but different perspectives.

Before I go back to Gopee and Deane (2013), let me use argument template II in a lighthearted example. The bold words are abstracted from the template.

> **When it comes to the topic of** cats and dogs, most of us (including psychologists) will readily agree that it is good to have a furry companion. **Where this agreement usually ends, however, is on the question of** which is the better pet, a dog or a cat.

Figure 2.1 Templates for introducing an argument around a topic

---

Argument template I: A controversial issue

In discussions of _____A_____, one controversial issue has been _____A1_____.

On one hand, _____B_____ argues _____B1_____.

On the other hand, _____C_____ contends _____C1_____.

Others _____D_____, even maintain _____D1_____.

My own view is _____E_____. (or, The purpose of my work is _____E_____.)

Argument template II: An issue where there are differences but something is missing

When it comes to the topic of _____A_____, most of us will readily agree that _____A1_____.

Where this agreement usually ends, however, is on the question of _____A2_____.

Whereas <u>B</u> is convinced that _____B1_____, _____C_____ offers another viewpoint that _____C1_____, while _____D_____ adds _____D1_____ to the conversation.

My own view is _____E_____. (or, The purpose of my work is _____E_____.)

A, A1, and A2 are about the topic or different perspectives on the topic.

B, B1; C, C1; and D, D1 are the names of the authors you cited (B, C, D) and their works (B1, C1, D1) that offer different viewpoints on the argument.

E is the writer's position on this argument. This can be expressed as a viewpoint or in the purpose statement.

Adapted from Graff, G., & Birkenstein, C. (2010). *They say/I say: The moves that matter in academic writing* (2nd ed.). New York, NY: W.W. Norton.

Shepherd (1918) argued that dogs are better because they obey you and force you to get exercise every day by taking them out for a walk. **Persian (1922) asserted** that cats are better because you do not have to walk a cat. In fact, if you try, you will end up dragging a cat, which is a particularly humiliating exercise for both owner and cat. You alone can determine when you want exercise. **My own viewpoint is** that cats are better because their lifestyle allows both the owner and the pet to be independent.

What you may notice about the argument is that there is really no right or wrong answer for owners and pets, just different perspectives. In constructing an argument, after I have acknowledged these different viewpoints, my job as a writer, even an academic writer, is to persuade you to read on because my work contributes to the conversation about this topic.

When working with the argument templates, I suggest you initially use the phrasing that Graff and Birkenstein (2010) have developed and fill in the blanks with your own ideas. The argument in the Gopee and Deane (2013) article previously presented seems to fit more readily into argument template II. As an example, I've inserted text of the Gopee and Deane article within the template (shown in bold) so you can see how, even though their argument does not use the exact template words, it follows the structure of argument template II.

> **When it comes to the topic of writing development for university students, most people would agree that** there is a wealth of literature on writing development. **Where this agreement usually ends, however, is on the question of how do we know which method works best.**
>
> **Some have demonstrated that** there is a wealth of literature on writing development for university students (e.g.[,] Murray, 2009), textbooks on writing strategies (e.g.[,] Cottrell, 2008), and online resources designed specifically for university students (e.g.[,] Purdue Writing Lab, 2012); **[a]nd, others have studied the** . . . various models for writing development such as one-to-one writing tutorials (Borg [&] Deane, 2011), group sessions, short courses, and writing groups (Rickard et al., 2009; Jackson, 2009), as well as self-study resources.
>
> **Given all the work done on this topic, our own view is that** surprisingly little attention has been paid to what students have to say about the support that they need to improve their academic writing. . . . **The aim of this article is to offer nurse educators an analysis of academic writing experiences of health and social care students on higher education courses to be able to identify which methods students say work well for them.** (p. 1624) (Template framework added as bold.)

Gopee and Deane's rhetorical moves in developing their argument are that, even though there has been a lot of work done on student writing development, the gap in the literature is that no one has sought out what students think about academic writing. The aim of their work is to describe how students respond to these academic writing programs so that nurse educators can design better programs to meet student needs.

As a caveat, I recognize that I have distilled a very complex topic, argumentation, into two seemingly simple templates. Chapter 9 has further examples and one additional template. Rhetoricians Graff and Birkenstein (2010) assert that the basic elements of argument can serve as a starting point in developing a more complex argument. Gopee and Deane (2013) didn't use the exact language of the template but constructed an approach to succinctly present existing viewpoints and conclude by identifying a significant gap.

By illuminating the not-so-obvious construction of arguments, I show you that you can also "mine" the scholarly publications you read for how to build an argument based on how others do it. There are many excellent books on writing a persuasive argument as well (e.g., Heinrichs, 2013).

The ability to make an argument is critical in getting your work published. Yet, for many of us, it is still a challenge. My hope is that after reading this section you can identify the structure of the arguments in the literature as well as use the argument template to craft your own persuasive arguments. Whether you are writing a book review (chapter 7), conference proposal (chapter 8), journal article (chapter 9), or book or book chapter (chapter 10), you may want to refer back to this chapter to create the secret sauce in making an appealing argument for your work. Similar to the key textual feature of making an argument, in the next section, I focus on developing an often important textual feature, a clear and compelling purpose statement.

Strategy III: Clarifying Your Purpose: Purpose Statement Template

Strategy III is about writing a clear and compelling purpose statement. The purpose statement is often the last sentence at the end of the introduction in journal articles. The purpose statement is the fulcrum around which your whole paper revolves. Because the purpose statement typically is just one sentence, it may seem to be an inconsequential part of your writing. Yet, many readers and reviewers home in on it and appreciate the purpose statement as a way to figure out what exactly the author(s) are writing about.

Faculty work centers on studying complex constructs within a variety of distinct disciplines, such as creativity, electrical magnetism, or neighborhood diversity. As a writer, you can assist readers in comprehending how you are approaching these constructs by writing a clear and direct purpose statement that tells readers why you are studying and writing about a particular phenomenon.

When writing your purpose statement, remember this is not creative writing where you want to express the purpose in a variety of ways. This is academic writing, which means you need to be direct and clear in your explanations. I have read dissertations where doctoral students write "I want to understand . . ." Then, because they are following the admonitions of previous writing instruction, they want to mix it up and not repeat themselves, so they continue, "I intend to learn more about . . ." or, "This paper explores the . . . ." Those are fine sentences, and they do vary the phrasing. However, readers of academic writing want to know in one sentence the purpose of the study or work without a lot of stylistic permutations.

Goodson (2017) tells the story of a colleague who always first looked for the purpose statement in the paper he was reviewing. If he could not immediately locate it, he considered it a signal that the author lacked clear purpose from the outset; thus, it was an indication the paper would not be worth reading and, therefore, as a reviewer, a reason for immediate rejection. Though extreme, the story illustrates that you can save yourself from potential rejection by simply including a statement such as, "The purpose of the study was to . . ." or, "The aim of the research was to . . . ." Some journal articles do not have purpose statements. By doing the TSA template you can find out what is typically expected by the journal.

A purpose statement needs to include the following components: who is involved (subjects, participants), what actions are being taken, and what is the topic you are writing about. I have adapted Goodson's (2017) purpose statement exercise to show you how to dig deeper into your goals and develop a clear and compelling purpose statement. To complete the exercise, you will need to give yourself permission to brainstorm a variety of ways to write your purpose so that you can narrow your statement down to one that expresses the real purpose of your work.

Here are examples that will illustrate a variety of ways to write a purpose statement. When I was brainstorming the purpose statements for chapter 11 on responding to a request to R & R, I wrote the following sentences:

> The purpose of this chapter is **to help** faculty respond to feedback on their work.
> The purpose of this chapter is **to show** faculty a variety of ways to complete an R & R request.
> The purpose of this chapter is **to assist** faculty in completing a request to R & R.
> The purpose of this chapter is **to give** faculty hope and not ignore the publication opportunity in an R & R request.
> The purpose of this chapter is **to illuminate** the R & R process and offer faculty ideas about how to handle it.

As you can see from these examples, I progressively changed the action—the verb—and the scope from responding to feedback to the completion of an R & R request. After completing this first set of purpose statements, I asked myself, "Am I focusing on how faculty can respond to feedback or on the whole context of the R & R process, or both?" Before I undertook the exercise, I hadn't realized the two possible purposes of the chapter.

The purpose statement exercise (Exercise 2.1) will guide you in writing a series of purpose statements about your work. Undertaking this exercise over several days will help you refine your focus; clarify where your work is going and who is going to be involved; and, finally, craft the best purpose statement. After doing this exercise and developing a clear purpose statement, some faculty have found it helpful to print out the final and best purpose statement and post it in a prominent place in their writing space. Clarifying your purpose and posting it prominently will help you make sure that all your reading, research, and writing lead you toward accomplishing that purpose. In the next section, I show how to use your argument and purpose statement, along with the title of the work, to add cohesion to the manuscript.

Strategy IV: Finding Textual Connections: Title-Argument-Gap Purpose Patterns

Strategy IV focuses on a structural analysis that involves the title, argument, and purpose statement in one journal article. Making explicit the textual connections across these features makes it easier for the reader to understand your manuscript.

EXERCISE 2.1
Writing a purpose statement

1. First practice session: Set the timer for eight minutes and write as many variations as you can to this question: What is the purpose of this proposal/study? Do not edit as you go. You will have a chance to do that later. Try to write rapidly without judgment. Be sure to write the sentence stem, "The purpose of the study is . . ." each time. It will let your brain rest in between and then find a unique response each time. Some faculty have found it useful to use the verbs in the following list to launch this brainstorming activity. You do not have to worry about editing your purpose statements; just write them in as many different ways as you can.

The purpose of the study is _____.
The purpose of the study is _____.

Remember that the purpose is to *do* something, an action you can observe. Here are some examples of action verbs to complete the sentence stem:

answer a question   *assess* the relationship between
test a hypothesis   *identify*
compare findings   *describe and explain*
argue for a better solution   *tell* the story
examine a problem in depth   *evaluate* the responses
analyze data in a new way   *analyze* a self-reflection
observe a situation

DO NOT USE THE VERBS "UNDERSTAND," "THINK," "KNOW," "LEARN"

Try not to use words such as "study," "understand," "think," "know," and "learn." These are vague actions that are hard to observe.

2. Second practice session: Review your purpose statements from session one. Then, star two or three that seem most direct. Set your timer for eight minutes again and rewrite the hopeful ones but add more to the page. You will think of other ways to craft the statement during the day, for sure! You can add another practice session if you wish.
3. Reread all your purpose statements from two or three practice sessions and decide on one that seems to work for you. For additional feedback, you can have a colleague read them as well. After you have decided on the best one, print it out or put it in your journal. Some people post it on their computer to remember that is exactly what they seek to accomplish in this work. Of course, you can revise later. The purpose statement can guide your selection of appropriate literature to accomplish that purpose. And, by doing this exercise, you are closer to targeting the works you want to cite and to accomplishing your purpose.

Adapted from Goodson, P. (2017). *Becoming an academic writer: 50 exercises for paced, productive, and powerful writing.* Thousand Oaks, CA: SAGE.

TABLE 2.3

Content links among title, gap, and purpose statement in journal articles

Title	Example of gap (key words in bold and underlined)	Purpose	Key words across title, gap, and purpose
1. Blending Health Literacy With an English as a Second Language Curriculum: A Systematic Literature Review (Chen, Goodson, & Acosta, 2015)	"**No systematic examination** of these curricula has yet been conducted to facilitate reflecting on where we are and how we are doing regarding the goal of improving health literacy for LEP populations through ESL classes" (p. 101).	"The **purpose of this systematic review** is to assess the characteristics and effectiveness of English as a second language health literacy curricula that are currently available in English-dominant countries" (p. 101).	Systematic review or examination ESL Curricula(um) Health literacy
2. An Investigation of Research Self-Efficacy Beliefs and Research Productivity Among Faculty Members at an Emerging Research University in the USA. (Pasupathy & Siwatu, 2014)	"However, there is a **dearth of information** on research self-efficacy and the sources of research self-efficacy within educational environments" (p. 728).	"Thus, the **primary purpose of this study** is to investigate research self-efficacy beliefs among faculty members, their influence on research productivity, and the relationship between research self-efficacy beliefs and research productivity" (p. 729).	Research self-efficacy (beliefs) Research productivity
3. Publish or Perish: A Systematic Review of Interventions to Increase Academic Publication Rates (McGrail, Rickard, & Jones, 2006)	"However, to our knowledge, there has been **no prior review** of the effectiveness of interventions that have been used in order to increase academic publication rates" (p. 21).	"The **aim of this paper** is therefore to review published literature that reports the effectiveness of measures designed to promote publication. It is hoped that this may identify strategies that can be used by university departments and their staff to meet their publication targets."	Review Increase (or meet) (academic) publication rates (targets)
4. Supporting Academic Publication: Evaluation of a Writing Course Combined With Writers' Support Group (Rickard, McGrail, Jones, O'Meara, Robinson, Burley, & Ray-Barruel, 2009)	"Although the literature review described above suggests that a writing course, writing support group, or writing coach increases publication rates, it is not known which aspects of these programs are most facilitative" (p. 516).	"The **aim of this project** was to explore the experiential aspects and the effectiveness of a combined approach—structured writing course plus writing support group—on academic publication rates" (p. 517).	Writing course Writing (writers) support group Academic publication rates

In the first three columns in Table 2.3 the title, argument, and purpose statement for four research articles are quoted directly from the work. In the last column, I list the key words that are present across all three key textual features. For example, in study #1, the authors have used the words "systematic" and "review" in the title, the gap, and the purpose. In addition, they have the topics and exact words "health literacy," "ESL," and "curriculum" in all three. By using the same words across all three features, the reader has to grapple only with these constructs. Instead of ESL, if the authors had used "emergent bilinguals," "English language learners," "speakers of other languages than English," or "limited language proficient" randomly across the title, gap, and purpose, the reader might become confused and ask about the difference between these descriptors. At this point of confusion, many readers stop reading. Making these consistent textual connections is an engaging rhetorical move.

What can you do with this knowledge? If you have completed the argument template (refer to Figure 2.1) and the purpose statement exercise (Exercise 2.1), you have an initial set of textual features to begin to craft the textual connections across your paper just like these authors have done in Table 2.3. Read the four examples carefully and then begin the exercise "Linking title, gap, and purpose" in Exercise 2.2.

I designed Strategy IV to heighten your awareness of some of the not-so-obvious textual connections. Strategy V introduces you to an invaluable website that distills key rhetorical moves into sentence starters across academic research articles.

Strategy V: Making Rhetorical Moves: Common Academic Writing Phrase Templates

The rhetoricians Graff and Birkenstein (2010) have done academic writers a great favor by identifying recurring and useful phrases found in academic writing. I have already introduced you to some of these in the argument and purpose statement templates. Besides Graff and Birkenstein (2010), another resource is the Manchester University Academic Phrasebank, created by Morley (2014).

Figure 2.2a is a screenshot of the home page on the academic phrasebank. The bubble on the top focuses your attention on the list of links you can open, from "Introducing Work" to "Writing Conclusions," that are typical sections of a research article, dissertation, or thesis. The lower bubble points to hot links where you can see phrases for typical rhetorical "moves" in academic writing such as "Signaling Transitions," "Being Critical," and "Writing About the Past."

Figure 2.2b is a screenshot of the web page linked from the "Writing Conclusions" tab. This is only the first of about five pages on how to approach writing a conclusion. You may notice the box at the top of the web page where Professor Morley defines *writing conclusions* and describes its use in academic writing. These boxes are at the top of all the pages with hot links.

I introduce faculty to this website because it offers a vast array of sentence-starters to stimulate their thinking. Some may find that writing the introduction stymies them; others balk at starting to write up the results. Phrasebank has suggestions for

EXERCISE 2.2

Linking title, gap, and purpose

The purpose of this exercise is to heighten your awareness of how you can make content links among your title, gap, and purpose statement, just as the authors of the journal articles did in Table 2.3.

STEP 1: Copy and fill in both the argument templates. Just write what comes to mind as you read the sentence stems. Do not worry about whether you have read enough literature to make the argument. Write what makes sense. You can use the argument template to identify the kind of literature you need to gather to make the argument. After you do this, you will see which one seems to fit the work you are now doing.

Argument template I: A controversial issue

In discussions of _____A_____, one controversial issue has been _____A1_____.
On one hand, _____B_____ argues _____B1_____.
On the other hand, _____C_____ contends _____C1_____.
Others _____D_____, even maintain _____A1_____.
My own view is _____E_____. (or, The purpose of my work is _____E_____.)

Argument template II: An issue where there are differences but something is missing

When it comes to the topic of _____A_____, most of us will readily agree that _____A1_____
Where this agreement usually ends, however, is on the question of _____A2_____.
Whereas _____b_____ is convinced that _____B1_____, _____C_____ offers another viewpoint, _____C1_____,
while _____D_____ adds _____D1_____ to the conversation.
My own view is _____E_____. (or, The purpose of my work is _____E_____.)

STEP 2: After you have completed the purpose statement exercise (Exercise 2.1), write out your purpose statement.

_____

STEP 3: List three or four key words found in your argument and your purpose statement.

_____, _____, _____, _____

Review column 4 in Table 2.3. Note how the authors have repeated key words in the title, argument, and purpose. Rewrite and redraft your purpose and argument so that you are using at least two or three similar words as well.

_____

STEP 4: Once you have those similar words, begin to craft the title of your paper, making sure there are some content links across all three essential structures found in your study. It might be helpful to once again review how other authors have done this in Table 2.3.

Figure 2.2a Screenshot of University of Manchester Phrasebank: Home page

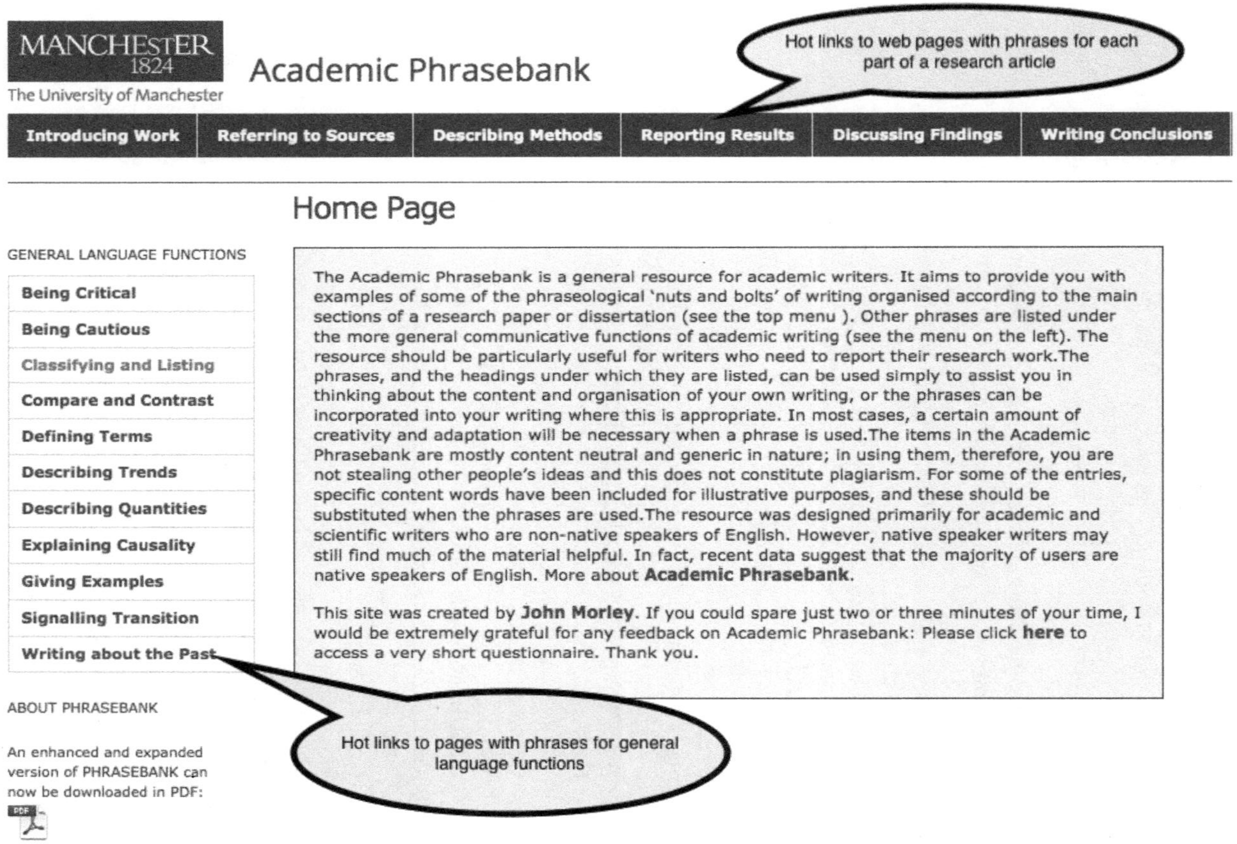

MANCHESTER
1824

The University of Manchester

Academic Phrasebank

| Introducing Work | Referring to Sources | Describing Methods | Reporting Results | Discussing Findings | Writing Conclusions |

Hot links to web pages with phrases for each part of a research article

Home Page

The Academic Phrasebank is a general resource for academic writers. It aims to provide you with examples of some of the phraseological 'nuts and bolts' of writing organised according to the main sections of a research paper or dissertation (see the top menu). Other phrases are listed under the more general communicative functions of academic writing (see the menu on the left). The resource should be particularly useful for writers who need to report their research work. The phrases, and the headings under which they are listed, can be used simply to assist you in thinking about the content and organisation of your own writing, or the phrases can be incorporated into your writing where this is appropriate. In most cases, a certain amount of creativity and adaptation will be necessary when a phrase is used. The items in the Academic Phrasebank are mostly content neutral and generic in nature; in using them, therefore, you are not stealing other people's ideas and this does not constitute plagiarism. For some of the entries, specific content words have been included for illustrative purposes, and these should be substituted when the phrases are used. The resource was designed primarily for academic and scientific writers who are non-native speakers of English. However, native speaker writers may still find much of the material helpful. In fact, recent data suggest that the majority of users are native speakers of English. More about **Academic Phrasebank.**

This site was created by **John Morley.** If you could spare just two or three minutes of your time, I would be extremely grateful for any feedback on Academic Phrasebank: Please click **here** to access a very short questionnaire. Thank you.

GENERAL LANGUAGE FUNCTIONS

| Being Critical |
| Being Cautious |
| Classifying and Listing |
| Compare and Contrast |
| Defining Terms |
| Describing Trends |
| Describing Quantities |
| Explaining Causality |
| Giving Examples |
| Signalling Transition |
| Writing about the Past |

Hot links to pages with phrases for general language functions

ABOUT PHRASEBANK

An enhanced and expanded version of PHRASEBANK can now be downloaded in PDF:

Source. http://www.phrasebank.manchester.ac.uk/

Figure 2.2b Screenshot of University of Manchester Phrasebank: Writing Conclusions page

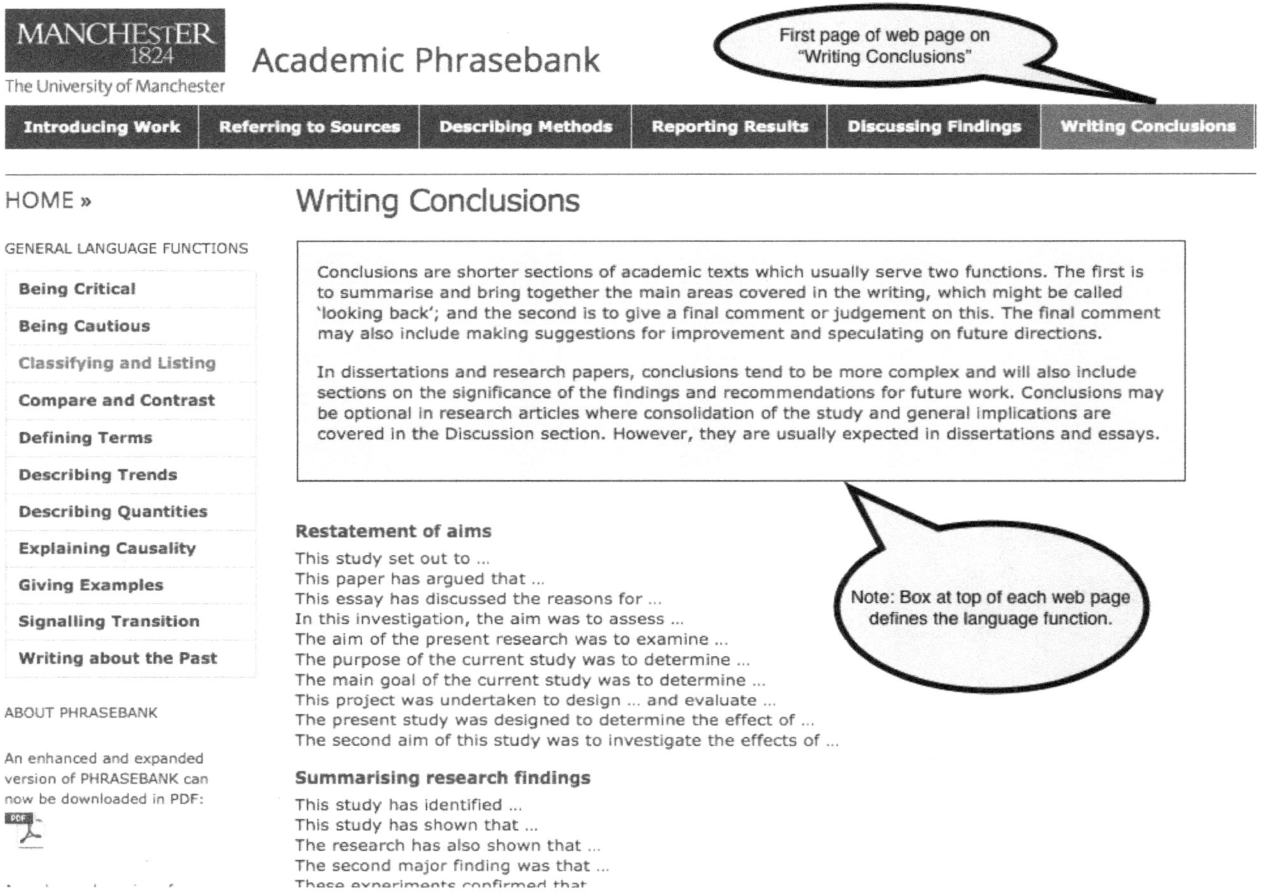

First page of web page on "Writing Conclusions"

MANCHESTER
1824
The University of Manchester

Academic Phrasebank

| Introducing Work | Referring to Sources | Describing Methods | Reporting Results | Discussing Findings | Writing Conclusions |

HOME »

Writing Conclusions

Conclusions are shorter sections of academic texts which usually serve two functions. The first is to summarise and bring together the main areas covered in the writing, which might be called 'looking back'; and the second is to give a final comment or judgement on this. The final comment may also include making suggestions for improvement and speculating on future directions.

In dissertations and research papers, conclusions tend to be more complex and will also include sections on the significance of the findings and recommendations for future work. Conclusions may be optional in research articles where consolidation of the study and general implications are covered in the Discussion section. However, they are usually expected in dissertations and essays.

Note: Box at top of each web page defines the language function.

Restatement of aims

This study set out to ...
This paper has argued that ...
This essay has discussed the reasons for ...
In this investigation, the aim was to assess ...
The aim of the present research was to examine ...
The purpose of the current study was to determine ...
The main goal of the current study was to determine ...
This project was undertaken to design ... and evaluate ...
The present study was designed to determine the effect of ...
The second aim of this study was to investigate the effects of ...

Summarising research findings

This study has identified ...
This study has shown that ...
The research has also shown that ...
The second major finding was that ...
These experiments confirmed that

GENERAL LANGUAGE FUNCTIONS

Being Critical

Being Cautious

Classifying and Listing

Compare and Contrast

Defining Terms

Describing Trends

Describing Quantities

Explaining Causality

Giving Examples

Signalling Transition

Writing about the Past

ABOUT PHRASEBANK

An enhanced and expanded version of PHRASEBANK can now be downloaded in PDF:

Source: http://www.phrasebank.manchester.ac.uk/

all parts of a research paper as well as typical academic moves such as "being critical." What I have found is that these phrases are a good starting place in structuring a manuscript or part of a manuscript. Often in the revision process the phrases get modified and revised and are totally unrecognizable from the original phrase. Speakers of languages other than English find the phrases in the bank invaluable in varying their writing and keying in on the essential rhetorical move in English.

A Caveat: The Tension Between Structure and Creativity

Some of you may be bristling at the words "structure," "template," and "patterns" in reference to academic writing, thinking, "If I write this way, it will dampen my creativity, deaden my writing and make it formulaic." In referring to the IMRAD (introduction, methods, results, and discussion) pattern of many research articles, Sword (2016) in *Stylish Academic Writing* acknowledges the value of structures but offers her own caveat:

> This paint-by-numbers approach prompts researchers to plan their research methodically, conduct it rigorously, and present it coherently, without leaving out any crucial information. Moreover, a conventional structure is relatively easy for new academics to learn; all they have to do is follow the models established by others before them. Readers, meanwhile, know exactly where to look for key findings. They can skim the abstract, mine the literature review, scan the data and grab the conclusions without wasting valuable time actually *reading*.
>
> However, conventional structures also have some significant drawbacks. . . . Another disadvantage of identically structured articles is that they all end up looking and sounding more or less alike, thus offering the subliminal impression that they all say more or less the same thing. Even more worryingly, academics who always plan, research and write to a template risk thinking to a template as well. (pp. 123–125)

In contrast to the admonitions of Sword (2012), Graff and Birkenstein (2010) argue for the use of templates and writing structures in academic writing. In reference to one of their templates that I have adapted in this chapter (Figure 2.1), they note, "In our view, this template represents the deep, underlying structure, the internal DNA as it were, of all effective arguments" (Graff & Birkenstein, 2010, p. xiv). They continue with the idea that some may view the focus on templates and structure work as "formulaic." However, many faculty members, including me, have not discovered these structures on their own. "While seasoned writers may pick up these moves unconsciously through . . . reading, many [academics] do not" (Graff & Birkenstein, 2010, p. xvii). "The aim of the templates is not to stifle critical thinking but to be direct . . . about the key rhetorical moves that comprise it. . . . Our templates do . . . provide concrete prompts that stimulate and shape such thought" (Graff & Birkenstein, 2010, p. xvii). Therefore, knowing the internal

DNA of the academic writing genre gives academic writers a place to start their writing. In my experience and that of other faculty members, yes, the templates are a place to begin; however, the final revised, rewritten, and edited version contains the structure of an argument with few, if any, of the words found in the template.

Conclusion

This chapter offers you five different strategies to help you become aware of often-unrecognized text structures found in academic writing. Strategy I, "Analyzing text structures," illustrates how to analyze three different works to shape your manuscript. Strategy II, "'Mining' persuasive arguments," focuses your attention on the structure of common templates to use when writing an academic argument. Strategy III, "Clarifying your purpose," shows you how to develop a clear and direct purpose statement, the fulcrum of any work. Strategy IV, "Finding textual connections," illustrates how the words used across the title, argument, and purpose can work together to reinforce each other and provide cohesion in the text. Strategy V, "Making rhetorical moves," introduces you to a very useful website that includes sentence-starters for accomplishing common tasks in academic writing.

The main goal of principle two is to increase your awareness of text structures and patterns within the academic writing genre. Some of you may have discovered these structures on your own. Many of you may have already unconsciously incorporated them into your writing. From becoming a student of the genre of academic writing, I know so much more about the structures and patterns in academic writing. I understand I need to persuade my reader that my work fits in with, contradicts, or adds to the conversation of prior work. I know I need to make clear connections among the title, argument, and purpose. I feel more confident about my writing, and I have less stress. I read like a writer now, gleaning ideas from my fellow scholars, not only about content but also, most certainly, about structure. I am looking at the map of the academic writing territory as well as the territory itself. "A map is **not** the territory it represents, but, if correct, it has a similar **structure** to the territory, which accounts for its usefulness" (Korzybski, 1933, p. 58, emphasis added).

Using this map guides me and my faculty colleagues toward a smoother, less stressful, and more successful academic writing journey.

CHAPTER 3

Be Strategic to Build a Sustainable Writing Practice

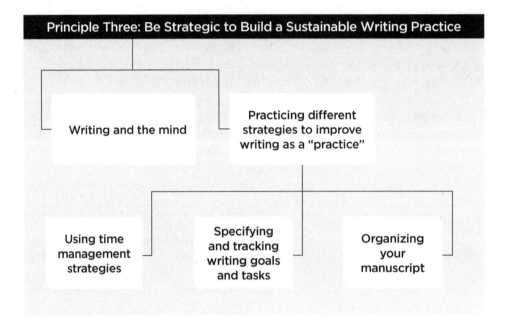

Principle Three: Be Strategic to Build a Sustainable Writing Practice

- Writing and the mind
- Practicing different strategies to improve writing as a "practice"
  - Using time management strategies
  - Specifying and tracking writing goals and tasks
  - Organizing your manuscript

Just write. Right? We've all experienced that gap between intention and action and felt the guilt. It is so easy to utter the words "just write," and another thing entirely to sit down and write. To have a consistent and productive writing practice, of course, I have to write. On the one hand, there's a choice: By not writing, I actually become quite accomplished at "not writing." On the other hand, by writing, I become accomplished at writing as well as develop a sustainable writing practice. The trick is to find ways to rewire my not-writing habits to spark my writing practice. To have a "writing practice," I must move into action; in other words, like any other practice, from going to the gym or learning to play piano, I must practice. But, how, when, and what should I practice?

In this chapter, I offer a buffet of strategies to help nourish your current writing practice to make it more doable, sustainable, and satisfying. By using some of these strategies, writing for publication becomes something you practice, regularly. This chapter provides several approaches to establish a fresh and healthy context for writing so that you write and then wave good-bye to guilt.

Chapters 1 and 2 provide a solid preparation for the key ideas in this chapter. "Know Yourself as a Writer," chapter 1, focused on where you are now and offered strategies designed to help you identify and challenge your writing gremlins, such as perfectionism and procrastination.

Chapter 2, "Understand the Genre of Academic Writing," lays out the rhetorical underpinnings of academic writing. From the text structure analysis activity, you may realize that the "bar" for publication in research journals is more attainable than you previously thought. You *can* easily write the expected 4 paragraphs as the introduction to a research article in the journal you analyzed. You only need 20 to 25 references, not the 150 you had for your dissertation. You discovered that knowing the structure of research articles (or whatever you are writing), helps you envision the parameters of the task and makes it more doable. Using the writing templates, you found how to quickly identify and create the secret sauce in academic writing: the argument. You now know more about yourself and more about academic writing.

This chapter introduces you to an array of practical strategies to help you set up a positive context for your writing, where you can try out some of the strategies described in chapters 1 and 2. This chapter begins with an overview section on being mindful as you write, followed by three sections that outline strategies to use to increase your writing time and output.

Writing and the Mind

Habits are formed through repetition and practice. To change a habit, you have to change your approach with mindfulness and intentionally. Brain research (Hanson, 2009) tells us that our habitual behavior patterns create neural pathways where "triggers" cue a certain routine. Every time we do the same thing over again, we reinforce that experience. We gradually react unconsciously. The more experiences around an activity, the more neurons are excited, the deeper the rut, and the more automatic the unconscious response becomes. In some cases, the unconscious response can include guilt and anxieties. For example, if you are feeling anxious and you don't write, that may induce guilt, resulting in another neural pathway being formed. Writing gets associated with unpleasant feelings of shame, embarrassment, and guilt.

To change a neural pathway that is inhibiting you from accomplishing a goal, you can stop before you start the activity, observe, and think. You can choose to act mindfully, not unconsciously. As Rick Hanson (2009) in *Buddah's Brain: The Practical Neuroscience of Happiness, Love, and Wisdom* reminds us, "*Mindfulness* involves the skillful use of attention to both your inner and outer worlds. Since your brain learns mainly from what you attend to, mindfulness is the doorway to taking in good experiences and making them a part of yourself" (p. 13).

Being mindful about your academic writing practice means observing what you are doing now and reflecting on it, while not judging it. Observation and reflection lead to changing current behavior. Experimenting with new behaviors leads to changing a neural pathway. As you practice new approaches, the power of old neural triggers is diminished. You glide along a new writing pathway toward a new sustainable writing habit.

Another way to think about this analysis of your current practice is to see yourself as a detective. Your current practice contains "clues" of what your patterns and preferences are. Taking the time to observe what you do now can be very interesting. Try to approach this self-study without judgment. Like a detective, you are just analyzing and taking note of what you do and what preferences you have. By paying attention, gathering evidence, and then making specific, strategic changes, you are laying a foundation for creating a different neural pathway. In the section that follows, you can see how I used the "evidence" from the analysis of my current practice to make strategic changes to add more writing time. Behavioral change can help increase the number of pages you write, the number of manuscripts you submit, your resilience, your level of confidence, and decrease your stress (Murray, Thow, Moore, & Murphy, 2008). This chapter presents insights and strategies that reinforce the practice of principle three in writing more, publishing more, and stressing less.

> **Principle three: Be strategic as you develop your writing manuscripts to create a sustainable writing practice.**

Practice Different Strategies to Improve Writing as a "Practice"

The following sets of strategies highlight some ways to manage your time and organize your writing life to make sure you accomplish your writing goals. As you practice these strategies, you are building a foundation for a fresh approach to your writing practice. I focus on ways to allocate time for writing, to set and track specific goals, and to organize your writing for efficient access:

> Strategy set I: Use time management strategies
> Strategy set II: Specify and track writing goals, tasks, and rewards
> Strategy set III: Organize and store your manuscripts

Strategy Set I: Use Time Management Strategies

Strategy set I includes seven strategies to make time work in your favor. Even though we are expected to write, lack of time is the most frequently cited reason to explain why faculty members have trouble getting the writing done that they want to do (Grant & Knowles, 2000; MacLeod, Steckley, & Murray, 2012). I start with this typical faculty concern.

As academics, our lives are filled with many pressing and often urgent expectations such as teaching, grading papers, advising students, writing reports, writing letters of recommendation, and attending meetings. When I was an early career faculty member, I knew that the most important thing I needed to do was to write. Yet, there were many days when, as I scurried about, I felt like I had no time to even think about writing. I kept admonishing myself that I just had to figure out how to manage my time better and not have it manage me. I realized that I was not alone in facing the challenge of planning to reach my goals in a set time period and not getting there. Here is a scenario described by Buehler, Griffin, and Ross (1994):

> Academics who carry home a stuffed briefcase full of work on Fridays, fully intending to complete every task, are often aware that they have never gone beyond the first one or two jobs on any previous weekend. The intriguing aspect of this phenomenon is the ability of people to hold two seemingly contradictory beliefs: Although aware that most of their previous predictions were overly optimistic, they believe that their current forecasts are realistic. (p. 366)

This is the *planning fallacy*. It is confounded by the optimism bias, that is, we are hopeful that we will actually get these things done. To tackle the planning fallacy we first have to know how much time we are spending on various tasks.

My doctorate in educational psychology with an emphasis in cognition led me to study my own behavior and try to figure out some strategies to improve my writing practice and productivity. As MacLeod and colleagues (2012) observe, the "[i]nability to make adequate time and space for writing can elicit feelings of guilt and dread towards uncompleted writing projects" (p. 644). By not making time for writing, you don't meet career expectations, but you also increase our stress (Moore, 2003). If you want to make adequate time for writing, build a new neural pathway to productive academic writing, as well as lower your anxiety, even fear, of putting words on the page, think about "allotting" time for writing rather than "finding" time for writing. Figure out how to have your life fit around your writing. Here is where you can start your detective work, and examine how you are spending your time now. Look for the clues to solve this mystery of why, on one hand, you know you should write and yet, on the other, you don't seem to meet your own expectations.

There is not a single formula that instantly moves a faculty member from languishing in the world of not writing to flourishing in the world of the prolific. To build the foundation of productive, satisfying, and rewarding writing, a good first step is to address the amount of time you allocate for writing as well as consider some of the issues associated with making those allocations. I offer seven strategies that can help you adjust your current writing practice to "tip" your writing time in your favor.

Strategy 1: Ask Yourself: How Do I Spend My Time Now?
Your first step begins with a blank calendar. Record on a weekly calendar how you spend each half hour, for each day, from early morning to bedtime. If you use Google Calendar or Outlook, you can print a weekly schedule for this exercise. I admit, it is not necessarily easy to track all these details, but the more details you include, the better information you have on how you are spending your time. The end goal is to figure out where you can fit in some writing. What did you do this week? Did you surf the Web? How long did you spend on e-mail? Did you have lunch with a colleague? Did you work with a student? Did you prepare for your classes? Did you buy groceries? Or exercise? How long did each event take? Just begin to write down exactly how you spent your time for each half hour, every day for a week.

By plotting your week in half-hour time chunks, you will have evidence of how you spend your days. The faculty members I have coached often notice how full their days are. Many find that teaching, and especially preparation for teaching, consumes a lot of time. To their surprise, answering e-mails eats up at least an hour, maybe more, each day. Others observe that one committee gobbles up several hours a week. Other administrative, secretarial tasks leak into our time. Because most of us do not have secretaries anymore, we have to buy our own tickets to conferences; fill out travel authorization forms; and, when we return, fill out travel reimbursement forms. More time. What about the survival and life balance basics? Buying groceries, going to the gym, even sleeping? Taking children to the dentist? Or soccer? What about working with colleagues on program assessment, writing recommendation letters, reviewing a promotion file for a colleague from another campus, and reviewing journal articles?

After you have filled out a calendar that contains the specific details of what you have done for one week, review the activities. Your analytical skills will come in handy now. This is like doing a research project on you. Withholding judgment, analyze your patterns, especially those with a higher time cost but little long-term benefit. How much time did you spend on preparing for your classes? Advising students? Attending meetings? E-mail? Writing? Grocery shopping? Observe. Gather the data. Step back. Analyze.

Because most of us teach, teaching/advising/grading consumes a lot of time. Teaching is engaging, worthwhile, and immediate. I don't want to discourage you from being prepared for your classes or giving feedback to your students. But, as my colleague Lynn points out, "You don't always have to be an A teacher. You can be a B teacher." Maybe you don't have to use a new textbook next year. Maybe you need to work with your department chair so that you don't have to take on new classes for next year. Maybe you want to review the number of assignments in your classes to narrow them down to those that are the most important so that you spend less grading time. Maybe you have students submit drafts and go through student peer review before you read their papers. Maybe you learn how to create rubrics for grading because they really do save grading time (Peat, 2006; Stevens & Levi, 2013). As Boice (2000) suggests, faculty should seek to balance teaching with publishing and community contributions. Getting a handle on how much time you need to prepare for teaching and your service contributions is very important, largely because you *also* want to write. (In strategy set III in this chapter, I suggest further ways to get control of the time you spend teaching and preparing for teaching, so that you can balance that with your writing goals.)

Strategy 2: Allocate Writing Time on Your Calendar for the Whole Week
Make a half-hour to an hour appointment with yourself each week just to allocate your writing time for the following week. Some people do this on Sunday night; others choose Friday afternoon. Fill in your calendar for the upcoming week with your commitments: meetings, teaching responsibilities, and appointments. Then, see where there might be a half hour here and another there that you can do some tasks associated with writing.

After I did some detective work and analyzed how I spent a typical week in October, I discovered, to my surprise, I was spending over 20 hours attending and preparing for meetings, and over 2 hours a day almost every day managing my e-mail, adding up to 12 hours on e-mail in a single week. Even though I used some time management practices, such as clustering my student advising and appointment times to a 3-hour block once a week and limiting my time in preparing for my classes, I was still not very efficient with meeting preparation and e-mails.

What could I do to be more efficient? I will start with meetings. I had administrative duties as the director of the doctoral program, but was there some way to claw back some time? I decided to set the agenda for the next meeting right at the end of the present meeting to reduce start-up time for the next meeting in two weeks. Right after the meeting I also created a to-do list on a Post-it in the front of my handwritten journal so I didn't have to recall all that I needed to do between now and the next meeting. Some colleagues put these notes in their Google Calendar on the date of the next meeting. By clustering my thinking about this committee to the time immediately before and after a meeting, I did not have to allocate other time in the week. Another trick I used when I ran a meeting was to spend half the meeting doing some of the ensuing committee work together in small groups rather than expecting people to meet at another time to do the work before the next meeting. Everyone liked that.

After filling in commitments, I make sure that I have blocked writing "appointments" with myself, even in small half-hour blocks. In this shared, digital calendar world we live in, my calendar with writing blocks set in place is a "closed landscape"; that is, there is little room for me *or anyone else* to add appointments to it. (A warning here: I have heard from a new faculty member that her department chair advised her not to close all available meeting slots on her calendar. The chair warned, "Keep some time slots open so that you are perceived to be available to participate in the department governance.") After consideration of department needs, then, I knew that I had a plan to write. I allocated time to my highest priority—writing—and I implemented ways to be more efficient in my other work as well.

One question I often get from faculty is, "How much time should I allocate to writing each week?" Following his years of research on faculty productivity, Boice (1987) argued that brief, daily writing sessions of 30 to 60 minutes offer the greatest likelihood of producing more writing over time. However, largely because Boice's results were derived under experimental conditions and based on her own surveys with 1,323 faculty and interviews with over 100 faculty, Sword (2016) challenged Boice's mantra of brief daily writing:

> For the vast majority of colleagues I interviewed, writing is neither a daily routine nor a rare occurrence, neither an immovable constant nor a random event, neither a public activity nor a rigidly sequestered one; writing is the work that gets done in the interstices between teaching, office hours, faculty meetings, administration, email, family events, and all the other messy sprawling demands of academic life. The secret to their academic success lies not in any specific element of their daily routine but in a complex cluster of attributes and attitudes. (p. 320)

Sword (2016) concludes that a productive scholar does more than just schedule writing on a calendar. There are also certain attributes, such as the "behavioral habits of discipline and persistence" and "emotional habits of positivity and resilience" (p. 320) that cement a solid and successful writing practice. In all, she notes that a cluster of behaviors and traits leads to productivity. She underscores that you can still be a prolific writer even if you do not write every day, as Boice urges. For now, though, it is best to start scheduling several blocks of time on your calendar to write each week.

Many faculty members are not committed to half-hour segments daily and instead vary their daily time commitment to writing. Others, like Silvia (2007), recommend 2 hours every morning devoted to writing and all the things associated with writing, such as reading and taking notes on references. Even a half hour, however, will give you enough time to get some real planning, as well as writing, done. Then, gradually you can add another 30 minutes. The benefits of approaching writing in small time chunks are real: You stay in touch with your ideas. You can pick up where you left off the day before. You don't have to try to remember what you wanted to do next. You are making a commitment. You are breaking an old habit of not writing and feeling guilty about and instead are writing and feeling positive about your commitment to change. You are creating a new neural pathway and garnering the positive feelings that come with meeting your writing goals.

Strategy 3: Be "Ferocious" in Protecting Your Writing Time

Scheduling writing time on your calendar is a big step in the right direction. I am sure you are aware that there are many competing commitments. Think of your writing time as making an appointment with a very important person: you. You cannot double book. You cannot cancel without making a new appointment. At times, you will have to be ferocious in saving time for writing. You make it a time that you do not look at your e-mail and do not answer your phone. On your computer system preferences, find the notifications icon and set it up to not bother you with e-mail, news, or any other notifications during your writing time. This is your time to stay in touch with your writing and your scholarship.

Strategy 4: Practice Ways to Say "No"

One way to avoid involvement in other demands is to practice saying "no." If someone scheduled a meeting during the time you are teaching, you would say, "No way! I have a class at that time." Similarly, you can assign the same inviolability to your writing time, and it can take on that quality of commitment. Here are some lines to practice when responding to a request to get involved in something that could interfere with your writing time or could result in a conflicting long-term commitment:

"Let me think about it, and I'll get back to you."
"I can't commit to this as I have other priorities at the moment."
"Now is not a good time. I am in the middle of something. How can we connect later?"
"I'd love to do this, but . . ."

"This doesn't meet my priorities now, but I'll be sure to keep you in mind."
"It turns out that I won't be able to do that."

Generally, your colleagues will accept these phrases. You may have even heard some of them use these statements. The last statement that I learned from a writing coach and friend, Meggin McIntosh, I particularly like: "It turns out that I won't be able to do that." "It" is vague, and the phrase implies that other pressing events popped up that were beyond my control.

Strategy 5: Set Up Your Environment With Physical and Mental Cues to Reinforce Your Writing Practice

Think about how you set up your environment for writing. By being mindful about your writing place, you are establishing a series of physical and mental cues that reinforce your practice. Some find that writing at home makes it more probable that they will write. Others find that washing dishes, doing the laundry, and dusting the floor magically seem much more inviting than sitting down to write. Perhaps, they have to choose another strategy. Some work in coffee shops. Others regularly close their office door and post a sign. Figure 3.1 is an example of a sign created by a Portland State University (PSU) faculty member to make sure she is not disturbed during her writing time in her office. She finds that her students respect her commitment to research. After reading the sign, some students even ask her about it. Some faculty find that if they clear their desk of other distractions, it is easier to focus. Some set aside a certain desk at home that is just for writing. All of these suggestions go back to observing and reflecting on your current patterns, taking action to change these patterns, and creating an environment that signals this is when and where you write.

Strategy 6: Reflect on and Challenge Your Old Beliefs About Writing

Some faculty members have said to me that they cannot write in half-hour time chunks; they need four or five hours in one sitting. "Writing all day Friday is really the only way I have done it." My suggestion would be to observe how well that practice is working for you. If you are not meeting your writing goals, then tweak your practice a little bit to see if that helps you meet your goals. Add two or three short chunks of writing during the week.

I, too, find some benefit in writing for four to five hours at one time when I have decided I just want to get a publication submitted by a certain deadline. When I go to a one- to five-day writing retreat, I write for long periods as well. However, I've learned that after this intensive writing, I feel tired and just don't want to think about my writing anymore. I may take a couple of days off before I come back to it. Sometimes those few days of rest after intensive writing have the benefit of allowing my ideas to incubate, and I find myself making fresh connections. Yet, at other times those few days make it difficult to get started again.

Even though having the four or five hours of writing in one sitting works for some faculty, for others this behavior actually turns into what has been called "binge writing." Binge writing is when the writer waits for that long chunk of time or

Figure 3.1 Faculty door sign

procrastinates until a deadline looms, and then writes for four to eight or more hours. One problem with bingeing is that large chunks of time on the calendar can be easily co-opted by an urgent demand. In addition, large chunks may only appear two or three times in a term. Furthermore, when a writer accomplishes a lot during a binge, binge writing is reinforced as a worthwhile strategy with a well-developed neural pathway with its cues and rewards. Binge writing can lead to a hurried product. Ideas usually need time to evolve in the brain as well as on the page. A hurried product generally is not going to be the writer's best work, whereas when the writer writes regularly in small chunks, she is in touch with her ideas and can refine and develop them more thoughtfully.

Writing regularly in small time chunks has other outcomes as well. First, "snack" writing, as it is also called, is less stressful (Murray, 2014). After your writing snack, you have done your writing for the day, and you can relax and enjoy the fact that you don't need to feel guilty for not writing. Second, when you stay in touch with your ideas on the topic through regular practice, you do not have to recall where you were last time when you sit down to write. Third, putting your writing time on your calendar even for short time chunks reminds you that part of your job as an academic is to write. As Matt Carlson, full professor at PSU, notes,

> Among the most helpful strategies I have learned in Jumpstart [PSU faculty writing program] is to plan one to two weeks ahead by putting writing time on my calendar each day. It has helped in two ways. First, I have learned through this approach that I do have time in my day to write, there is time each day on my calendar that I can reserve for writing time, even if it's only 30 minutes. Second, I have learned that by doing this it reinforces that writing is part of my job, and I should schedule the time each day to do it.

An excellent online resource for supporting snack writing and reducing binge writing is The Pomodoro Technique (Cirillo, n.d.). The Pomodoro Technique involves using a timer when you write, in this case, a kitchen timer in the shape of a tomato (*pomodoro* being Italian for tomato). It could be any timer, of course. The Pomodoro creators' key idea is that during those 25 minutes you do not allow yourself to be distracted by anything and all you do is write. When the timer goes off after 25 minutes, you have completed one "pom," and then you take a break. One benefit of this method is that you begin to see how many poms it takes to complete a task. The Pomodoro people are not alone in offering methods for timing and charting your writing. If you search for "habit tracker" in the applications on your smartphone or other device, you will see that there are many different habit trackers that help you set time goals and monitor your accomplishment of those goals.

Strategy 7: Manage the Time-Gobbler: E-mail
The last strategy in this first set of strategies is to pay attention to how much time you spend on e-mail. Calculating how much time you spend reading and responding to e-mail is another activity that benefits from observation, reflection, and action. Opening an e-mail invariably leads to some thinking, let alone responding and maybe taking action. Even just seeing a notification that you have an e-mail can distract and derail your focus. By simply managing your time on e-mail more efficiently, you can accumulate more writing time.

As responsible faculty members, e-mails have to be answered, at some point. However, as Perry (2012) describes in *The Art of Procrastination: A Guide to Effective Dawdling, Lollygagging and Postponing,* if you wait long enough, sometimes the expectation that you accomplish the thing you are avoiding just evaporates. You open an e-mail feeling guilty that you didn't immediately address the prior request when you read the e-mail last week only to discover "Oh, we really don't need that report on how you will convert your class to an online format after all. The provost changed her mind about putting funding into online learning this year." Whew! Perry calls this "structured procrastination," that is, "the art of making this negative trait work for you" (p. 2). Perry's corollary is "Never do today any task that may disappear by tomorrow" (p. 65). Of course, we cannot always wait for the gods and goddesses of structured procrastination to bless us with this happy circumstance. We generally have little choice but to respond to e-mail. Here are several strategies gleaned from research, faculty, and my own experience that can corral the time you spend on e-mail and open more writing time blocks:

- Silvia (2007) recommends that you do not even open e-mail until after you have done your writing in the morning. There is always something urgent, and even important, in e-mails that distracts, dismays, and delights but has nothing to do with your writing.

- I recommend that you turn off the computer feature that notifies you when you receive a new e-mail. As said earlier, go to the notifications icon in your settings to change notifications such as the news, or e-mails or appointments. Though this is a brief distraction, after looking at it, it takes a valuable minute or two to get back to your work.

- I keep a notepad next to my keyboard. If I interrupt my thinking with the realization that I need to write an urgent e-mail, I just write "e-mail Joanne about syllabus" on the notepad. That way the fear I might forget does not bug me while I am writing. I can take care of it later.

- I include advice to students in the syllabus about my e-mail practices. "If I do not respond in a day or two, just write me again. Sometimes e-mails just fall off the page." Then, they usually nod, acknowledging that it happens to them, too. "Don't feel bad about writing and reminding me again." If it is urgent, like they need a signature on a document that day, I tell them to write "URGENT" in the subject line.

- When I am reading e-mail and I realize I cannot answer the question now, I put a star next to the message. That makes it easy to find because when I sort that column all the stars come up.

- Make a subject heading that contains an abbreviated version of all the vital information about a meeting. For example, "CI Masters Com Mtg Nov. 13, Thur. 9:00, ED 604," translated as "Curriculum and Instruction Masters Committee Meeting November 13, Thursday, 9:00, Room ED 604." As a committee member, I appreciate getting this kind of message in the e-mail subject line because sometimes I forget to write down the room or the exact time in my calendar. I also like to know the day along with the date. Also, for you as a sender, it takes less time to send out a reminder by putting all of these details in the subject line.

- Write EOM (end of message) at the end of the subject line. That communicates to the reader that what is in the subject line is all there is to the message and they do not even have to open it. While this will take some training of your peers about the practice of using EOM in the subject line, you'll appreciate the benefits.

- Other faculty add a message along the lines of "I will respond to e-mail for one and a half hours a day, usually in the morning. If you have something that requires urgent attention, state so in the subject line, with the prefix "URGENT, NEED RESPONSE TODAY."
- Keep your responses to e-mails brief. Following your greeting, lead straight into "I am writing to you because . . ." and use bullet points to highlight the key ideas. I do not hesitate to use bold font or other ways to flag the key message in the e-mail. Often people do not read the whole e-mail "beyond the fold," which means they may not scroll down the page, so try to keep your message within the opening frame.

Because lack of time tends to be the most cited reason for not writing, spending some time observing, reflecting, and acting to allocate time for writing is beneficial, of course. However, the next question is, "Given that you have allocated time to writing, what is the best thing to do during the precious time that you have allocated to writing?"

Strategy Set II: Specify and Track Writing Goals and Tasks

As we move from the last section on allocating time, let us turn to what you can do during that allocated time. One valuable thing is to write out your goals. Strategy set II describes three strategies for writing goals: Write specific goals, analyze the task, and track your progress. The value of setting and writing down goals accrues as you begin to change habitual patterns (Moore, 2003; Silvia, 2007). A goal without a plan becomes just a wish. By writing your goals you are visualizing specific plans, not vague wishes. You are reinforcing a new neural pathway that leads to the creation of a more sustainable writing practice.

I bet you already make a daily to-do list for your writing, teaching, committee work, and personal life. One of the big benefits of a to-do list is that you are able to accomplish more by having a written list. When I have one, it is less likely that I will get distracted. I plan ahead of time to gather resources. I don't have to pull from memory what I was supposed to do, and, finally, I can select and pace my activities based on the amount of time I have. Have you ever gone to the grocery store without a list? It is very easy to buy things you don't need. If you have a list, it is more likely what you buy is what you need and you will use what you buy. You are more in control of your purchases.

Making a written to-do list for academic writing accrues similar benefits. You can feel you are more in control of your writing practice. You can document and reward your progress, which also leads to decreasing the guilt and stress associated with not writing. The strategies in strategy set II offer insights into writing goals that sustain and bolster your writing practice.

Strategy 8: Make Yearly, Term or Semester, Monthly, Weekly, Daily Goals

In my September writing workshops, I have faculty start with writing a goal for the end of the school year. Several years ago one faculty member said to me, "I just wrote, 'two journal articles' as my goal this year. But I don't know what to do next." The answer to this lies in funneling from that big goal for the end of the year to the very little goal that addresses the question, "What do I do tomorrow?"

One way to begin to craft specific actionable goals is to think of all your goals as nested within your big, end-of-the-year goal. Figure 3.2 illustrates how long-term goals are nested and broken down into monthly, weekly, and daily goals. The smallest goal is the daily goal. The next level, which contains all the daily goals, is the weekly goal. The level above is the monthly goal, which includes all the daily goals and weekly goals. Finally, the nest holds all the goals for the entire year.

But, how do we write that daily goal and feel confident that it will help us accomplish the long-term goal? I found that I needed to learn how to write goals that I could visualize and actually do. I am not alone in having had to learn how to write good goals. Esperanza writes about her experience learning how to write weekly goals in Sidebar 3.1, "Writing down weekly goals: Esperanza."

Sidebar 3.1 Writing down weekly goals: Esperanza

Setting goals has been huge for me. At a weeklong jump-start writing retreat, Dannelle shared the research, which showed how much more productive scholars were IF they wrote down a goal. That moment was an "aha" for me that helped me BEGIN to be more deliberative in writing my weekly goals. After several months, I began to realize that my intentions were always too grand and too general to actually do! So, I had to learn how to write goals that were "specific" instead of vague and general.

Esperanza De La Vega, Portland State University

Over the years I have improved at writing doable goals. Recently, I shared my daily writing goals with a colleague. I knew I had only 45 minutes to work on my paper the next day. My goals were, "Find the paper. Print it. Read it through. Take notes on first three pages." She was surprised that I had "find" and "print it" as daily goals. In this case, I had not worked on this paper for three weeks and I knew it would take a little time to locate it; I wanted to visualize those steps and then give myself credit for accomplishing them.

Well-written goals that have certain characteristics are referred to as SMART goals:

Specific (you clearly describe the task)
Measureable (it is stated in such a way that you can tell if you did it or not)
Action-oriented (you use a verb that is an observable, such as "write," "list," "print")
Realistic (it is possible that you will get it done in the time allotted)
Time-bound (you set a time frame to accomplish the goal)

Figure 3.2 Writing goals nest

TABLE 3.1
Analysis of written goals: SMART or not?

What you write as a goal on your to-do list	*Specific*	*Measureable*	*Action-oriented*	*Realistic*	*Time-bound*
Journal article	No	No	No	No	No
Work on journal article	Sort of—the project is identified	No	"Work on" is an action verb, but what does the work entail?	No	How long will it take?
Print current draft of journal article: Five minutes	Yes	Yes	Yes	Yes	Yes
Read and take notes on two journal articles: Two hours	Yes	Yes	Yes	Yes	Yes

Table 3.1 illustrates how to take a general goal and make it a SMART goal. Column 1 contains several examples of written goals from a to-do list. In the next five columns, I assess the written goal to see if it is a SMART goal. Just the words "journal article" as a goal do not fit the characteristics of a SMART goal. However, "Read and take notes on two journal articles: Two hours" is a SMART goal. Writing goals with these SMART goal characteristics helps you visualize the task as well as begin to learn how long tasks actually take so that next time you can feel more confident about the amount of time to allocate to a certain task.

Strategy 9: Analyze the Task to Visualize the Steps
Another step in writing goals is to think about all the tasks associated with your writing project. Doing a task analysis of a writing project will further your writing SMART goals and accomplishing the task. A task analysis is "a systematic identification of the fundamental elements of a job, and examination of the knowledge and skills required for the job's performance" (Business Dictionary, n.d.).

To complete a task analysis, you identify the fundamental elements (steps and products) that go into accomplishing the final task as well as examine the preparatory skills needed to complete it. Table 3.2 is a list of many of the tasks associated with writing the literature review section of a journal article found in the introduction section of a journal article. I have also included in this table references to figures in this book that can assist you in completing the task. This is certainly not an exhaustive task analysis of finding the literature for an introduction. However, it can show you what a task analysis for this complex task looks like. Each one of these tasks can take a different amount of time depending on your resources, knowledge, and skills, and subtasks are even embedded in these tasks.

TABLE 3.2
Task analysis of writing a literature review for a journal article

Task Analysis: *Writing a Literature Review for a Journal Article*
STEP I: IDENTIFYING A JOURNAL FOR SUBMISSION
Select an appropriate journal for this manuscript. Review reference list from other articles I have written on this topic. Identify the one journal most often cited. Select three recent journal articles from one journal. Complete the TSA template (description: chapter 2; appendix A: blank TSA for journal articles) for three articles from one journal.
Look at the last column in the TSA. Identify patterns across the three articles and take notes to shape the overall structure of your manuscript.
STEP II: GENERATING IDEAS
Write out several versions of the purpose statement (Exercise 2.1).
Develop the rationale and argument for the paper, based on the literature. Complete the argument template (Figure 2.1).
Do a focused free-write (Exercise 5.2).
Keep a list of key words for database searches.
STEP III: FINDING AND READING JOURNAL ARTICLES
Use library databases and collect at least 15 articles.
Set up a citation management system (CMS) such as Zotero (appendix D), Endnote, or RefWorks.
Read journal articles and take notes. Make sure articles are in CMS as a "collection" for this one manuscript.
STEP IV: STRUCTURING AND WRITING THE LITERATURE REVIEW
Given what I have read from some of the articles, complete the argument template again.
Do another focused free-write to see how the literature contributes to my thinking.
Write another series of purpose statements to refocus and clarify the purpose.
Review "Reffering to Sources" on Manchester Phrasebank to use typical academic language (Figures 2.2a and 2.2b).
Write the first sentence for each paragraph as a "reverse outline" to see how my ideas are flowing for the review.
Edit text.

Note. Items in parentheses can be found in this book. The first number is the chapter in which the element resides.

From this task analysis, you can identify and write SMART goals for specific writing sessions. For example, the first task of identifying an appropriate journal could be accomplished over several writing sessions of 30 to 60 minutes. Reviewing chapters 2 and 9 on selecting an appropriate journal will orient you to some of the steps you can take. Each of these steps can be a SMART goal. Because certain journals tend to focus on certain topics, one step I suggested earlier is to look at the reference list of one of your previous publications and highlight the journals. The journals you most frequently cite are candidates for potential submission. Your SMART goals for one writing session could be "Find my last three manuscripts on this topic. Highlight the journals cited. Go to the websites of two journals that appear most frequently and read the journal's scope. Thirty-minute session." Note that this set of daily goals meets the criteria for well-written goals. It is *specific* about what needs to be done (identify a journal for submission), *action-oriented* (check out the verbs: "find," "highlight," "go"), *measureable* (list of frequently cited journals), *realistic* (could be done in one time block), and *time-bound* (completed in one daily session). It may be that I won't get it all done in one time block. That is just fine. Just move the incomplete task to your next writing session.

Strategy 10: Chart, Count, and Track Your Progress
Why should you track your progress? Creating a visual chart of your progress and reflecting on it is motivating. You can see where you were and where you need to go. In addition, you can reward yourself as you accomplish your goals.

What are some ways to track your progress toward your goals? Some faculty prefer to track with paper and pencil; others prefer applications such as Google Sheets. Just like the Fitbit can track your steps, computer applications can remind you to write, set writing goals, and record your progress. I just downloaded one called Wordly that allows you to set daily word goals and track your daily output of words written. You can easily see how close you are to meeting your goal.

When I work with faculty at PSU in September, I give them a calendar for the whole school year, set up with small monthly calendars over two pages and space to put Post-its, with a single goal on each one. Their first goal is the one for the end of the year; they stick it on the last month. Then, given this long-range goal, we start backward using the notes to begin to think about what they could accomplish in one term. Then, they write that goal on a Post-it Note and place it at the end of the term. Now, how about a month? What do they imagine they could accomplish in a month? They keep narrowing their goals down to this next week and, finally, to what they could do tomorrow. After they have begun to get an idea of how to funnel down to weekly goals, I suggest that we look at only one term and count the number of weeks left in the term. Since we are on the quarter system, 1 term of 3 months feels a lot longer than 12 weeks. This energizes them to think about what they need to accomplish in the immediate week.

Faculty members use a variety of ways to track progress toward their goals. One way is writing goals and documenting progress on a daily goal sheet. Table 3.3 is a daily goal sheet that Daniel Sullivan, a colleague in the sociology department, kept as a Microsoft Word file. In the final column on the right you can see that he has given himself a 1, .5, or 0 for his completion of the task. Besides logging every bit of writing he did every day, he kept a list of ongoing projects and thoughts about projects at the bottom of his daily goal sheet. Included in that list are his

TABLE 3.3
Excerpts from Daniel's writing log
Writing Log (started 9/19/11; updated 8/29/12)

September	28	Wednesday	Edited survey assignment again, did lots of things and **SUBMITTED to TRAILS!!**	1
September	30	Friday	NSF initial draft—entered participants and their info; met with L&Ds *qua* RAs	1
October	3	Monday	NSF report—wrote project activities and training and development	1
October	5	Wednesday	NSF: Wrote outreach activities; found the # of LT orgs.; looked at 2007 report to get ideas how to write the 2011 one; started updating SPSS data set	1
October	7	Friday	Black butte	0
October	10	Monday	Worked on updating SPSS, own, black, local, stay, public space	1
October	12	Wednesday	Looked at Eliot business report to see how to include interviews into it	.5
October	14	Friday	Read and edited Alberta business report	1
			FALL: Although busy, need to write MS for ASA 2013 in NYC	
			FALL: Submit ASA 2012 to journal	
			FALL: Sabbatical application for Spring 2014/15/16	
			FALL: Finish up and submit urban studies MS	

Notes about current and future writing projects:

Ideas for sabbatical: (1) eligible Spring 2014 (I would like three consecutive spring sabbaticals); (2) find out when I need to submit application to PSU.

Teaching and learning: (1) publish in TRAILS [submitted 9/28/11]; **published in November 2011**; (2) check out "Quick Fix" in *College Teaching* to see if appropriate for any of my ideas. (3) 420-neighborhoods submission to TRAILS **published in May 2012**. (4) IDEA FOR T&L MS; (4a) importance of formative assessment, not just summative assessment (Weimer, 2010).

accomplishments. An additional benefit of this method is that he can easily add his publications to his curriculum vitae (CV).

Besides a daily goal sheet, another way to track progress is to count words. When I am in the early stages of a manuscript, I count words. I set a goal of 500 words a day to just generate text. Figure 3.3 shows part of my daily word count chart. Figure 3.4 is the way Lynn, a colleague in applied linguistics, tracks the number of words she produces in a week over one quarter term. She adds the words she has written each day over a week with a different texture. In Sidebar 3.2 "Words written and edited: Winter 2015—Lynn Santelmann," Lynn describes the benefits she receives by simply counting words.

Figure 3.3 Counting words: Graph, Dannelle

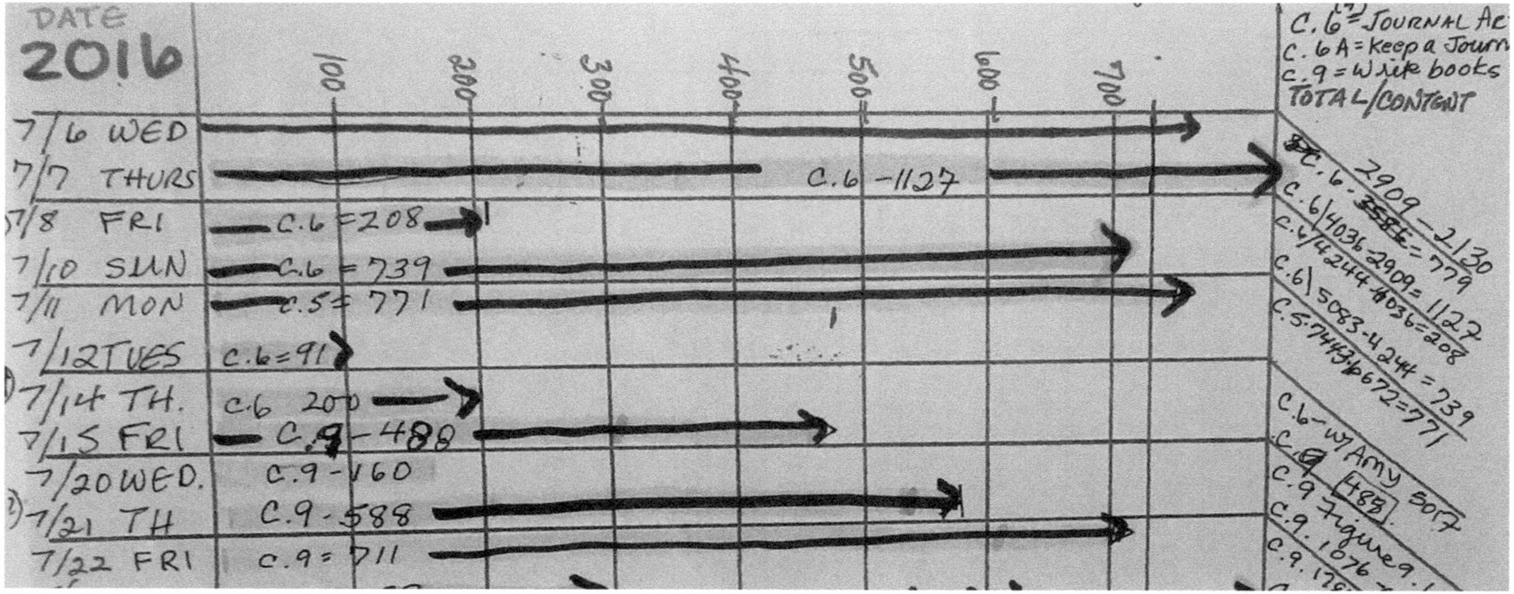

Figure 3.4 Words written and edited: Winter 2015, Lynn Santelmann

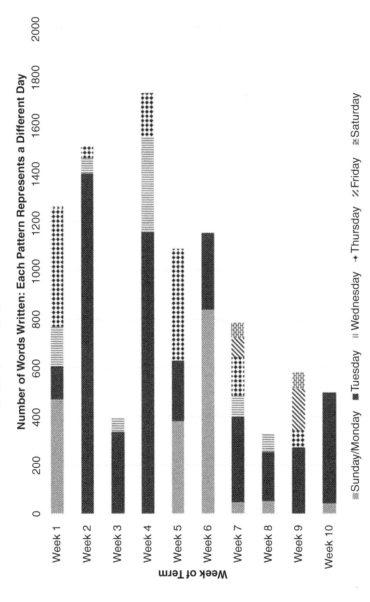

Sidebar 3.2 Words Written and Edited: Winter 2015: Lynn Santelmann

Planning out my writing times at the beginning of the term is essential. If I don't do that, my schedule fills up and then I no longer have time to write when I'm at my intellectual best.

Writing specific daily goals helps me the most in terms of goals—if I don't have both a goal for the term and daily goals, I put off writing because I don't have a good sense of where to start.

When I'm dealing with multiple projects, laying out goals for each day and labeling them for each project helps. So, I create a table that looks like this:

Day	Project	Goal	Completed?
Tuesday	Ripple effect	Write two paragraphs of results for writing plans	Yes
Tuesday	UG reading	Find and analyze pretests for new data	No

All these actions—listing, counting, and tracking progress—document your writing day by day. In the appendices you will find some blank charts for listing daily goals, charting, and counting words written each day. All these charts were made with the table feature in Microsoft Word. In the charts, I have found it is helpful to have the date as well as the day of the week. You can look back over a week to see which days you were most productive, as well as easily tell how long it has been since you worked on the manuscript. As an alternative, some faculty use Google Sheets to track and chart their progress.

In summary, after allocating time to writing on your calendar using the strategies in strategy set I, strategy set II includes several strategies to write meaningful goals, and then, by tracking your progress toward those goals by listing or counting, you are taking charge of your goals and identifying what you need to do. Try out one strategy and reflect on how it works for you. Most of us tend to think that writing should go faster than it does. Reflecting on your work in this systematic way, by listing, counting, and tracking, helps you to be more realistic and patient with yourself. In addition, you are accumulating some knowledge about how much time and effort it takes to accomplish complex writing tasks. By visualizing a specific goal and documenting its accomplishment, you can reward yourself. Pat yourself on the back and push on.

Derived from years of practice, strategy set III includes some little tricks with big payoffs in "buying" more writing time and spending less time looking for things.

Strategy Set III: Organize and Store Your Manuscripts

Lucky you, the conference paper you submitted six months ago was accepted! However, that was six months ago! Where is it? In which computer folder did you store it? You may have found yourself in this situation. If so, by attending to consistent organizational patterns suggested in strategy set III, you can avoid the stress of spending a lot of time looking for things.

Strategy set III consists of three action steps that help you reduce the stress of scrolling through your computer files, scratching your head, scanning Google Drive, and peering into all your devices to find a misplaced project. Organizational strategies are related closely to time management strategies. On one hand, when you are organized, it saves time. There is a trade-off, of course, as organizing takes some time, and you are not getting any writing done when you are organizing. On the other hand, if you spend no time on organization, you may waste a lot of time looking for things. If you spend 10 minutes a day searching for something for 7 days, you will have spent over an hour looking. In a month, you would have lost over 4 hours just trying to find something you need. Over a year, that's close to 7 working days! Here are several strategies designed to help you spend less time looking for things and more time writing.

Strategy 11: Organizing Files on the Computer: File Naming
The idea that you pay close attention to how you name your computer files may seem trivial. It is not. Using a consistent pattern for naming each file gives you more time to write rather than engage in a frustrating and sometimes fruitless search.

Every time you open a document to write on it, put a new date in the file name. This will keep the last document intact but allow you to write on a new one. Should something happen and you lose that day's work, such as your cat going to sleep on your computer delete key, you will still have the previous day's work.

Ch3BeStrategic9Jan2018dds.docx
Ch3BeStrategic12Jan2018dds.docx
Ch3BeStrategic15Jan2018dds.docx
Ch3BeStrategic16jan2018dds.docx

The previous list is part of the list of documents in my computer file for this chapter. It illustrates my file organization system for this book. Each time I open the same document to work on it, I save it with a new date within the file name. I do not depend on the date the computer gives it, because each time I open a document, the computer assigns it a new date whether I write on it or not. By the time I complete the final draft of a document, I will have stored a long list of versions. One great advantage of this system is that if I get interrupted or my computer crashes, all I will lose is the work from one day. I have all the previous files saved. For this book, as you can see, I have used the convention of chapter number, short title, date (day first, month, year; it does not always have to include the year, but the few times it was important, I was very glad I had the year in the file name).

If I am collaborating with someone, I use the same system, except I put my initials at the end. Then, because of the initials, I know that I was the last person to touch this document. If my collaborator or copy editor had worked on the draft, his or her initials would be added at the end. For Apple computer users, one advantage to having the initials at the end is that they are close to the file type like ".docx." The initials will not get lost in the middle of the file name when the computer shortens it.

Strategy 12: Storing Working Drafts: Options
You have several options for storing your drafts. If you are writing by yourself, you do not have to worry about sharing drafts with other authors. However, given we have so many options for computer storage, such as Google Drive, Dropbox, a flash drive, an external hard drive, the hard drive on your computer, or cloud-based storage such as iCloud, you do have to remember in which file system the document is stored. In addition, if you are coauthoring, you will need some consistent way to share drafts and keep track of which draft is which, who worked on it last, and where is it located.

Today, there are several storage options that have different advantages and disadvantages. I have listed them in Table 3.4 so that you can evaluate which one is suited to your needs. They include storing on your hard drive, on a flash drive, in Dropbox, or in Google Drive.

I do not necessarily recommend one over another because each has its own upsides and downsides.

Strategy 13: Creating a To-Do List at the Top of Your Paper
Another trick is to place a to-do list at the top of your manuscript when you are working on it. You could write it at the beginning or at the end of the writing session for the next time. By updating the to-do list each time you work on a manuscript, you will be immediately reminded of what you want to work on next and have much less start-up time. This is especially helpful if you have several projects going on at once. The to-do list also contains your specific daily goals for your next work session. It is also handy when you have several people collaborating on a paper. You can assign tasks this way to remind your collaborators what they are supposed to contribute when they open the paper. When you complete your part of the task, you can use the strikethrough feature to tell others that you have finished your part, as shown:

> TO DO:
> ~~Read the article itself: DDS & MMC~~
> Read about worldwide attrition: DDS & MMC
> Cite Peter Felton, 5 principles of good practice in SOTL: MMC
>   Describe use of Plus/Delta, CIQs, questionnaire—cycle of inquiry (SOTL)
> ~~Get data from Stefanie about # of applicants in 2012 cohort; time of completion between milestones=core; dissertation proposal, dissertation=past and with CI 2012 cohort: DDS~~
> Read "lack of progress": Ahearn and Manathunga: ~~DDS~~ & MMC

Organization in our writing life is critical to making the most efficient use of the time you have allotted to writing. I am sure you have developed some of your own strategies as well. The most important message is recognizing that time spent on being organized is a time-gainer not a time-waster.

TABLE 3.4

Advantages and disadvantages of different file storage systems

Storage option	Where it is stored	Ease of storage	Ease of sharing with others	Ease of retrieving	Ease of editing	Potential of losing	Connection to smartphones	Ease of writing together on the same document
Hard drive on computer	On computer itself, unless you have link to "cloud" or back-up on a server.	Click to save or save as.	Need to upload to e-mail or Google Drive and share.	Click "hard drive" and select.	Use editing program on Word program.	Possibility of losing with damage to computer or hard disk.	Not on smartphone.	Not possible.
Flash drive (thumb drive)	On physical device plugged into USB port.	Select external drive and move document into flash drive. Save is same as in hard drive.	Plug physical device into another computer.	Once plugged into USB port, retrieve with a click.	Once on computer becomes editable document.	Just don't lose this physical device.	Not possible to plug into a smartphone.	Not possible.
Dropbox	In the cloud, accessible when connected to Internet only.	From document on computer, select "Dropbox" for storage.	Files can easily be shared with colleagues.	Click document in Dropbox. You can nest files in folders. Create consistent labeling convention for folder names.	No editing in Dropbox. Once retrieved, download to edit.	Files are in the cloud. You will not lose if your computer crashes.	Dropbox can be an application on your phone.	Both share the document in Dropbox. Download, edit elsewhere.
Google Drive	In the cloud, accessible when connected to Internet only.	Files and documents are uploaded into Google Drive.	Very easy to share with others who have Google Drive. Tracks each person's contributions when collaborating	Very easy to view. You can nest files in folders. Create consistent labeling convention for folder names.	Very easy. Google Drive also tracks history of editing.	Files are in the cloud. You will not lose if your computer crashes.	Accessible on smartphone.	Best-selling point for Google Drive. Several can edit document at same time.

Conclusion

Principle three, "Be strategic to build a sustainable writing practice," as described in this chapter, offers three sets of strategies for how to escape the cycle of guilt and dread that so many academics experience about writing. By being more mindful and strategic, you are creating a supportive environment for yourself as a writer. From allocating more time for writing; to listing, counting, and tracking progress; to being more organized, you are creating a more sustainable writing practice as well. Through observing what you are doing now, reflecting on how you might want to change, and taking strategic action to meet your goals, you are also creating a new neural pathway that can be self-reinforcing. The more you consciously and intentionally practice new strategies, the more likely your writing practice will weave itself seamlessly into your daily activities. Yet, these changes take time. Besides your own commitment, another way to reinforce and sustain change in your writing practice is to work with others. In the next chapter, I present principle four, "Be social," which is another essential principle for success: how to work with others in a writing group.

CHAPTER 4

Be Social

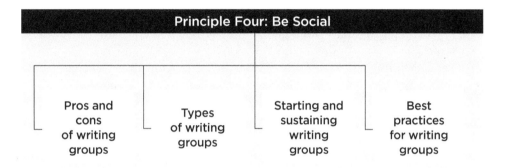

Principle Four: Be Social

| Pros and cons of writing groups | Types of writing groups | Starting and sustaining writing groups | Best practices for writing groups |

Academic conversations . . . take place over time, draw in people from different institutions, at different points in their academic careers. They move from individual to joint work, from private to public. Any one conversation won't affect all participants' work—but our endeavors are indelibly shaped by ongoing interaction among colleagues.

—A.S. Huff, 1999, p. 4

Academics belong to a community of teachers, thinkers, researchers, and writers. From our collaborative work on committees to face-to-face discussions with our peers, we share our ideas. In our writing, we get feedback, and engage in different types and levels of "conversation" as well. As Aitchison and Lee (2006) observed, "Despite enduring romantic notions of writing as a solitary pursuit (Grant & Knowles, 2000; Moore, 2003), writing in specific contexts always enters into a more or explicit network of social, institutional and peer relations—of readers, reviewers, teachers, examiners, editors, publishers" (pp. 271–272).

When our "conversations" are motivating, supportive, and informed, our thinking and writing soar (Boice, 1992; Devlin & Radloff, 2014; Faulconer, Atkinson, Griffith, Matusevich, & Swaggerty, 2010). Writing groups are one way to converse with colleagues about our work, about both the process of writing and the manuscript itself.

The previous chapter offered you a buffet of strategies to change your current writing habits and experiment with some new strategic approaches. You learned about the value of practice. This is not just any practice, but intentional, focused, and timely practice to break some old ways of doing things. Some of these changes involve closing your office door and focusing on your writing to create writing time. In contrast, in this chapter I suggest that strategically opening your office door and working with others accrues a considerable number of advantages on your path to increasing your productivity and lowering the stress that can be closely associated with writing (Faulconer et al., 2010). As a number of researchers over the years have found, working together in large and small writing groups reduces isolation, adds the element of accountability, and builds confidence (Boice, 1987; Devlin & Radloff, 2014; Lee & Boud, 2003; McGrail, Rickard, & Jones, 2006; Moore, 2003; Murray, 2012). When you are in a writing group, you are not alone or lonely as you craft your work.

Academic writing is often framed as an isolated, competitive, and individual activity (Aitchison & Lee, 2006; Roberts & Weston, 2014). Grant and Knowles (2000) suggest that "while the act of writing is most often performed in private (hence perhaps the unrealistic ideas about how others write), it may usefully be rethought as a social act" (p. 10).

Some faculty might wonder what it means to make their writing more social. Given all the levels of peer review for conference proposals, journal articles, and book proposals, other faculty might feel that academic writing is already quite social and public enough. For those who are skeptical about writing groups, reframing academic writing as more social may not allay their fears. Perhaps they worry that their uneven writing habits and lack of confidence will be exposed. Perhaps they worry that others might see how long it takes for them to craft a manuscript. All of this might become a source of embarrassment, or even shame, which could lead to exacerbating their guilt and anxiety. Thus, they cannot imagine themselves in a writing group.

You may ask, "Why not keep my office door closed and figure out how to improve my writing all by myself?" The answer is, if what you are doing now is not working as well as you would like, bravely go forth and try something else, such as joining a writing group. Change takes courage. Combine courage with a dash of curiosity and humor and, as Dr. Seuss says, "[Y]ou have brains in your head. You have feet in your shoes. You can steer yourself in any direction you choose" (Dr. Seuss, 1990, p. 2). In this chapter, I share ways that you can steer yourself toward gleaning the research-based impressive advantages of being in a writing group.

My experience setting up and participating in writing groups at PSU has cemented my own commitment to being in a writing group. Over the past five years in our PSU Jumpstart Writing Program, writing groups are a key feature. When faculty members join Jumpstart, they have the option to participate in a writing group. Then, by random selection, as facilitator, I assign them to a group of two to three other faculty members who are not in their department or discipline. After I identify a "lead" convener in the group, they go forth and meet. I give the newly formed group Figures 4.1a and 4.1b, the decision tree, so that they can use it to have a conversation about how they want their group to function.

Other than this initial assignment of members and giving each group the decision tree, I do no other additional monitoring of the groups. From informal feedback, I would say there are anywhere from 10 to 15 cross-disciplinary groups meeting each week. Most groups meet weekly for one hour. Some groups have figured out how to meet two hours every week, every term, and over several years. Most groups are cross-disciplinary and cross-rank. Some faculty form their own groups within their departments. Others form groups with their students. Some people engage with two or three groups in one week because they know that, for sure, they will get their writing time in. Some groups dissolve after one term because they cannot schedule a common time for the next term. Some dissolve because one member becomes an administrator with no time to write. Yet, these wonderful writing groups gather together to interact in a variety of ways—from traditional feedback to basic accountability, to write-on-site groups. In this chapter, I will tell you about the broad array of types for writing groups that includes those at PSU, as well as those described in the literature.

This chapter offers you several choices about how to work with others on your writing so that you can receive the tangible and intangible rewards each can offer. For all groups, I describe the steps for starting and sustaining a writing group and suggest the best practices for any type of writing group.

This chapter is divided into four sections. Each section covers a certain aspect of writing groups:

1. Pros and cons of writing groups
2. Types of writing groups
3. Starting and sustaining writing groups
4. Best practices for writing groups

Principle four: Be social. Because the foundation of academic writing is a "conversation," writing groups can be a haven for conversations about writing that reduce isolation and anxiety . . . and increase productivity.

Pros and Cons of Writing Groups

Even with all the good news about writing groups in the research literature (Devlin & Radloff, 2014; McGrail et al., 2006), they do come with their challenges. If you decide you want to be in a writing group, here is another time block that has to be scheduled during your busy week; and, by the way, it has to be coordinated with others who are also busy. In addition, deciding with whom to work has consequences. Being in a writing group with your department colleagues may be stressful because you don't want those who sit on promotion and tenure committees to know what questions and concerns you have about your own writing. Then again, working in cross-disciplinary groups may have its challenges because you worry that these colleagues may not understand your content and may not be able to give helpful feedback. Giving feedback to

Figure 4.1a Decision tree for writing groups: Part I

DECISION TREE FOR WRITING GROUPS: Part I

* Questions to discuss to set up your group.... *

WHO LEADS?
- ☐ FACILITATOR
- ☐ CONVENER
- ☐ ROTATING LEADERSHIP

HOW MANY PEOPLE?
- ☐ TWO
- ☐ THREE *optimal
- ☐ FOUR-FIVE
- ☐ MORE
- *easier to schedule

WHERE TO MEET?
- ☐ ON CAMPUS
  - ○ Office
  - ○ Meeting Room
  - ○ Library Room
  - ○ Coffee Shop
- ☐ OFF CAMPUS
  - ○ Coffee Shop
  - ○ Homes

WHEN TO MEET?

DURATION?
- ☐ ONE TERM
- ☐ ONE PROJECT
- ☐ ONE YEAR
- ☐ SUMMER

FREQUENCY?
- ☐ WEEKLY
- ☐ BI-WEEKLY
- ☐ MONTHLY

HOW LONG?
- ☐ 1 HOUR
- ☐ 2 HOURS
- ☐ 3+ HOURS

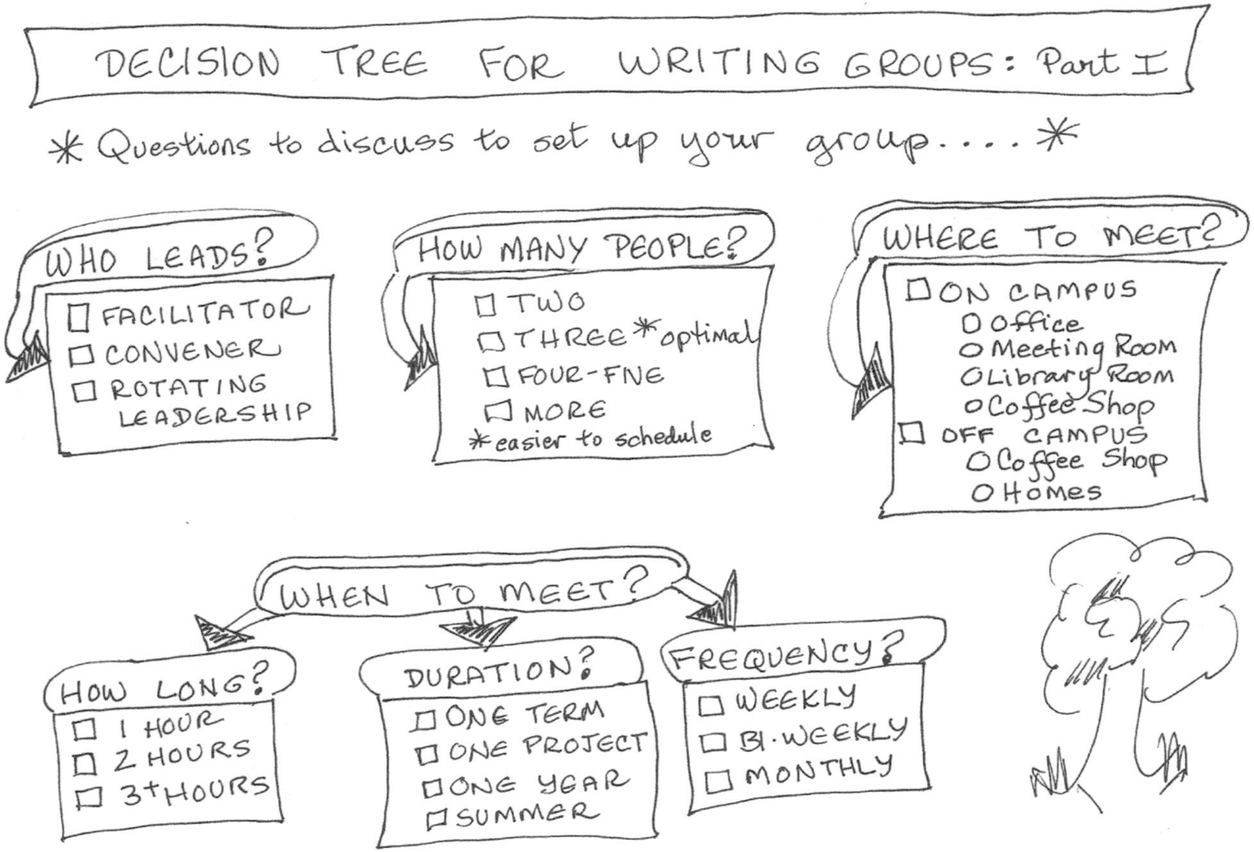

Figure 4.1b Decision tree for writing groups: Part II

DECISION TREE FOR WRITING GROUPS: Part II

* What kind of activities will your group do?

🐝 Remember to set aside time to build rapport! 🐝

WHAT IS THE TYPE OF GROUP YOU WANT?

☐ WRITE·ON·SITE?

☐ ACCOUNTABILITY?

☐ FEEDBACK: Traditional editing groups?

HOW WILL THE GROUP MAINTAIN MOMENTUM?

☐ SHARED ACCOUNTABILITY? (Chapter 4)

☐ REFLECTIVE WRITING PROMPTS? (Chapter 6)

☐ REWARDS FOR PROGRESS? (Chapter 4)

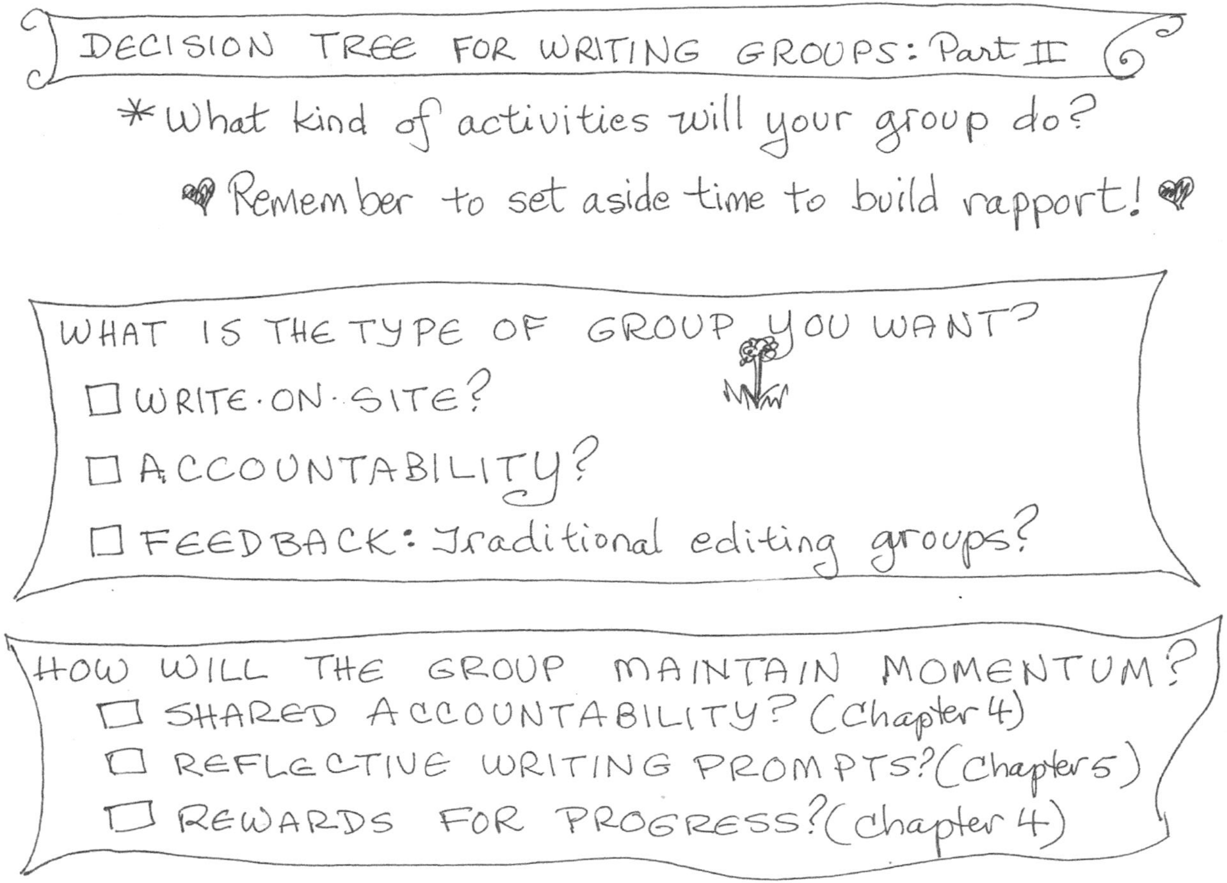

another writer can be stressful as you seek to be honest and respectful but not demoti-vating. And, getting feedback may make you feel nervous and vulnerable. You may ask, "Given all these issues, why join a writing group?" Understanding the advantages and disadvantages of writing groups will help you make an informed decision.

Not all writing groups are the same. You can choose one to meet your needs. Many people assume that a writing group is a feedback group where each person submits work and gets feedback from others. Yet, a writing group can be just a group of faculty who write together in the same room, a write-on-site group, like parallel play, if you will. A writing group can be a group of colleagues who went through graduate school together and meet virtually once a week to check in. Or, it can be a specialized group working on one paper or project together. I just formed a small writing group with a colleague for writing an Institutional Review Board (IRB) proposal. I was having trouble getting traction on getting the IRB done, and she had never written one. I can teach her about the submission process, and I can get my IRB done at the same time. This was a short-term, focused writing group. We talked, and then each wrote on our proposal over two time blocks.

For some, writing groups have left a bad taste, leading to a great reluctance to join one. A newly hired faculty member told me that her department started a writing group with senior and new faculty. While the senior faculty member read her work, the new faculty member did not have much work to read. She felt embarrassed, and gradually dropped out. As suggested in principle one, chapter 1, past negative experiences can affect how you approach writing now.

Selecting what kind of writing group you want offers a modicum of control over how far you open your metaphorical office door, as well as how long you keep it open. With more knowledge about the variety and outcomes of different kinds of writing groups derived from this chapter, you can find a way of being social, that is, entering the academic conversation with others, while creating healthy boundaries where you feel safe.

Despite the potential disadvantages associated with writing groups, research lauds their short- and long-term advantages. In an experimental setting, Boice (1987) noted that, after setting goals, belonging to a writing group that meets regularly can significantly increase productivity. Boice's foundational research is echoed by Lee and Boud (2003), Moore (2003), Roberts and Weston (2014), and Devlin and Radloff (2014).

Another advantage of writing groups is that you reduce your isolation. You join a community of writers sharing best strategies and offering suggestions to those who are stuck (Roberts & Weston, 2014). Moreover, research indicates,

> People writing as part of a community of writers are more likely to learn faster about the conventions and challenges of writing, to support each other at times of block-age and to demystify the process of writing by sharing each other's successes and failures. This approach challenges many of the cultural and competitive conventions of academic life. (Moore, 2003, p. 334)

As Moore (2003) notes, by being in a writing group, you are challenging the conventional notions of the independent scholar grinding out brilliant contributions in isolation.

Finally, academic writing involves many skill sets. In traditional writing feedback groups, when members share their individual work, writers can learn about the rhetorical moves that other group members use in their manuscripts. Some members may be more skilled at writing abstracts. Others may impart their greater experience writing qualitative results. Still others may be adept at creating tables and figures. We each bring a different set of skills and experiences to the group discussion about our writing practices.

As Aitchison and Lee (2006) note, "[W]riting groups are self determining; that is, research writing groups are, on the whole, explicitly negotiated, self-directed, evolving and dynamic and inherently responsive to group agendas and articulated needs" (p. 271). Working together in a writing group takes many forms. There is not just one way to do it.

Types of Writing Groups

Knowing what kind of writing groups are possible helps you be informed before you make a commitment (Haas, 2014). Writing groups vary by their purpose, participants, activities, and time commitment. Finding and choosing the right writing group may take some time. You may have to create one yourself with your peers or you may find one that others have created. While I discuss six different formats for writing groups (see Table 4.1 for a summary of purposes, participants, activities, and time commitments across these writing groups), this list is not exhaustive.

1. Traditional feedback groups
2. Accountability writing groups, including online writing clubs
3. Write-on-site groups
4. Writing retreats
5. Pop-up writing groups
6. Writing workshops: short and long term

I hope this section will get you started in thinking about what kind of writing group might suit your needs.

Traditional Feedback Groups

The purpose of a *feedback group* is to get feedback on your writing as well as to give feedback to other group members. The feedback gives you an opportunity to get peer review before you send a paper off for publication. In addition, members get practice at giving feedback to others and refining their skills to assist other writers.

TABLE 4.1
Types of writing groups

Type	Purpose	Participants	Activities	Time commitment
Traditional feedback groups	To get and give feedback on writing from peers.	Limit size to three to five people.	Model 1: Each participant presents short piece each week in limited time for reading aloud and feedback. Model 2: Rotating among participants with one per week.	Once a week for an hour or two. For reading, the work is done during group time.
Accountability writing groups, including online writing clubs	Public accountability to accomplish self-selected goals.	Can be larger than traditional feedback groups. But, may be difficult to schedule common time, if too large.	Write out goals for the next week in a common folder or online. Check in every week to see if goals were accomplished.	Once a week for an hour or two.
Write-on-site groups	To write for a block of time with others in one space.	Can be larger than other groups because there is no sharing of goals or getting feedback.	Write in the same space together. Practice not letting yourself be interrupted by e-mail, etc.	Once a week for an hour or two.
Writing retreats	To spend a day or several days writing in a remote location.	Depends on the size of the facility used for the retreat.	Focus on writing over a full day or several days. Food and coffee provided. No distractions.	One full day or even up to five days.
Pop-up writing groups	To accomplish a specific shared writing task with others.	Depends on the task that needs to be done.	Build rapport, set goals, complete specific tasks with collaborators.	Varies.
Writing workshops: Short and long term	To tap expertise on campus or from elsewhere to build skills in academic writing.	Usually 10 to 45 people attend; size depends on the content and instructor preferences.	Activities will vary depending on the instructor and content.	One morning workshop or full day, or once a week over a term.

The composition of the group can vary. Some feedback groups are limited to faculty from the same discipline, the advantage being that they are all familiar with the technical terms in the discipline. Other groups mix disciplines, which demands that writers have to be crystal clear about their ideas and express them clearly enough for a novice in the field to understand.

The size of the group has to be limited because it takes time to discuss each other's writing. I suggest three to five members. At PSU, we limited our feedback groups to 3 members so that each week everyone could get 20 minutes of "air time" at each hourlong meeting. Participants brought in three pages of their writing, and during the 20 minutes set aside for that writer, the group read the piece and provided feedback. One person also took on the role of time-keeper so that everyone received equal feedback. Even though limited to only 3 pages, faculty have commented on the usefulness of the feedback for the rest of the manuscript.

Other groups focus on only one writer during the hourlong meeting. Each week the writer changes, so that the group cycles through the writers over a three- to five-week time frame, depending how many writers are in the group. Groups larger than five can be demotivating for members because of the lapse of time between individual feedback sessions. Yet, for some writers, this model works well because they have plenty of time to apply the copious feedback given after one hour of review.

Feedback can leave us feeling buoyant and encouraged or deflated and discouraged about our writing. All writers experience some apprehension about getting feedback on their writing, even to the level of anxiety (Cameron et al., 2009; Devlin & Radloff, 2014). Feedback can heighten those feelings. The writer is putting her ideas and self out there for scrutiny and critique. Pile on top of that the emotions surrounding writing, the potential for unhelpful, even hurtful, feedback, and that can destroy confidence! However, quality feedback facilitates communication and shows the writer more about capturing audience attention. After all, the writing group is an audience. Box 4.1 provides some guidance for giving constructive feedback that addresses the writer's concerns. What are some of the specific advantages and disadvantages of feedback groups?

Advantage: Using model 1 of a feedback group where everyone shares each week, the expectation of writing three pages a week can push you to keep on writing each week, even if you don't feel ready. Writing before you feel ready can cement the idea that you can produce something, and you can get some benefit from sharing it, even in its infancy, or what I refer to as a "sloppy copy." Meeting the expectation to produce three pages a week militates against your perfectionist. You cannot procrastinate. You just have to write. Often your fears are unfounded because the writing group can spot some gems in your writing that you just did not see. If the writing group adopts the cycle of giving feedback to only one writer each week, model 2, the advantage is focused attention to your work with copious feedback.

Disadvantage: The fact that faculty may have varied skills in giving feedback on writing is one of the challenges of feedback groups. I am sure you want to give feedback that is constructively received. Some of you have received blind

BOX 4.1
A variety of ways to give and get constructive feedback on writing

Academic writing is a "conversation" at many different levels. One level is the conversation the author has with the reader. As an author, of course, we want our work to be read. Getting feedback early on from readers can lead to our work being more widely read. Yet, feedback can be motivating or discouraging. To avoid some of the dangers of inappropriate and enervating feedback, I offer some starting points for giving and getting feedback on writing. Items I, II, III, and IV are different ways to approach feedback.

I. **Three basic qualities to look for when reading or hearing text**: The author may ask: "What parts of the text were . . . ?"

   Velcro ideas: As a reader, what ideas from the text stuck in your head? What words or even sentences seemed to be memorable? Interesting? Important?
   Confusing: As a reader, what parts seemed unclear to you?
   Needing elaboration: As a reader, what did you want to hear more about?

II. **Author requests**: One way to manage feedback is for the author to ask the group to read for something specific as he or she is reading. This helps the group focus their attention on the issues the author considers the most important.

   The author could say: "As you are reading, please look for places where my writing . . .

   is not clear,
   is confusing,
   is too technical,
   does not persuade you that the topic is important,
   belabors the point, or
   works well and makes a clear point."

   For example, I had someone read a draft of a chapter I was writing, and I asked the person to give me feedback on the parts where I might have sounded "preachy."

III. **Early draft questions** (adapted from Goodson, 2017, p. 84). At this early stage, most authors are looking for the viability of the basic ideas presented in the paper. The author first tells the readers about the intended audience, then either reads the text aloud slowly or lets the group read it to themselves, and finally asks questions, such as the following:

   1. What do you think of the idea?
   2. Can you tell who the audience is? Will it work for the audience I have in mind?

(*Continues*)

BOX 4.1 (*Continued*)

3. What am I missing? Any suggestions for readings or other ideas?
4. In what ways can I improve the introduction? What other approach might I take? Do I need a better argument?
5. What about the methods? The results? The conclusion/discussion?
6. What sticks in your mind after reading this? What jumps out at you in need of improvement?
7. What should I really keep in the manuscript?

IV. **Middle draft questions** (adapted from Goodson, 2017, p. 86). At this stage of writing the paper, most authors have the basic thesis in place and the structure of the piece is clear. What authors might need from the audience is feedback on the high points, the ideas that seem most important to the reader. Also, at this stage, the author needs to know how the transitions work between sections so that the piece is cohesive. The questions that follow focus on smooth transitions and the clarity of individual sentences:

1. What did you learn from reading this piece?
2. What impressed you the most?
3. Could you tell who the audience was? How interested will the audience be in this topic?
4. Are there places where you stumble? Sentences you read more than once to grasp the idea?
5. Does the text flow coherently? Do I need better transitions between sections?
6. Can you think of something (author, citation, transition sentences) I am missing?

reviews from journal reviewers that were devastating. Receiving and giving feedback are skills that often need to be developed. When PSU faculty members form editorial feedback groups, they spend several meetings establishing rapport and building relationships before they start the feedback meetings. This practice makes the group a safer environment for feedback.

Accountability Writing Groups, Including Online Writing Clubs

The purpose of an accountability group is to increase productivity by sharing, discussing, and being accountable for accomplishing writing goals. In both a face-to-face and an online accountability group such as AcademicLadder.com, writers begin by writing down goals for a set period of time, usually for a week. In addition, AcademicLadder.com has a writing club. You can select to be involved for four weeks

($115) or longer. You check in weekly, join group chats with a coach, and receive some content on topics such as increasing your productivity through better planning. Whether you choose to work with an online organization that provides this service or build a group on your own campus, group members make a public declaration of goals for a time period and hold themselves accountable for accomplishing those goals. The accountability comes in the reporting at the next meeting about whether or not each group member has met his or her stated goals.

The composition of an accountability group is less critical than in traditional feedback groups where group members might want to share writing with disciplinary peers. Accountability groups can be larger than feedback groups because group members are not sharing their writing and seeking feedback; they are only sharing their goals and accomplishments. The only constraint on group size is finding a common meeting time for face-to-face groups: the larger the group, the more difficult to find a common meeting time. Generally, at PSU, we keep our groups at three to four people. Over the years we have found that groups of five or more don't seem to be able to meet regularly and consistently.

In accountability groups, it is best to not only state out loud but also write down weekly goals. The recording of the goals can be in a common folder where everyone writes their own goals for the week, or online where others can see the goal. Many are motivated by telling others they are going to accomplish something. Groups can also offer support to writers in terms of advice and encouragement.

As one of the members of the PSU Jumpstart Writing Program said, "[Public accountability] has a psychological effect that works for me in part because I am naturally a 'people pleaser' and I try to honor my commitments." Another reported, "I've also learned that I *need* a community of writers that keep me encouraged and moving forward in my writing. It makes the process less lonely for me." Envisioning writing goals that are doable over a week also takes practice. As noted in chapter 3, writing goals and the tasks that are associated with those goals is another skill set associated with writing. Finally, others can offer support and strategies about how you can accomplish your goals. For example, Sarah, Naomi, and Jake have been in the same writing accountability group for two years. When Sarah wrote her goal for the following week, Naomi asked, "Sarah, are you sure you can accomplish that writing goal this week? Isn't your daughter coming into town? Maybe just pare it down to one small, more doable goal?"

> Advantage: By sharing writing goals with others, you get better at setting doable, reasonable goals and defining the tasks associated with them. The group becomes a support group for meeting self-imposed expectations. Group members also learn how others manage to meet their goals. You learn more about the goal-setting process.
>
> Disadvantage: Public accountability for accomplishing goals is important, but you may find that accountability is not enough to keep you motivated. It takes group time to write down and discuss goals. You may just rather be writing.

Write-on-Site Groups

These groups share one purpose: writing at the same time with others in the same space. This resembles the "coffee shop phenomenon" where people take their computer to a coffee shop with free Internet access and work away at their separate tasks, benefiting by being in the same room with others, even strangers. In faculty writing groups, each member brings his or her computer or other materials, spends an hour or more together, and just writes. Some people do this in a coffee shop; others find space in the library, department meeting rooms, or even someone's home. The goal is to focus on writing for a set time period. No e-mail. No texting. No talking. Just writing. Some faculty members combine this with the goal-setting and accountability activity. However, for many groups, write on site is quite enough. Adding accountability to write on site reduces the time for writing but may increase writers' commitment and motivation.

> Advantage: If your week is a mess with far too many meetings, too much class preparation, and too many letters of recommendation to be written, then, by participating in a write-on-site group, you have at least carved out an hour for writing. You have the combined energy of others in the room. You can practice how to not get distracted by e-mail or other tasks. Others will be pleased that you showed up, and there is a sense of shared struggle and support. Just writing on-site can reset your motivation.
>
> Disadvantage: Initially, you may be skeptical that this could work. You will not learn about setting goals. You will get no feedback on your work. To get the most out of this approach, consider combining it with other writing group methods to foster development of other skills such as writing goals, and doing free-writes. However, for many faculty, just showing up every week at a set time and writing with others is quite energizing.

Writing Retreats

Writing retreats accomplish one purpose: a time commitment to writing over a day or several days. Retreats support patterns of productivity (Moore, 2003), improve well-being, and increase motivation to write (Grant, 2006; MacLeod et al., 2012). An individual can create his or her own writing retreat by getting away for a weekend or longer. Yet, more and more institutions are offering a day- or weeklong option for faculty. Usually writing retreats are off campus or at a remote location on campus. By moving the event to an unfamiliar location, faculty members feel a sense of mission and commitment away from the daily routine and its demands (Murray & Newton, 2009). The institution might provide food, a quiet space, and extension cords so that writers can easily keep their computer charged up. Some retreats combine feedback and coaching from an outside expert.

Our daily and weeklong writing retreats at PSU are at a remote location on campus. On the first day of the weeklong retreat, we assign faculty buddies. Each person writes down his or her goal for the next day and then discusses his or her success in accomplishing that goal with the buddy at noon on the next day. We also offer one-hour mini-lessons on academic writing for those who choose to participate.

> Advantage: When you are working quietly in a room with other faculty for an extended time, you may feel a sense of shared energy. Writing retreats also offer the opportunity to connect with other writers across campus who have a common commitment to writing. MacLeod and colleagues (2012) found a boost in confidence from those attending a five-day retreat. Participants in Grant and Knowles's (2000) retreats noted that they began to see themselves as writers when many unconscious forces in their lives told them otherwise.
>
> Disadvantage: With all the demands on your time, a daily or five-day retreat is admittedly a serious chunk of time. For those who tend toward binge writing, the retreat format can reinforce notions that the best writing gets done in large chunks of time. To counter the possible reinforcement of binge writing from attending a retreat, I suggest combining retreats with a weekly writing group and putting small blocks of writing time on the calendar every week before you attend a retreat.

Pop-up Writing Groups

Pop-up writing groups have a very specific purpose; that is, accomplish a short-term task. Many of you may not think of this as a real writing group. When I am collaborating with a peer on a conference proposal, that is a writing group. When I work with others on a grant, that is another kind of pop-up (or short-term) writing group. Many of the skills we have been discussing can be used to good effect in these groups: setting goals, sharing expertise, and giving and receiving feedback.

> Advantage: You can accomplish a particular task through a concentrated effort in these short-term writing groups. Successful pop-up groups can lead to making more writing friends on campus and can grow into more formal groups, such as accountability groups or feedback groups.
>
> Disadvantage: Pop-up groups can derail a larger project for which you need momentum. Because you might have several writing projects you are working on in your own research area, getting involved in another writing project with others in a related but different area may take time and energy away from your original work.

Writing Workshops: Short and Long Term

Professional development writing workshops are a focused opportunity to hear from experts while working with others to learn more about academic writing and the components that undergird its success. Some campuses have writing experts who can run workshops from the writing center, the Office of Teaching and Learning, or the English department, whereas other campuses may have the funds to bring in outside experts. Some campuses also offer a series of workshops on one topic, such as writing and publishing about your teaching.

Although most would not think of a writing workshop as a writing group, if you reframe it as a large, onetime writing group, you can see its potential. When I start a workshop, I congratulate the participants for choosing to attend. After all, these faculty participants have made a time commitment to focus on their writing and develop the skills surrounding their writing. They are building their knowledge base about writing and learning from their peers as well. As Roberts and Weston (2014) note, "The experience of attending workshops had a surprising effect on rapidly establishing a sense of collegiality amongst our novice writers and in moving participants towards their writing goals" (p. 710). Participants can quickly see that they are not alone in the pursuit of writing improvement and can perhaps find others with whom they can collaborate after the workshop.

> Advantage: Workshops are a place to learn new writing strategies as well as reflect on current practices. In addition, when attending a writing workshop, you may look around the room at the other workshop participants and appreciate that you are not alone in facing the challenges of academic writing. You may find some colleagues with whom you can collaborate in the future. Depending on how the presenter structures the workshop, you may be able to start working on a current writing project. When I conduct a workshop, I always make sure the faculty leave with several strategies that they implement immediately after the workshop.
>
> Disadvantage: Attending a workshop is a time commitment. The workshop can generate excitement, but, without follow-up, you can easily fall back into old patterns.

In summary, writing groups come in a variety of forms and meet a variety of needs. Several faculty at PSU like the writing groups so much that they have created more than one. Maude Hines, in the English department, has three hourlong writing groups during the week. Two are accountability groups with different colleagues; one is a small feedback group. She found that the groups keep her writing regularly.

Starting and Sustaining Writing Groups

Once you have decided it is worthwhile to participate in a writing group, it is worth taking a bit of time to reflect on the decisions needed to start, set up, and sustain your group. Figures 4.1a and 4.1b, the decision trees, presented earlier in the chapter, are check sheets with a number of questions about the nitty-gritty of starting a writing group. Faculty have found that the conversation that follows the completion of the decision tree helps them sort out some of their individual expectations for joining a writing group. Five key questions need to be addressed when forming a group: Who leads? How large is the group? Where will you meet? When will you meet? What will you do at the meeting?

Who Leads?

One of the initial questions when starting a group is who will "lead" the group. To launch a writing group, someone will need to take the lead; that is, bring up the topic at lunch with colleagues, distribute a broadcast statement to the department or college, or write an e-mail invitation. The lead or convener collects the names and the e-mails and, when he or she has the volunteers, works with the group to set the date and time for the first meeting.

At the first meeting, the members need to think about the leader. The most important part in the early stage of group formation is this conversation about leadership. Each person needs to evaluate what role he or she wants to play in the group. What kind of leader does the group want? Individuals might ask who is going to be the "chief worrier" for the group—someone who makes sure scheduling and logistics are in place. This person is also the chief "warrior"—battling all the distractions that might interfere with attendance at the group meeting. The leader could be the convener for the first meeting and take on the task of e-mailing to schedule subsequent meetings. Some groups have found that rotating leadership works. Other groups prefer to be leaderless. They collectively set the meeting times for the whole term or semester and meet and get to the task at hand: sharing goals, writing-on-site, or giving/getting writing feedback. The leader could take the role of being more of a facilitator, that is, keeping the writing goals folder, suggesting writing prompts, and prompting conversation about writing strategies. In Figure 4.1b, check out the box at the bottom on how to maintain momentum. The facilitator could take charge of managing these activities. A member of a writing group may have very good reasons for not wanting to take a leadership role. She may be slammed this term with several committees, two new courses, and a conference proposal to submit. This person would just as soon have someone else send out the e-mail reminders and carry the group writing goals folder to the meeting every week.

How Large Is the Group?

This seems like a no-brainer—find the people who are interested and get them together—but the number of people involved in a writing group is another important decision to make. There are three factors to think about when you consider size: scheduling, group activities, and the importance of regular attendance. First, as previously noted, scheduling is a challenge, especially if the groups are interdisciplinary, because departments have different meeting schedules. Groups larger than four find it extremely difficult to schedule a common meeting time every week. Second, the size will depend on the kind of activities in which the group engages. Bear in mind that if a writing feedback group will need to have "air time" for each faculty participant, in that case, six people are too many. Again, three to four people seem optimal in a writing feedback group. However, if it is a write-on-site group or accountability group, the group may be larger. The third factor to consider is the importance of regular attendance. Members need to ask themselves, "How high do I place this writing group on my priority list?" Regular attendance indicates commitment and shared interest in each other's success. Whatever happens, groups should establish that each member has strong commitment to regular attendance.

Where Will You Meet?

Again, this decision seems trivial; yet, location can affect people's ability to be regular participants. A frank discussion will be very helpful. When we have so much on our plate, consistency of location is important. PSU faculty writing groups meet in a variety of locations: a faculty office (although most of ours are too small these days), a library conference room, department meeting rooms, or a local coffee shop. Some find an off-campus location is suitable. Wherever the group meets, consistency of location and accessibility are important.

When Will You Meet?

Several factors come into play when the group considers when to meet: How long are the meetings, what is the duration of the group, and how frequently will the group meet? Typically, groups meet for one hour. Yet, one PSU write-on-site group met for two hours a week and found it quite successful. What are the group members thinking about for the duration of the group: one term, one specific project, or even the year? To what length of time can the members commit? Some members might be dipping their toes into the river of writing groups and are willing to commit for just one semester. That is just fine. Others have experience and want to commit for the year. The third area for decision-making is the frequency of the meetings. Some are quite happy to meet every week; others want to meet biweekly, whereas some prefer once a month. Once a week seems to keep the writing momentum of the group at a high level. If a member is at a conference, he or she could even Skype into the meeting.

What Will You Do at the Meeting?

What will happen at the meeting is probably the most important decision that the group will make.

How Will You Build Relationships?

Even if you are a group of colleagues who have known each other for several years, take some time to talk about writing. More than likely writing has not been a hot topic of discussion at the watercooler or the copier. Discuss your experiences with academic writing—successes and challenges. Also, talk about your goals for the group and your vision for your writing during the time you will be meeting. Particularly if the group is a feedback group, share your experiences with getting and giving feedback.

What Kind of Writing Group?

Accountability, writing feedback, write on site, or other type of group? Use the descriptions of the groups provided earlier in the chapter and in Table 4.1 to assess what kind of group you and your colleagues want. See Figures 4.1a and 4.1b for a to-do list for setting up each type of group. I would like to emphasize, especially for the writing feedback groups, the importance of setting some guidelines and ground rules, especially around the topic of feedback.

How Can the Group Activities Foster Momentum?
By writing your goals in a shared document each week, you are fostering momentum. The shared document can be as simple as a file folder with a blank chart for writing down goals. One group member is responsible for bringing the folder to the regular meeting. Because it is easy to lose the folder in a stack of folders, I give the groups at PSU their own folders and make sure the folder is colorful.

The online chart of progress in Table 4.2 is an example of another shared goals document. This online form is from a faculty writing group who started face-to-face when they were in graduate school and who now find themselves on four different campuses. They have had a meeting with Google Hangout every Friday at 3:00 p.m. for five years to review the chart and each other's writing progress. You can see from the chart that they are interested in specific goals for the week as well as in "seat time," projecting how much time they will spend accomplishing that goal this week. Also included is a column for a short reflection where they can write about what worked and what didn't in accomplishing their weekly goals. Online they can see each other's charts and offer support and inspiration for each other. I like the reflection column because that is where the writer can assess the type of activities in which he or she engaged and how they worked in meeting his or her goals.

This chart can be kept in Google Drive as a Google Sheet or Google Doc, allowing easy access for everyone. Even though you can create a writing chart using the table function in Microsoft Word or Excel, you would have to share the file via e-mail. An alternative is to share a Microsoft file through Dropbox to give everyone access.

Review and Reward Progress
The loneliness of this work can be daunting. Even when good things happen, your non–writing group colleagues and department colleagues may not celebrate with you because of lack of knowledge, neglect, or just plain jealousy. Having members in your writing group celebrate your accomplishments can be a positive force for you and the whole group as well!

Business research shows that groups can go through several stages as they become cohesive and committed (Tuckman, 1965). After you invest the initial energy to get a group going and establish norms, it's very common for groups to experience a bit of a "stormy" period or go through some internal tension as members confront the lived

TABLE 4.2
Online chart of writing progress

Week	Goals this week	Projected writing time	Actual writing time	Percent of completion	Reflection

reality and expectations of the group. Members may realize that they need to make adjustments to the rules of the group for the process of using a writing group to work for them. Building rapport during the first and even second meeting will establish an open and safe environment for members to air their concerns. Once those adjustments have been made, called *norming* by Tuckman (1965), the group often then will proceed and run quite smoothly for an extended period of time. The bottom line is that the group is either writing, learning about writing, or learning about how other faculty approach writing. Writing groups help faculty realize that they are not alone in their struggles to find the time, as well as the motivation, to write and that this knowledge in itself can be encouraging.

Best Practices for Writing Groups

What is a best practice? Gleaned from the research literature and my years of experience with writing groups, I identify practices that groups need to consider no matter what kind of group is formed. Best practices will give you a foundation for what needs to happen to have a successful writing group.

Figure 4.2 presents best practices for writing groups under five main themes. First, writing groups need organization and consistency. Second, writing groups should not ignore fundamental communication and relationship-building among the members. Third, writing group members should try to generate a common vision and share their accomplishments. Fourth, each member of a writing group is personally responsible for fostering positive ongoing interactions that meet member goals and contribute to constructive interactions among the members. Fifth, writing groups should celebrate accomplishments. Let us look at each of these in turn.

Figure 4.2 Best practices for writing groups

Be Organized and Consistent

One important role in a writing group is that of a "leader." I call this "the lead" instead of the leader for two reasons. First, many faculty don't have time to take on what they feel is the very full responsibility of being a leader. Second, faculty may feel that they don't know enough about academic writing to be able to "lead" a writing group. The lead can be the instigator for the group, but the group members themselves need to decide how to handle the jobs associated with this key role: making announcements, setting the schedule, and running the group. Leadership is associated with the decision-making the group has to do. The elements in the decision tree highlight many of the key decisions a group has to make to function well.

Build Personal and Professional Relationships

Build trust, lay out ground rules, and establish positive communication using active listening strategies. As mentioned earlier, it helps to spend at least one session building trust and having a conversation around the ground rules. Using the decision tree in Figures 4.1a and b can foster a more focused conversation. These conversations lead to rapport-building with a shared sense of mission for each member in meeting his or her individual writing goals.

Develop Shared Vision

With decisions made about leadership and the establishment of positive relationships, the group can focus on being goal oriented for the group members and for the group itself. Pay attention to time limits so that members feel that the time is not wasted or overextended. In addition, seek to be consistent about expectations for accountability.

Celebrate Accomplishments

Devising ways to reward progress encourages more progress. What are some rewards that individuals have used? Some faculty say they spend some time at a local bookstore. Others give themselves permission to buy a special pair of shoes. Some may go for a walk in the woods. Others browse an antiques mall (my favorite). Rewards are things that members like to do but often don't because they are too busy. Yet, if members reframe them as rewards for meeting writing goals, these can be seen as more enjoyable. For groups, the reward might be a box of candy at a meeting, a meal, or happy hour at a local restaurant.

Foster Positive Interactions

Be supportive. Check in on ground rules. Offer constructive feedback. Initial excitement for the group may waver as time passes. The group may wander away from the ground rules established early on. By being supportive of and respectful to each other, the group works well. It is not a bad idea to check in on the initial ground rules about midway through the term. For feedback groups, talk about how the process of giving and receiving feedback on goals or on writing is working. Some members may need encouragement in commenting on how the group is working for them.

Conclusion

The essence of principle four is be social. Because the research on the advantages of writing groups is so compelling (Devlin & Radloff, 2014; Lee & Boud, 2003; McGrail et al., 2006; Moore, 2003; Murray, 2012) and my own experience in coordinating and participating in writing groups has been so positive, principle four sets forth the idea that it is worthwhile to make writing groups an addition to your repertoire of writing strategies. From feedback to accountability, to pop-up groups to writing retreats and workshops, when faculty meet and talk about their writing, they reduce isolation and improve their craft. As a consequence, over time, faculty become more productive and less stressed because they are accomplishing their goals. In addition, they become part of a community of writers. Moore (2003) aptly summarizes the benefits of writing groups:

> [A]cademic writing needs to be reframed. Instead of a solitary, isolated, solely competitive activity, it is more useful to approach it as a community-based, collaborative, social act. The benefits of viewing writing through such a lens are based on the same principles that have been found to prevail in research on collaborative and cooperative learning (see, for example, Cohen, 1986; Kagan, 1988; Slavin, 1996). (p. 334)

As I was finishing this chapter, Christina Gildersleeve-Neumann from PSU's speech and hearing sciences department sent me an unsolicited e-mail that summarizes the value and results of her work with other faculty in a writing group:

> I just wanted to let you know that my coauthor and I just submitted our textbook! It has been two years in the making but it is now with the copy-editor. I could barely say hi when I saw you Tuesday because that was my last day before the midnight deadline—I think I would have started crying right then and there if I'd said anything!
>
> 576 pages, 230 figures, 39 tables. But who's counting? :)
>
> Thank you so much for all you do, for having writing groups and retreats and for supporting us in our writing journey. Writing is so hard, but so fun, and having your support, Janelle's support, and our groups to cheer us on is the only reason this thing is done!

Explore Creative Elements in Academic Writing

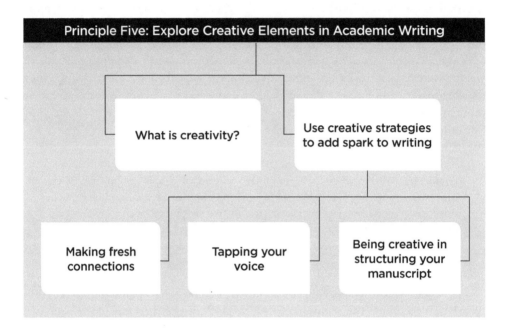

What does creativity have to do with academic writing? Some people might view academic writing as merely "writing up" their research or transferring their finished thinking from the brain to the page. However, developing your material for an audience and getting it to the page demands reflection, analysis, synthesis, and a dash of risk-taking—the underpinnings of creative thinking.

For many of us, being an academic means adhering to the conventions of our discipline. Terms such as *rigor*, *scientific*, *systematic investigation*, and *objectivity* loom large in our consciousness. To have legitimacy, we may feel that our work needs to be seen as a "straightforward, intellectually-driven and logically-ordered process" (Antoniou & Moriarty, 2008, p. 159). To be published and respected, we may feel that we must take care not to violate the methods and procedures established in our disciplines. If we violate those often hard-edged descriptions of valued academic work, we fear we may hear from our reviewers terms such as *sloppy*, *inconsistent*, and *subjective*. Will engaging in creative thinking lead us down the path to subjectivity and unpublishable work?

Antoniou and Moriarty (2008) argue that, beginning with problem identifica-tion, hypothesis creation, and data selection, academic research and writing are crea-tive acts. They continue, "[L]ittle attention has been paid to the more holistic aspects, such as the lecturer-writer's sense of self and identity, their emotional orientation to their writing and their creative process" (p. 159). Further, they argue that the con-sequences of not paying attention to the self, emotions, and creative influences that thread through work are significant:

> [M]aintaining the notion that academic writing is an intellectual and professional task, rather than one which involves the whole of the writer's self, leads to difficulty and disenchantment with the writing process and makes many academics resentful at having to write. (Antoniou & Moriarty, 2008, p. 159)

Allowing ourselves to take risks, be more playful, and be open to the serendipitous leads us to refreshing insights that spring forth from our whole self. The repertoire of creative strategies in this chapter offer you a series of exercises that you can do when you feel disengaged with your topic, when you don't know where to go next, or when you want to challenge yourself to approach your topic from a different viewpoint.

The purpose of this chapter is to describe some creative strategies to generate more ideas and to learn more about yourself as a creative thinker while reducing your stress. The first four chapters in this book highlight four key principles of academic writing: principle one: Know yourself; principle two: Understand the genre of academic writing; principle three: Be strategic; and principle four: Be social. Following the strategies and suggestions from these four principles will move you toward building a solid, sustainable academic writing foundation. This chapter suggests you turn inward and practice some exercises to let your more creative side feed your curiosity, fuel your momentum, and even generate some new, original perspectives on your work.

The first of two major sections in this chapter defines *creativity* in the context of academic work to build a deeper appreciation of the fundamental role creativity plays in our academic life. The second section includes three sets of strategies, each with writing exercises. The first set of strategies describes the exercises of freewriting and focused freewriting where you can tame your inner editor and generate some surprising and valuable connections among your ideas by writing before you have your manuscript planned out. The second set of strategies helps you uncover the voices in your head as well as understand your audience better through dialogue with others. Finally, after you have gathered some fresh perspectives from the exercises in the first two sets of strategies, the third strategy shows you a way to initially structure your manuscript with a concept map made up of Post-its. The ultimate goal of these creative approaches is to increase your commitment and excitement as you work on any manuscript at any stage of the writing process.

Principle five: Explore creative elements in academic writing to generate fresh connections and move academic writing from the formulaic to that which is more engaging for the reader and more personally meaningful for the writer.

What Is Creativity?

The Association of American Colleges & Universities (AAC&U) (n.d.) defines *creativity* as "both the *capacity to combine or synthesize* existing ideas, images, or expertise in original ways and the *experience of thinking, reacting, and working* in an imaginative way characterized by a high degree of innovation, divergent thinking, and risk taking" (emphasis added). This AAC&U definition emphasizes two elements involved in being creative. The first is a capacity to take one thing and transform it into something else. The second is the experience of being creative; that is, the feeling you get when you are using your imagination imbued with innovation, divergent thinking, and risk-taking.

Even though we may find ourselves challenged to approach new projects from a fresh perspective, the creative elements in academic work are not necessarily obvious. Creativity in academe is about reacting to and even incorporating other perspectives into our work, rather than creating something totally new. Being creative is often about synthesizing and moving knowledge forward, sometimes in small steps.

In academic work, we are in "conversation" with existing concepts and understandings. Because experience leads us to question existing concepts, our natural creativity leads us to find ways to build on these concepts or refute them. Scholars engage with the literature of their disciplines or make connections with others in and outside their field. Artists respond to and build on or reject what has gone before. The bottom line is that creativity is not an isolated, solitary act, but is often a response to a stimulus. Research and academic writing become the process of creating new pieces to a puzzle that is already in the making.

The opportunity to recognize an unusual and creative connection can appear at any time. One opportunity came to me when I started working for PSU. My job was to broker opportunities for faculty and public school teachers to work together. After several weeks in the schools and on campus, I casually mentioned to my dean that I felt like I was in the middle of a surreal painting. The offhand comment captured my imagination. I found a painting by Magritte called *personal values* (Magritte, 1952) and shared it at a faculty meeting as a way to illustrate the miscommunications between the worldview of the schools and that of the university. Next, I stretched the metaphor further and wrote an article using the metaphor "The Real, Ideal, and Surreal in School–University Partnerships: Reflections of a Boundary Spanner" (Stevens, 1999). By pursuing that casual remark and writing about it, I found a metaphor that made sense to other academics as well.

A key ingredient in being creative is developing a set of dispositions. These include our willingness to take risks; to make mistakes; and, even in the light of seemingly disconfirming evidence, to keep forging on. Over time, through practice with creative strategies, we begin to trust our own creativity and even turn to creative strategies to make sense of our current work and to spark our imagination.

When I ask faculty to engage in a creative exercise such as writing out a dialogue with perfectionism (Exercise 5.3), I suggest that they "suspend their disbelief" for a little while, follow the directions, and set up the dialogue on their paper, starting with "How are you_____?" In one of my conference workshops, Stephen

Yandell wrote a dialogue with his perfectionist tendency (Sidebar 5.2). Stephen had not ever thought of perfectionism as a dialogue partner. As he wrote, though, and let the dialogue flow, his very judgmental perfectionist introduced him to a younger brother, "good enough." After writing the dialogue, he said that, when he becomes aware of his perfectionist judging his writing, he now knows to stop and tell himself to allow his writing to be "good enough" in order to get a manuscript out the door.

As Stephen found out, creative writing exercises loosen up the tight hinges of his judgments and expectations about the way the world should work, and open the doors of possibility.

Use Creative Strategies to Add Spark to Writing

Strategy I: Making Fresh Connections

Creative writing activities can prompt you to generate text in a nonjudgmental way without editing, thus overcoming the stress of facing the dreaded blank page. In this section, we will be working on making fresh connections and generating text through two exercises, freewriting and focused freewriting.

Freewriting

What is freewriting? Freewriting is a reflective writing strategy that has a very simple prompt: "Put your pen to paper or fingers to the keyboard and write for a set period of time." Once you set the timer, you begin writing without a topic or question in mind.

Elbow (1973), the pioneer in the use of freewriting, recommends that you spend 15 to 20 minutes freewriting just to get what is on your mind out of your mind. After about 15 minutes, you will typically dig deeper to the ideas that were not readily accessible before. It is an unusual kind of writing where there are no rules. No grammar rules. No spelling rules. No sentence rules. Not even rules that require that you need to stick to a topic. What you produce may be disorganized and may be illogical, but more often than not there are surprising and valuable connections among the ideas.

When I free-write, I like the image of letting the words tumble out onto the page. Of course, because the hand is slower than the brain, I cannot write every word. However, during freewriting, I push on, writing and writing and not stopping for any reason. If I don't know where I am going with an idea, I ask myself, "Where am I going with this idea?" The more I get into the spirit of freewriting, the more I allow myself to put down anything that crosses my mind. I generally seem to glean something useful from the process. The best part, the very best part, is when I make a connection in my writing that I have not thought about before. My mind makes a leap and I am surprised! How motivating! How affirming!

Here is an example of a free-write from my journal from several years ago when I was working on my book *Journal Keeping* (Stevens & Cooper, 2009):

July 7, 2007 (Context: writing a free-write at the beginning of class while my students also do one. Ten-minute free-write in action research class—I start with comments about the sounds in the hallway): lighter steps, flip flops, "go-aheads," rubber sandals, yes, doors closing. Be here now, be hear now, be hear now. The noises of the college hallway clunch, chuck, thump doors close flip flops scrunk, squnk flip, growl of buses, urgent push of engines. How come I can hear it but I cannot put it in a language? Now I feel obsessed with the sounds in the hallway. Soft chatter, but rapid—Is that what poets do? They work to get a sound you cannot even say easily—broil it down to its sound essence. Hey, how are you? Having a good summer? Good to see you—conversational lubricants—just easy, summer-lite conversations like lite milk, lite cottage cheese, lite ice cream, light like lite like lonely being alone listening. . . . (Journal 2007, #2)

You may read this and think, "That is a lot of gibberish." I understand that response. When I free-write, I just relax with the English language and let my busy brain rumble along without judgment. Faculty have told me that freewriting for even five minutes before working on a manuscript helps them get things off their mind so that they can be more present and focused. Freewriting develops fluency, gets words on the page, even if the words do not make much sense. It is like stretching your "word-production muscle." The directions for doing a free-write are included in Exercise 5.1.

Sometimes faculty have a hard time getting started on a free-write. They wonder, "Well, if I just put pen to paper right this minute, what do I write about?" If you feel stuck, try writing all the words that come into your head as they appear in your brain. You do not have to use sentences; phrases will work. If you still feel unsure about what to write and those are the words in your head, you write, "I don't know what to write," over and over again. Your busy brain will get tired of writing that one sentence, and something will break loose in your wonderful and creative brain, and other words and sentences and connections will start appearing. Then, you write those. I hope you try out freewriting and enjoy seeing what your brain comes up with.

Focused Freewriting

A focused free-write starts with a focus on a topic, phrase, or question and follows many of the directions for doing a free-write with one constraint—the writer starts with a focus on a topic. Freewriting does not require you to have a topic. Focused freewriting helps you start your writing on a topic or question that interests you, even before you have your outline or have your ideas formed.

How do you select a topic or question for a focused free-write? Don't spend too much time on deciding on the *best* topic. Select one that is related to your current work. The topic could be the main theme of your work or a question with which you are struggling. The topic could be about research you want to do in the future. The focused free-write is really a written brainstorm about what you know, want to know, and would like to do about this topic. Perhaps you are fascinated about the idea and think you might be able to write about it because you care about it. Or, you know you should write about this topic because it was part of your dissertation. Or, you are expected to write about this topic because you are on a collaborative team who is

EXERCISE 5.1
Free-write

Step 1: Open your journal to a blank page or start with a new document on your computer.

Step 2: Write for a set period of time: 6 to 20 minutes.

Set a timer for 6 to 20 minutes. A free-write is a type of writing where you do not necessarily start with a topic in mind. You just start writing. There is only one rule in a free-write: Set your pen to the paper or fingers to the keyboard and write. No one else will read the free-write. There are no grammar rules, punctuation rules, sentence rules, or even sense-making rules. There is only one way to go wrong in a free-write and that is not to write. Otherwise, all you need to do is write and keep on writing.

If you get stuck and don't know what to write, you write, "I don't know what to write" and then write it again. Your busy brain will eventually get tired of writing that and give you something to write. Some people keep on writing by asking themselves questions.

Freewriting gives you practice in producing text without editing, an invaluable skill. When you edit as you write, you stifle your voice, verve, and energy in your writing. Some people find that if they free-write before they write regularly, their other writing flows more easily and is more expressive. Stop when the timer rings.

Step 3: Draw a line under what you have written. Read what you have just written. Write a meta-reflection about what you have written.

A meta-reflection is two or three sentences about what you have just written. After you have read what you just wrote, think about what insights you have about what you wrote. What thoughts do you have about doing a free-write? Was it helpful? Interesting? Difficult? Easy? Comment on any insights you have about what you wrote about as well.

working on this research project. Whatever your motivation, this activity is designed to further your thinking about the topic, foster production of text, and get the ideas out of your head and onto paper. A focused free-write generates kernels of thought that deserve your attention. For pop-up writing groups (chapter 4), that is, when a group of faculty are collaborating on a paper or proposal, I suggest the whole team can do individual, focused free-writes when you first meet to identify what interests, perspective, and knowledge each team member brings to the project. The group discussion following the focused free-writes can be rich and rewarding because focused freewriting can bring forth each individual's perspective and some new ideas.

EXERCISE 5.2
Focused free-write

Step 1: Identify a topic or a question about a topic that you want to write about. Write it on the top of a blank page in your journal or on the computer.

Think about your recent work and select a topic related to that work. If you are working on issues about women as wives during the suffragette movement, you could write about women as wives, or the suffragette movement, or a combination of the two. The process of doing the focused free-write will help you narrow down the topic to what you really care about in the topic. The topic could easily be a question about the topic that particularly interests you, such as, "What do we know about the relationships the suffragettes had with their husbands?" Don't worry too much about finding a perfect topic because in the process of doing the focused free-write, you will narrow it down and refine it.

Step 2: Write for a set period of time: 8 to 20 minutes.

Set a timer for 8 to 20 minutes. This type of writing is similar to a free-write, except you start with a topic. The freewriting part includes keeping your pen on the paper, or fingers on the keyboard, and writing as fast as you can without stopping to fret, think, and wonder. No grammar rules, no punctuation rules, no sentence rules. If you get bogged down, look at the prompt questions and answer another one. No judgment here. No right or wrong way to address these questions. In fact, you don't even have to answer these questions. Make up some of your own. These questions are here as prompts for your thinking.

- What is **the topic**?
- Why do **I care** about this topic?
- Why should **others care**?
- What is **interesting** about this topic?
- What **do I know** about this topic?
- What else do I **need to know**?
- **Who** can help me with this topic?
- What are **key words** associated with this topic?
- What are the **next steps** I need to take to get going on this work?

Step 3: Draw a line under what you have written. Read what you have just written. Write a meta-reflection about what you have written.

A meta-reflection is two or three sentences about what you have just written. There are two types of reflection you can engage in following a free-write. First, a *process reflection*: After you have read what you just wrote, what thoughts do you have about the process of doing a focused free-write? Was it helpful? Interesting? Difficult? Easy? Second, a *product reflection*: Comment on any insights you have about your topic from doing the focused free-write. Did you think of some new connections? Do you have some ideas about what you might do next to get into the topic?

I often do focused free-writes on various parts of a new manuscript. As I developed this chapter, I did four focused free-writes:

1. Value of creativity in academic writing
2. Emotions and creativity in academic writing
3. The relationship between creativity and academic writing
4. Faculty responses to creative activities

For each topic on different days I wrote for 10 minutes using the prompts found in the directions for the focused free-write. The focused free-write helped me elicit what I already know, what else I need to know, and how important each topic was to the whole chapter. In addition, often the ideas generated were entirely brand new, so I made fresh connections that I had not thought of before! I savor those surprises!

Exercise 5.2 has a step-by-step description of how to do a focused free-write. Note how there is a series of questions. You do not have to answer these questions one by one. Use them as prompts. If no ideas come to mind right away about your answer to a question, move on to the next. Just like any free-write, the most important part is to keep on writing for a set period of time. The first time you do a focused free-write, 15 minutes is quite adequate to get your writing juices flowing. Later, you might want to set your timer for a bit longer.

Martha, in Sidebar 5.1, writes about how she has modified the focused free-write to use the questions for editing her manuscripts. She took the basic prompts out of the focused free-write exercise and rewrote them as a way to have a conversation with the text she was writing. She benefited from this type of dialogue with her own text because she got a "surprise," a new way of looking at what she was writing. After being in several workshops with me, I appreciate the fact that Martha took the basic focused free-write and modified it (creatively!) so that the exercise made sense in her own writing.

Sidebar 5.1 Freewriting: Martha

Once I learned and embraced freewriting, I gravitated on my own to a regular practice, similar to "focused freewriting." I designed a set of my own prompts. These prompts are my free-flowing, "talk-back" prompts, such as, "Well, how come this is so important to you anyway?" or "What makes you think people should be interested in this?" or "What's your point here?"

The structure of my prompts is designed to bring out a bit of my feisty adolescent. At some point in a free-write, there comes a big surprise as I write something down that makes me almost say aloud, "There it is!" I have broken through a logjam. I either highlight or circle the "thing" that surprised me . . . feeling fresh, lighter, and more confident to return to my formal writing.

Martha McCarthy, Portland State University

After you have responded to the prompts, draw a line across the page. Now, go back and reread what you have written. Rereading what you have written is called a *meta-reflection*. Think about what you have put down. What surprised you? What did you learn about this process? Would you do this again? What will you do next? What insights did you gain about your content? After reading what you have written, write out two or three sentences about what you learned about your topic or the process from doing this focused free-write. Because meta-reflections can be used with any type of writing, I give a more detailed description of how to do a meta-reflection in a later section (see Exercise 5.6).

Benefits of Freewriting and Focused Freewriting
Freewriting itself has many benefits. As Elbow (1973) explains,

> The main thing about freewriting is that it is *nonediting*. It is an exercise in bringing together the process of producing words and putting them down on the page. Practiced regularly, it undoes the ingrained habit of editing at the same time you are trying to produce. By unblocking your writing you'll find words will come more easily. You will use up more paper, but chew up fewer pencils.
>
> The habit of compulsive, premature editing doesn't just make writing hard. It also deadens it. Your voice is damped out by all the interruptions, changes and hesitations between consciousness and the page (as you produce and edit at the same time). (p. 6)

Freewriting challenges the writer to stop editing as he or she writes because, as Elbow says, editing dampens the flow of the words on the page. In addition, the words are lifeless and you lose your voice. Freewriting is at the heart of good writing precisely because it gives voice back to the writer. No one is watching over your shoulder when you free-write. No judgment. No editing, just the free flow of words, sentences, and ideas. Freewriting builds fluency with the written language and acquaints you with your voice, your rhythm with words, and your unique expression and observations.

Faculty are genuinely surprised by how much information they can write down in a short period of time during a 10-minute focused free-write. Faculty are also surprised by how much they already know about a topic, maybe even before going too deeply into the research literature. They also tell me that when they consider the prompt questions "Why do I care about this work? Why should others care about this work?" they reconnect with their vision, their larger purpose, and the long-term value of their work. In the daily-ness of writing journal articles, analyzing data, grading papers, teaching classes, and negotiating office politics, we can often forget where a piece of work fits into our larger life scheme. The focused free-write can lead to an affirmation of our values, or even a realization that maybe the current work deviates from what we really care about. And, that can lead to deeper reflection about what we are doing, why we are doing it, and what steps we might take to better align our work with our values.

Strategy II: Tapping Your Voice

Academic writing can be viewed as a conversation. This conversation can occur in different contexts. In this section, I invite you to try out four exercises that are based on "having a conversation." Each of these exercises are conversations with imagined others or the self. When you write out a dialogue (Exercise 5.3), you have to imagine the other person who will be responding to you. When you write an "unsent" letter (Exercise 5.4), you conjure up the recipient and craft your letter to that audience. When you respond to a question or prompt (Exercise 5.5), you are allowing the unconscious free rein to answer. Then, when you reread whatever you have written in these timed exercises and write a reflection on them through a meta-reflection (Exercise 5.6), you are affirming your voice and appreciating the insight that these kinds of exercises can offer—all of which can be free-flowing, spontaneous, and uncontrived. There is no right or wrong way. The goal is to practice writing with your authentic voice by simply writing the words that come into your head in response to a prompt generated by imagining a "conversation" with another.

Dialogue

Dialogue is an interaction between two entities. Because we have a lifetime of experience with dialogues, our brains are wired for dialogue. Ask a question; get a response. "How are you?"; "I am fine." Why would we write out a dialogue as part of our work? Writing a dialogue brings us closer to our natural way of interacting with others. We are familiar with the structure of dialogue and conversation with others.

Even though writing a dialogue is a powerful reflective activity, those of you who have not written one before may have to "suspend your disbelief" to begin and complete the activity, just like Stephen did at the beginning of the chapter. When I describe the dialogue activity to faculty, I see the knitted brows of disbelief. "That is crazy! Why would I write to such a thing? Why would I have a dialogue with perfectionism? Perfectionism is not a person. That makes no sense." This is the voice of your cautious self, your disbeliever and protector who saves you from embarrassing situations. For the length of the activity, try telling your disbeliever to suspend her or his judgment and let you jump right in. Then, when you have finished, you can make your final decision about the value of the activity. In all the years that I have been teaching this activity, I have found that almost all faculty have been able to suspend their disbelief and write a dialogue that surprises them.

With whom can you write a dialogue? Certainly people: a spouse, department chair, friend, parent, or others. What about dialoguing with your cat, dog, or other pet? Faculty typically nod at that; of course, they talk to their pets. That is easy. Let's think more broadly. What about your car? Your computer? Faculty say, "Of course, I have been known to talk to my computer." Now that we are in the realm of inanimate objects, how about a dialogue with abstract concepts? Stephen's dialogue with perfectionism in Sidebar 5.2 falls into this category.

Sidebar 5.2 A dialogue with perfectionism: Stephen

A Dialogue With Perfectionism

Steve: Hi Perfectionism; how are you doing?

Perfectionism: I'm perfect.

S: I get it; you don't have to be condescending.

P: I'm just being honest. I'm an abstract concept; I don't spend any time in the real world, so I can be anything I want.

S: You seem pretty real to me.

P: Yeah—I am a real idea that hangs around you, and I do make you feel inadequate most of the time, but I'm not something you actually encounter on a day-to-day basis . . . or ever. We have a lot of conversations, I know—usually when you want to tell me about the student papers you're grading, or when we spend time criticizing your own work; but all of our time together is spent in my "perfect" space, not the real world—it's on my terms. I see you've got your "writing" folder crammed into your satchel again. Is tonight the night you're going to finally buckle down and create that perfect draft?

S: Uh, yeah—I've got to get this article written.

P: You're kidding, right? You've taken so much time with it already, it doesn't have to just be perfect now, it's got to be *more* than perfect. The editors expect you to have turned it into the world's finest masterpiece with the time they've given you. You know who you need to meet? My uncle, More-Than-Perfect. If you think *I* get on your nerves, you're going to hate him.

S: Why can't you ever be supportive?

P: Because I know your habits so well: you carry the same writing folder for months and months and never get anything done. And you make the same entry into your to-do list every morning: "write article." It's so vague, I can't help but mock you. Plus, I know what your drafts look like—they're garbage.

S: This is why I never want to work on my writing: you begin criticizing the minute I start.

P: What do you mean? You rarely get anything down on paper, so I don't get a chance to judge. Don't blame me for learning how to have high standards!

S: High standards?—they're impossible standards. But I'm afraid if I stop hanging around with you, I won't have *any* standards. I need to produce quality work.

P: Oh, you really don't understand our relationship, do you? If you really cared about getting quality work done, you'd be spending time with my little sister, Pretty Good. Now *she* spends a lot of time in the real world. She's the one who will help you get to know people, move you ahead,

(*Continues*)

Sidebar 5.2 (*Continued*)

	and get your writing projects finished regularly. She has high standards, but she's encouraging, not judgmental; everybody loves her. Except me.
S:	She sounds great. Why don't you like her?
P:	She's taken too many of my friends. Once I introduce people to my sister, most of them stop spending time with me. I'll give you her number—but I guarantee it: once you get to know her, you and I will stop talking. You'll miss our conversations at first, but you'll get over me—they always do.
S:	But I'm so used to you. What about those last two pieces of writing I finished . . . a couple years ago. They turned out really great, even if they took a year to write. Didn't you help make that happen?
P:	Oh, I remember those late-night writing sessions. You got so good at saying the things I was whispering in your ear, I left you alone at my place. I was gone for two weeks—you spent it with my brother who was visiting for the holidays, Good Enough. Didn't you notice? We look a lot alike, but trust me, we're very different people. You must have been pretty focused. Good Enough is the most approachable sibling I have. He's super laid back, but also super productive. He'll help get any project done.
S:	Wait, what? That guy was your brother? He's the guy who talked me through the tough nights? That's it. From now on, I'm only hanging out with Pretty Good and Good Enough. They sound like they'll support me through my messy drafts. I need to stop talking to you so I can be happy moving through all the stages of writing that I know are inevitable . . . and I know are messy . . . and I know take time.

Stephen Yandell, Xavier College

Think about a dialogue with anger or frustration or love or joy or procrastination. Certainly you can also do that!

Exercise 5.3 gives a full step-by-step description of how to write a dialogue, starting with identifying the person or thing with whom you will converse. A few important pointers in doing this exercise are to start writing on a new line each time the speaker changes. It is also best to set a timer. The first time you write a dialogue it may seem contrived and difficult. By setting a short time to complete it, say six minutes, you will get the feel of the exercise. The next time you might want to extend the time. It will feel easier each time you practice.

Another activity that promotes an interaction with others is writing an unsent letter.

Unsent Letter

Have you ever wished you could just say everything you wanted to say to someone and not worry about what his or her response would be? The unsent letter exercise is

EXERCISE 5.3
Write a dialogue

Step 1: Identify a person or an entity with whom to have a dialogue.

Typically, we think of dialogue as a conversation between two people. However, there are some interesting opportunities to think of dialogue as a conversation between you and something else, such as a behavior, say, perfectionism. Faculty have had fruitful dialogues with the journal article they are writing or with people from whom they are collecting data. A dialogue is a conversation with a person, construct, place, or thing that has meaning for you. Some people play with having a dialogue with their computer or their car. All of these dialogue partners have meaning in your life. By creating a written dialogue with another person or entity, the writer can gain fresh insights about what role this entity plays.

Dialogue partners: Dialogue with persons, dialogue with events and circumstances, dialogue with works, dialogue with the body, dialogue with societies, dialogue with emotions/feelings, dialogue with material objects/possessions, dialogue with subpersonalities, dialogue with resistance, and dialogue with your inner mentor/wisdom.

Step 2: Set the timer for 10 to 20 minutes.

When first learning how to write a dialogue and to feel comfortable about it, it might be best to limit the time for the dialogue.

Step 3: Open a blank page in your journal or on the computer. Set up the dialogue so that you skip lines each time the speaker changes.

Be assured that at first it is normal to feel a little uncomfortable with this activity. Dialoguing with, say, an inanimate object, such as your computer, takes practice until it feels comfortable.

Before setting the timer, some people like to reflect on their dialogue partner and think about any questions they might have.

Your dialogue should be set up like a screenplay where you skip lines each time a new entity speaks. Start with your voice. Here is an example of an opening dialogue:

Dannelle: Hi, procrastination, how are you?

Procrastination: Well, I am fine. I know it feels like you are procrastinating. That makes me happy. However, I do note that you are making progress. . . .

Step 4: Draw a line under what you have written. Read what you have just written. Write a meta-reflection about what you have written.

After you have read what you just wrote, consider what insights it revealed. A meta-reflection is a two- or three-sentence reflection about what you have just written. What thoughts do you have about doing a dialogue? Was it helpful? Interesting? Difficult? Easy? What did you learn about your dialogue partner? Were there any surprises?

just that. It is a one-sided conversation. The recipient of the letter could be a person. Some faculty have found that they can also write a letter to a feeling, a project, or a paper they are crafting. Sidebar 5.3 is from a faculty member, Donna, who was stuck with the last part of getting her dissertation done. She mentioned to me that writing the letter to her dissertation opened the door for her to finish. Like Martha before, Donna also modified the exercise so that she wrote a short note to her dissertation and, then, her dissertation wrote a longer letter back to her.

Write the letter on a fresh page of your journal or on a piece of stationery just as if you were really writing the letter. Format it the way you would write a letter. Do you put the date in the upper right-hand corner? Do you start with "Dear . . ."? Do

---

Sidebar 5.3 An unsent letter to her dissertation: Donna

October 28, 2012

Dear Dissertation,

How are you? I have been thinking about you a lot, mostly how I don't know what to do with you because you are so large and complex. I've been researching for so long, I don't even know how to start!

Dear Donna,

I am certainly large and lumbering. I have many pieces and am just waiting for you to take me apart. I can help. Why not start with your original proposal and figure out where those pieces fit? Or, you could begin with the 1960s—by putting the numbers together, as well as the original affirmative action plans.

I know you think that sounds kind of boring. What is it that you think sounds fun? You do know you will need to do some of the boring pieces at some point—and laying it all out might make you feel more comfortable as you move into writing....

I think you should start by pulling those things—numbers, mandates, and so on—together beginning in the 1960s and bring yourself up to the 1980s, which is when most of the folks you've spoken with begin. Your documents start earlier, though, so you can untangle all of that while you continue to bring those other pieces—the backstory from the sixties—together. And here's my most important advice. Start writing now!

Meta-reflection: Wow, I found the heart of my work right here! By breaking the material into small pieces and writing daily, I completed a 549-page dissertation about civil rights in the Forest Service. I can't believe I did it in just two and a half years!

Donna Sineliar, Portland State University

EXERCISE 5.4
Unsent letter

Step 1: Identify a person or a thing to whom you would like to write a letter.

The unsent letter is a one-sided dialogue. The recipient of the unsent letter could come from the list of dialogue partners found in the dialogue exercise (Exercise 5.3). A letter is a more extended text and gives you more opportunity to express your ideas and feelings to the person or thing. An unsent letter is sometimes useful in defusing some negative feelings you have about the recipient. It can also be a place where you sort out some of those feelings and ideas and give them a cohesive form. Sometimes this helps clarify what you think and feel about the person or the situation. If you can imagine it, you can write a letter to it.

Letter recipients could be any of the following: persons, events and circumstances, a work in progress, the body, social groups, emotions/feelings, material objects/possessions, subpersonalities, abstract concepts such as resistance, or your inner mentor/wisdom.

Step 2: Open a blank page in your journal or on the computer. Set up the letter as if you are really writing the letter with the date and the greeting at the top. When you sign off, do it just as you would in a genuine letter.

You will probably feel more comfortable with the process of writing a letter. However, writing a letter that you will not send and expressing thoughts you would not openly say may be uncomfortable. Writing a letter to an inanimate thing, such as a journal article you are working on, may initially feel awkward or embarrassing. However, as you immerse yourself in the process and let your imagination go, you may find that you feel relief at getting some of these ideas that are swirling around in your mind down on paper or on the computer screen. Before setting the timer, some people like to reflect on the letter recipient and think about any particular thing they would want to make sure the person knows.

Step 3: Set the timer for 10 to 20 minutes.

This exercise really has a broad set of time limits because it is best not to exhaust yourself by feeling the need to write a long letter.

Step 4: Draw a line under what you have written. Read what you have just written. Write a meta-reflection about what you have written.

After you have read what you just wrote, what insights emerged from what you wrote? A meta-reflection is a two- or three-sentence reflection about what you have just written. What thoughts do you have about writing an unsent letter? Was it helpful? Interesting? Difficult? Easy? Were there any surprises?

you have a greeting paragraph, such as "How are you?" Yes! Set up the letter as if you were really going to send it to the person, the feeling, the project, or the paper. The more you set it up to appear as a "real" letter, the more likely your brain will surface unconscious ideas that are what you need to say to this person. Exercise 5.4 provides step-by-step instructions for writing an unsent letter.

Writing Prompts for Stuck Places

When faculty writers feel stuck, some find that having a list of writing prompts at hand often gets their writing juices flowing again. A prompt can be a sentence fragment or a question. Some people put the list in front of their journals and use the prompt as a warm-up activity before they go to their more structured writing. Exercise 5.5 contains a list of writing prompts that a faculty member uses. I have clustered the prompts into three sections based on writing challenges: prompts for clarifying your focus in the manuscipt, prompts for reinvigorating commitment, and prompts for exposing and dealing with the emotions of writing.

EXERCISE 5.5
Writing prompts for stuck places

Being stuck in your writing is often an opportunity to reflect more deeply on what is holding you back. Ask, "What is bothering me right now?" Pick one of these prompts to write about to understand more about the feeling of being "stuck" and unable to proceed with your writing. Which one of these prompts seems pertinent and appropriate right now? Which one of these seems to address a stuck place in your writing? A prompt is an opportunity to explore your thinking through writing and, by doing this exercise, you may advance to the happy place of not being stuck anymore! A good thing!

I have clustered the list of prompts that follow into groups about the content of your work, your commitment, and the emotions of writing, respectively. I suggest that you set a timer for five to six minutes when you are responding to a prompt. Write quickly. Remember there are no right or wrong responses to a prompt.

Prompts for clarifying your focus in the manuscript:

The most important thing about this manuscript is . . .
I just can't figure out what I want to say about . . .
The questions that I still have to address in this work are . . .
The next thing I need to write about is . . .
I am just confused about . . .
The list of questions I have about this manuscript is . . .

Prompts for reinvigorating commitment to this work:

I care about this work because . . .
I want people to know about the ideas in this article because . . .

(Continues)

EXERCISE 5.5 (*Continued*)

> People should care about my work on this topic because . . ..
> This work relates to work I have done in the past because . . .
>
> Prompts for exposing and dealing with the emotions related to writing:
>
> The thing that seems to be preventing me from getting this work done is . . .
> I feel the most guilty about . . . and I will do this about that guilt: . . .
> I am frustrated about this work because . . .
> I feel shy about making a presentation at the conference because . . .
> My inner mentor would address my fears as follows: . . .
> I feel more confident in my writing now that . . .
> The most dominant emotion I am feeling right now is . . .

Some writers like to use prompts at the beginning of a writing session. Others use them for a short break in the middle. One thing for sure is that they can take the pressure off, exercise your writing muscles, and get words on the page. This can build confidence and fluency with writing. Some glue a copy of these prompts inside their journals for easy access.

Another way to respond to text is through a meta-reflection; however, in a meta-reflection, your response or reflection is only to what you have just written.

Meta-Reflection

You may have noticed that after most writing exercises in this book, I have suggested that you draw a line, reread what you have just written, and write a reflection on it. To build fluency and tap your authentic voice when you undertake the exercises, such as focused freewriting and dialogue, I suggest that you write quickly and uncritically within a short time frame. The meta-reflection is different and is also an important activity in the creative process. If this is the first time you have written a dialogue, reading it after you have written it and then writing a meta-reflection on it will help you assess what worked and what didn't in doing the activity. Above the line, before the meta-reflection, is the text you generated so quickly. Buried in the text may be some ideas that you might want to think about more deeply or incorporate in your writing. As you reread the text, you might underline or put a star in the margin to highlight an appealing idea. Exercise 5.6 gives a full set of directions on writing a meta-reflection. In the meta-reflection, you are writing about what you just noticed in the reflection.

Benefits of Tapping Your Voice Through Dialogue, Unsent Letters, Prompts, and Meta-Reflections

The second set of strategies—dialogue, unsent letters, prompts, and meta-reflections—is designed to help you get to know yourself as a writer, as well as develop your authentic writing voice. Each is an unedited response. The more you

EXERCISE 5.6
Meta-reflection

A meta-reflection is an important step to follow a writing activity such as freewriting, focused freewriting, dialogue, or any other you have tried. It is an opportunity to read and reflect on what you wrote so spontaneously and mine some gems of wisdom and insight from your work.

Step 1: After you finish the writing exercise, draw a line under what you have written. Read what you have just written above the line.

Step 2: Write a meta-reflection about what you have written.

Think about what insights you gleaned from what you wrote above the line. A meta-reflection is a two- or three-sentence written reflection about what you have just written and is an opportunity for you to stand back from something you have just written and reflect on its meaning. There are two aspects to this reflection.

The first aspect of the meta-reflection is a reflection on the process *of doing the writing activity.* You could ask yourself, "Have I done this kind of writing before? How did I feel as I was writing? Did it feel awkward or uncomfortable because I was not paying attention to spelling, grammar, or sentence structure in the free-writes, for example? Did it actually feel good to be free from those structural constraints? Did I stop and think? What did I do to get myself writing again? Or did I just keep on writing knowing that I can do the editing later? How did that feel?"

The second aspect is on the content *of the writing.* You could ask yourself, "Have I thought about this topic this way before? What did I learn about the topic that I have not thought of before? Did I make any new connections between ideas? Were there any surprises from writing about the topic this way?"

let your writing flow and don't edit while writing, the more ideas you will elicit. When you write freely and openly about your perspectives and feelings, you learn more about others—the person, feelings, or project with which you interact. You take the "others" out from your brain where they are unexamined and probably not well understood and then imagine them in a dialogue or letter. The others become an "object," exposed and more fully comprehended. You are illuminating its role in your thinking and responses, just like Stephen, who did not know what a powerful and judgmental voice his perfectionism had. By exposing his perfectionist through dialogue, he found a way to neutralize its negative effect on his thinking about his writing.

Strategy III: Being Creative in Structuring Your Manuscript

Concept mapping is a way to illustrate relationships between your ideas. At the beginning of each chapter in this book is a concept map of the chapter content: The various sections of the chapter are nested under the chapter title. Concept maps are about not only relationships but also hierarchies among those relationships. What ideas cluster and what are the relationships among clusters?

EXERCISE 5.7

Post-it concept map

> **Materials: Two stacks of Post-its (small: 1″ by 1″ or so; large: 2″ by 2″). Blank sheet of paper on which to place the Post-its. I often use one of the pages in my journal, although you could use a white board.**
>
> **Step 1: Select a topic. Identify a topic that you are working on.**
>
> The topic could be something you are currently working on or it could be something that you want to work on in the future. Think a little bit about why this topic is important to you and about what you already know about the topic.
>
> **Step 2: Brainstorm ideas about the topic. Get a stack of at least 20 small Post-its. You are going to brainstorm as many ideas as you can about your topic and write each idea down on a small Post-it.**
>
> The rule is that you have only one idea per Post-its. The ideas could include questions or short phrases or sentences. Write as quickly as you can to generate a lot of ideas. Don't edit them now. You will have a chance to edit in the next step. After you have at least 20 Post-its or have run out of ideas, stop.
>
> **Step 3: Cluster similar ideas in groups. Read through the stack of Post-its. After reading, begin to cluster the individual Post-its in groups with ideas that seem to go together.**
>
> Because just reading the Post-its can generate more ideas, you may want to add some more ideas on new Post-its. Then, put the Post-its in a cluster with the others or create a new cluster. If any of the new ideas don't fit in clusters you have now, just set them aside. Don't worry if some of the Post-its within a cluster are repetitious. Usually these repetitions of ideas mean that the idea is very important to include in your manuscript.
>
> **Step 4: Label the clusters. Read all the Post-its in each cluster and get another stack of larger Post-its or Post-its of a different color. After you have read and reflected on what is common about these ideas in the cluster, write a label (a phrase or a sentence) for the cluster. The label needs to capture the essence of all the Post-its in the cluster.**
>
> **Step 5: Put the clusters with their labels in some logical order. Read all the cluster labels and begin to think about what would be the logical order for the clusters with their labels. You can number the clusters and reread them to see if they make sense in this order.**
>
> The clusters are the emerging sections of the text you are working on.

Concept Mapping With Post-its

The concept mapping with Post-its exercise (Exercise 5.7) is designed to generate a lot of ideas, as well as organize them into some logical flow. The steps of brainstorming and clustering push you to think about your topic in as many different ways that you can without constraints. Using Post-its allows you to reread and reorder the ideas as you work to cluster them. When you label the clusters, you have to reflect, analyze, and synthesize the ideas to reveal the logical connections and associations among them.

In 2007, I was working on the assessment of student journals chapter in my coauthored book *Journal Keeping* (Stevens & Cooper, 2009). I knew this chapter was essential because it addressed the question faculty often asked in my workshops: "How do you assess reflective writing in journals?" Because I had used journals in my classes and taught workshops on journal keeping for 11 years, I felt I had a foundation of experience to address many of the questions. Without editing I brainstormed on Post-its everything I could think of related to grading student reflective writing with one idea on each Post-it. The Post-its filled two journal pages and included answers to questions I asked myself: "Why grade reflective writing?" "What can you grade in reflective writing?" "Is it the quantity or quality of entries that is important?" I read all the Post-its and moved them around so that similar ideas were clustered together. Then, I started to make labels for each cluster that summarized the ideas in that cluster. Figure 5.1 is a photo from part of the page in my 2007 journal where I placed the Post-its. In the upper right-hand corner you will see the label "Types of feedback

Figure 5.1 Example of Post-it concept map in a journal used to structure a journal article

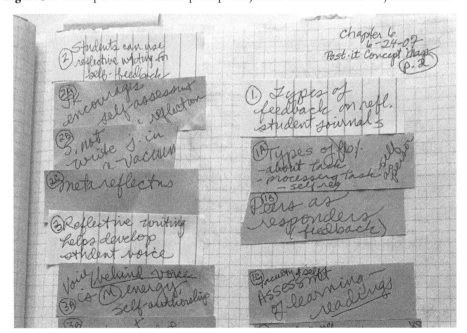

on refl. student journals." This label was made after reading the series of Post-its below the label. On the left, you will see another label, "Students can use reflective writing for self-feedback." Again, this label was created based on the cluster below the label. The numbering and ordering came later as I read and reread the notes and wrote labels for all the clusters. An outline for several sections of the chapter fell into place. It was as follows:

1. Types of feedback on reflective student journals:

   1a. Journals provide feedback to the self (the writer) through reflection on the process of writing the journal.

   1b. Peers can read another student's journal and give feedback.

   1c. Faculty give feedback on student journal entries on class readings.

2. Benefits of students using reflective writing as feedback for themselves:

   2a. Journal keeping encourages self-assessment and reflection.

   2b. Students can learn that they are not writing a journal in a vacuum. The journal reflects their authentic self.

   2c. Through meta-reflections, they can acknowledge and affirm the gems of wisdom in their own reflections.

The affirmation of the power of creating a concept map with Post-its came from a reviewer of *Journal Keeping* (Stevens & Cooper, 2009), who noted, "Indeed, I found the authors' discussion of grading classroom journals to be one of the best introductions to grading student work that I have read, quite apart from the specifics of journaling" (Hess, 2010, p. 385). I attribute the success of the chapter to the foundation that was built when I brainstormed everything I could think of about the assessment of reflective writing in journals, putting my ideas on Post-its, and then clustering and labeling them into logical sections to create an initial outline.

Conclusion

Principle five, explore creative elements in academic writing, is the last principle in this book before I move on to more specific applications of the ideas to different writing manuscripts. Combined with other principles, the creative exercises add several other benefits on your path to better and more engaged academic writing.

By doing these exercises, you tap your inner thinking without judgment. These creative strategies help you surface some new connections among your ideas. And, in some cases, because, for example, you have identified your deep feelings about why you care about the topic, the final manuscript can retain the tone, the flavor, and the verve of your individual voice, which readers find engaging.

Another benefit is that by letting ideas flow quickly on the page, you build your writing production muscles. You may increase your confidence when faced with any writing task because you know you can generate a lot of words without judgment before you start editing.

A final residual benefit is that engaging in creative thinking and writing reduces the stress associated with the wide range of your academic work that involves writing. Being an academic today is more stressful than it used to be with "high workloads, resource constraints, declines in government funding and the increasing pressure to publish" (Dickson-Swift et al., 2009, p. 229). Writers experience stress when the words are not coming on the page and when they do not meet their self- or outside-imposed expectations. Given this environment, it is important to take opportunities to reengage with your work, as well as find ways to affirm your unique contribution. Looking at your work as a creative process opens doors of new possibilities and builds trust in what you already know and in how your own thinking and writing processes work.

The next chapter starts with how to use a written or digital journal to organize, log, and interweave your research, writing, and professional life (chapter 6). Then, the next four chapters (chapters 7–10) focus on the application of the five principles to writing book reviews, conference proposals, journal articles, and book proposals. Because responding to reviewer comments is an important part of the publication process, chapter 11 describes several ways to make that response constructive and successful. Finally, because PSU has had a faculty writing program under the direction of this author and the center for teaching and learning director for the last five years, the director and I conclude the book with a chapter on what we have learned from instituting this program.

CHAPTER 6

Keep a Writing or Research Journal

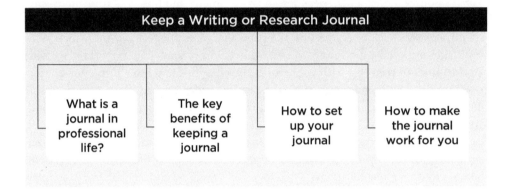

Why keep a journal in your professional life when you are an academic writer?

Academic life is complex. Academic life is full of different expectations, from preparing for teaching; working with others on teaching; being on committees; designing new courses; advising students; giving feedback on student work; reviewing faculty work; providing mentoring for students and, as you advance in your career, for junior faculty; and, when you can squeeze it in, writing.

A journal is an incredibly valuable tool that can help you be more organized; write more; create fodder for your writing and professional life; and, in the long run, fret and stress less. Keeping a professional journal helps you integrate the diverse facets of your professional life and manage its complexity.

The only other job that was similar to the intensity, immediacy, and complexity of being an academic was when I was 22 years old. In the summer of 1968, I was learning to be a breakfast waitress at the Essex Inn, a conference hotel in downtown Chicago. By 6:30 a.m. all 10 tables in my section were full with 2 to 6 people each. I had prepared for the rush. People must have coffee, which means cream and sugar bowls were full and coffee was ready. What I was not prepared for was the intensity and complexity of taking breakfast orders and getting the food and drinks to the table quickly. Because the conference had opening remarks at 8:00 a.m. in this hotel, each table needed immediate attention. Okay, take the order: How do they want their eggs: over easy, fried, no eggs? Do they want juice? What size? What about fresh fruit, grapefruit? Some do not want coffee. They want tea. That means getting a teapot and plate. What if they do not want eggs? Okay, pancakes mean syrup and margarine.

One person says no, not margarine, butter, please. What about toast? What kind of bread? White? Wheat? Sourdough? Another says no eggs, no pancakes, just hot cereal. More coffee. Eggs get cold quickly so they need to be served quickly. More coffee. Oh, is the coffeepot in the kitchen out of coffee? Refill the coffee grounds. Do not run out of coffee. The clock is ticking. They ask, "Where is the check?" Do they want different receipts for each person? Some use cash. Some credit. Eight o'clock is just two minutes away.

You may wonder how this little story of my life as a breakfast waitress could have anything at all to do with academic life or even the topic of this chapter: keeping a journal in professional life. In both jobs there appear to be some consistent routines. In addition, a waitress, like an academic, has to be focused and appear to move effortlessly and confidently within a demanding and somewhat unpredictable setting. For the breakfast waitress, she has to take the order correctly and quickly. In academe, faculty have office hours, but what do the students want when they come into the office? I don't know what to expect in any given appointment. Students may have concerns about a paper I gave comments on, or need information about the courses they need to complete for their degree, or a desire that I write them a letter of recommendation. I am expected to switch gears and know what to do no matter what they ask.

In giving me feedback on this chapter introduction, Lynn, a PSU colleague, sent me this e-mail about a day on campus as an associate professor in the applied linguistics department:

> Yesterday was a day I didn't teach in the classroom. Yet, I spent: 90 minutes writing, 1 hour fighting with technology, 1 hour advising a thesis student, 1 hour on [American Association of University Professors] business, 1 hour prepping for class, 1 hour grading papers, 1 hour meeting with colleagues about research, more than an hour answering e-mail, 30 minutes on departmental committee work, 15 minutes making sure that the student online academic record reflected exceptions we were making to a student's MA program, and that doesn't even start with family or personal stuff. . . . You get the idea—it's the notion that you have lots of things coming at you from unexpected directions. (personal communication, Lynn, April 29, 2017)

As you can see, across a single day in Lynn's life as an academic, she had to call forth her intellectual, social, and interpersonal skills to accomplish so many different tasks.

To be successful as a waitress and an academic requires some similar skills. In both, you have to be responsive within a very intense environment that has many performance expectations, make informed decisions, and keep track of what you need to do next, and next, and next, all while maintaining a pleasant demeanor. In addition, you have no particular training for the key job expectations of either one of these jobs. Waitresses do not go to school to become waitresses. Faculty are not trained in more than one of the key expectations of their job such as how to advise students, how to keep e-mail at bay, or how to write letters of recommendation or . . . even how to write a journal article.

Many things, of course, are different in the two jobs. As a waitress, you get immediate feedback about the quality of your work in the form of tips and smiles whereas faculty must wait weeks, months, and even years to get substantive feedback. You do not need an advanced degree to wait tables. Yet, as Rose (2004) notes waitressing does require stamina and memory, making it a physically and cognitively demanding job. In his book, *The Mind at Work: Valuing the Intelligence of the American Worker,* Rose celebrates the complex cognitive and interpersonal skills it takes to be a waitress, as well as several other seemingly "menial" jobs, such as being a plumber. Of course, to be a professor, you need many years of successful schooling and an advanced degree. Yet, the intensity, immediacy, and cognitive challenges are very similar.

There were times, especially in my early years in the academy, when I felt my professional life was out of control, the demands were too great, and the expectations were too unclear. Just like how I felt about being a breakfast waitress, in academe I also felt I could not move fast enough, or think fast enough, or organize well enough to be successful. I needed to get control of the paper flow and manage the daily demands while keeping my eye on the long-term goal of writing, researching, and publishing. As a way to manage my stress, I went back to an old practice from middle school, keeping a journal that was a location for conversations with myself about my life and future direction. After these initial reflective activities, my journal evolved and included a record of my day-by-day professional life, organized chronologically. I took notes at meetings, I made to-do lists, and I reflected on my research and writing projects, as well as made plans for the future—all in one location: my handwritten journal.

Some of you may describe yourself as one of my faculty colleagues did: a "failed journal keeper." Even if you start from the place of being discouraged about developing a regular practice of journal keeping, there is hope, largely because what I describe in this chapter is a different kind of journal. If you do not keep a journal now, my goal is to help you consider the real value in keeping a journal in your professional life as an organizational tool, a sketch pad for ideas, a location for reflection, and a companion on your journey as a writer. If you keep a journal now, I hope there may be some new ways of using your journal that you will find useful. I am so committed to this practice that I coauthored a book on journal keeping with a dear colleague, Joanne Cooper (Stevens & Cooper, 2009). The purpose of this chapter is to introduce you to the idea of keeping a journal for your professional life as a way to grapple with the intensity, immediacy, and complexity of academic life that we deal with every day.

What Is a Journal in Professional Life?

Because we all come to this idea of keeping a journal from different experiences and perspectives, I would like to define the key characteristics of a journal. For clarity, I am not thinking of a personal diary that contains reflections on your personal and emotional life. A typical professional journal is a collection of written entries that are kept in a bound blank book, a binder, or a virtual space that is centered around your professional life. A journal has certain characteristics that distinguish it from other kinds of collections of written notes and lists. Here is a list of the characteristics of a journal, drawn from our journal-keeping book mentioned previously (Stevens & Cooper, 2009).

- Dated
- Written (or drawn)
- Informal
- Flexible
- Private
- Archival

The characteristic that each journal entry is *dated* is on the top of the list because it is the essential defining characteristic of journals. Putting the date on the entry anchors the experience and the entry into the continuum of the author's life experience. When the journal writer seeks to review and reflect on his or her experiences over a period of time, the date is critical.

A journal is *written*. The author is the source of the text, either on the computer or in a blank book. Given that the journal is *private*, the author is the only one who has access to the text; so, really, the entries only have to make sense to the author and be of use to the author. The entries are generally *informal*, not using polished language. There is no need to spell correctly nor use complete sentences. The *flexible* aspect of a journal, both online and handwritten, is that it allows the author to draw, sketch, and organize in any way that makes sense (or not, if he or she is feeling creative). A journal is an *archival* document because it chronicles your day-to-day life as an academic and can be referred to in the future. Table 6.1 compares the key characteristics of a digital versus a handwritten journal.

A digital journal has some distinct advantages over the handwritten format. A digital journal can be kept in a file in Microsoft Word, either stored on your hard drive or maintained in the cloud or Google Drive. You can create subfiles, link to other documents, as well as import documents (such as meeting minutes) or photos. You may want to investigate online applications such as Evernote or Notability that can be accessed on your smartphone, iPad, or other tablet. In Notability you can write on top of photos submitted to your notes. Your entries become searchable through computer search engines. Over time, the digital journal-keeping applications have added more and more features that provide much of the flexibility of handwritten journals. Apple offers a stylus pen that lets you write on the iPad screen just as you would in a handwritten journal. Another advantage is that typing can be faster than handwriting. In addition, files can be protected with a password.

The handwritten journal, on the other hand, has some advantages over a digital journal. First, it does not need charging like a device, although a handwritten journal does entail carrying a writing instrument. Second, despite

TABLE 6.1

Comparison of key characteristics of digital versus handwritten journals

Characteristic	*Digital journal*	*Handwritten journal*
Portable	Must be charged Can access from smartphone	Must be with you Must have a writing implement Can be a size that doesn't fit in a pocket
Private	Can have secure password access	Can be kept in a secure place
Flexible	Can draw, write, and store images Can include photos Can import images and link to other sites and documents	Can draw, write, and keep entries Can add entries at any time Can paste in business cards and important documents Pages can be lined, gridded, or blank
Accessible	No random access Slow to move through pages Can access by key words	Random access at any time Can flip through pages quickly
Archival	Can be retrieved, especially if entries are in the cloud Cannot be retrieved if computer crashes or application is no longer available	Does not depend on latest computer application or program for retrieval Cannot be retrieved if the journal is lost

the great advances in digital applications, it's far easier to draw, sketch, write, and glue in relevant documents in a handwritten journal. You can put handouts in your journal that have meaning over the whole year, such as meeting schedules or calendars. I glue a yearly calendar in the back of my journal to track future conferences and meetings that I have every month. Third is random access to the content. That is, I can flip through the pages and find things. I can go back and color code the pages and the entries that are significant. Once I create the table of contents at the front of the journal and record the date, title, and page number of each entry, I can quickly find notes from meetings, conferences, and meetings with students. My colleague Micki, an associate dean, has her to-do list notes in the front of her journal with colored Post-its for each project she is working on. Because I take my journal to all meetings, I can access the notes from the last meeting quickly. It usually takes me 3 to 6 months to fill up a journal that has 90 pages and is 8″ × 11″ inches.

What I am suggesting is that the journal has inestimable value beyond your personal life for your professional life. I hope this chapter will stimulate your imagination about the utility of a journal and the key elements of your academic life you can track in your journal.

The Key Benefits of Keeping a Journal

I take my journal with me everywhere: at work, when teaching, in meetings or in my office; after work, in coffee shops; and at home. I record notes during department and committee meetings. Or, should I say, sometimes, when the department meeting topics do not catch my interest, I may look like I am taking notes. I may be doing something else in my journal (tsk, tsk!), such as sketching out the outline for a future conference presentation. I also take it to conferences along with a glue stick to keep business cards of colleagues as well as to paste in handouts. I record notes during conference presentations.

For academics, there are four key benefits of keeping a journal in professional life. First, it contributes to being more organized. Second, the journal can be used as a sketch pad for nascent ideas about future projects; this is the creative aspect of keeping a journal. Third, keeping a journal decreases the stress associated with the intensity, immediacy, and complexity of academic life. Fourth, reflecting and writing in a journal slows things down and enables the journal keeper to gain some distance from the expectations that may be overwhelming and confusing. Let us look at each of these in turn.

Organization

Over the years, I have developed a way to set up my journal that increases the chances of being much more organized than I would otherwise be. The chronological order of the entries helps me locate an event along a time line. Numbering the pages also helps me flip through the journal for instance access. By recording all meetings, notes, and musings in one place, I have an accounting of events as well as a record of my thinking. At the end of the year, if I need to update my CV, I can quickly tell what department and university committees I have been on from my meeting notes in my journal. I can tell what my contribution to these committees has been. I can see what conferences I attended. I have a log of my interactions with my department chair, students, and colleagues. All these data points are in real time.

Creativity

A journal is flexible. You can write, draw, doodle, and make lists in a journal; thus, it is a location for your creative thinking. A journal is a place to experiment, test out ideas, and make mistakes. A journal is a sketch pad and incubator of the rich experience that you bring to your work and to your life. After all, you are the audience for your journal. You can ask yourself questions and test out ideas. "From the types of entries, formatting of the pages, purposes for journal keeping, audience for whom it is intended, and benefits that accrue from keeping them, journals can vary tremendously" (Stevens & Cooper, 2009, p. 6).

When I am working on a writing project, I often brainstorm ideas in a list or on Post-its and then create a concept map of my ideas, as described in chapter 5 and illustrated in Figure 5.1. Because they are in my journal and I do not have to dig out a file folder, I can review my thinking at any time. Riding the bus to work, waiting for a meeting to start, or launching into the writing phase of the project, the seeds are there. I don't have to recall or reinvent them and I can find them.

Recently, to gather the initial ideas for chapter 11, handling an R & R request, I decided to try out another kind of brainstorming activity I learned from Meggin McIntosh (a writing coach) called "30 things." In my journal, I brainstormed a list of 30 things I know about responding to an R & R request. After reviewing the list, I wrote four or five of the main ideas from the list using one Post-it for each idea. On the next journal page, I put these ideas in order and discovered I had the basic outline for the chapter. When I started writing, I referred to my journal to make sure I would not forget anything.

Less Stress

Who is the audience for your journal? You. No one will critique your work in your journal. A journal is a place to have a conversation with yourself about your life and your work. By doing so, you can gain a healthy perspective. A journal is your place to experiment, explore, and play. A journal is a sketch pad, a doodle spot, a nonlinear space, and a flexible environment. What better place to record your sketches, diagrams, musings, wanderings, wonderings, and deliberations day by day about your professional (and personal) life?

Written expression has other benefits as well. Pennebaker (2000) has studied the value of writing short narratives. He concluded that writing reduces stress associated with dramatic life events.

> Through a series of experiments, my colleagues and I discovered that when people put their emotional upheavals into words, their physical and mental health improved markedly. Further, the act of constructing stories appeared to be a natural human process that helped individuals understand their experiences and themselves. (p. 4)

Pennebaker's work indicates that by summarizing our experiences with written language we can get some emotional and intellectual distance from the events. By externalizing with words all the events that pull on us every day, journal entries help us make sense of the world. In addition, keeping a journal gives us a greater sense of control and decreases the stress associated with dealing with the unexpected and sometimes overwhelming events in our professional life.

Reflection

A journal is a private place to have a conversation with yourself. It is a place to ask yourself questions about projects you are working on and on the future direction of your life. You may not have answers now, but it is a place to start teasing out the best approaches for the issues and opportunities presented to you. There are no reviewers. There are no critics in your journal. A journal is about you at a point in time. No one else should read it or comment on it. It is you working out what you want to do and say. Schneider (2003) remarks, "Your imaginings, your dreams, your life has significance" (p. 67). A journal marks that significance. No one else can create your journal. Journal writing is closest to the voice and, because of that, there tends to be a lack of self-consciousness in a journal. As Schneider (2003) asserts, "You don't have to [be] sensible, serious, subtle or sophisticated" (p. 66) to write in a journal. You just have to keep on writing, exploring, creating, and trusting in the process of written expression. Like any practice, the more you do it, the better you get at it and, therefore, derive deeper benefits.

How to Set Up Your Journal

The best way to approach setting up your journal is to think about how you are going to use it. Will you focus more on using it to track events and organize your professional life? If you want it to contain only to-do lists, then check out the Bullet Journal YouTube videos (Bullet Journal, 2015). The Bullet Journal approach is to make to-do lists for the year, for next month, for the week, and for the day over a series of journal pages. Those who use this method have found it quite helpful. It is a clever option because it helps the journal keeper focus on prioritizing and getting things done while tracking long-term goals.

If you want to go beyond to-do lists and incorporate more of the ideas suggested in this chapter, then consider setting up the whole journal, from formatting individual pages and creating a table of contents to having access to entries over time and adding enhancements in front and back pages attached to the cover. Box 6.1 has a brief summary of the key points about setting up your journal.

Formatting Individual Pages

For handwritten journals, I suggest that each page of the journal have two columns. One column is smaller (say 3/4″ to 1″) and the other takes up the rest of the page (5″ to 6″). In the smaller column, write the title of the entry found in the larger column. The title could be the name of a committee or meeting and a list of attendees. This smaller column is useful for summarizing the key points from the meeting. In addition, the smaller column has the date of the entry. Sometimes I write out a to-do list from the meeting in the smaller column. Because the title and date are in the smaller column, it makes it easier to find entries in the future. The larger column contains notes from the meeting, or the Post-its from a brainstorming activity. All pages are numbered from the front of the journal as well.

Creating a Table of Contents

When you start a new journal, it is important to leave the first three pages blank so you can put in your table of contents. When the journal is filled and the pages are numbered, I make a table of contents that allows me to review what I have been doing over the last six to eight months. This is a very important task because during the review I pick up some ideas that I had lost over time as well as make decisions

BOX 6.1
Setting up your handwritten journal

To maximize its potential for organization, reflection, and idea generation, pick and choose from the suggestions that make sense to you.

Setting Up Individual Pages

Draw a line to make two columns:

Smaller column metaphor: "bank of a river"	Large column metaphor: "river of experience"
Date of entry Attendees at meetings Other lists To-do lists from event	This column could contain any of the following: • Notes from a department or committee meeting • Conference presentation • Notes from a research team meeting • Post-its you generated from brainstorming • Concept maps, diagrams, sketches • Business cards from people met at a conference • Elaborated to-do lists • Free-writes or focused free-writes

Creating a Table of Contents

A table of contents is a chronological list of all the contents by page numbers. By reviewing the table of contents, you can scan all the different activities that you are involved in and make decisions about the long-term value of these commitments. You also have a log of activities that is useful when you write your narratives for promotion and tenure.

Step 1: Set aside three pages in the front of your journal for a table of contents.
Step 2: Number all the pages in your journal.
Step 3: Draw two to three vertical lines down the front pages set aside for the table of contents.
Step 4: Add entries to the table of contents in the following order (see Figure 6.1):
  • Date
  • Title of entry
  • Page number

Add enhancements inside the front and back covers
  • Front cover: To-do lists on Post-its; lists of articles submitted; list of items to add to your CV
  • Back cover: Lists of books recommended, websites; yearly calendar

about how I might want to spend my time over the next three months. I make three columns in the table of contents: the date, title of entry, and the page number. It is best to have the page number last because sometimes there is more than one entry per page. Figure 6.1 is a photo of one of my tables of contents.

Adding Enhancements Inside the Front and Back Covers

Another option is to use the inside covers in the front and back of your journal for other notes. On one page, I keep a list of all the kinds of activities I have been doing that I want to put on my CV, such as the dates of submissions of journal articles or conference presentations and committees I have worked on. In the busy-ness of my life, sometimes I forget all that I have done, and this is a quick and easy way to keep track. Inside the back cover, I keep lists of books and websites that others have recommended to me.

How to Make the Journal Work for You

The most important part of keeping a journal and using it consistently is to have it available all day and night. Take it with you as either a laptop computer, a phone, or as a hardbound handwritten volume. When you have your journal with you, you can start recording what is going on at meetings and conferences. Then, it is possible for you to make use of these ideas in the future. As you read this chapter, you may see that I use my journal in a variety of ways. Some of these foster organization and others contribute to formulating and creating ideas for my writing. All in all, organization, reflection, and expression lead to a better sense of control over my academic life and, most importantly, a reduction in stress. I don't have to remember it all. If I get a flash of insight about my work or my writing, I don't record it on a slip of paper. I put it in my journal. Figure 6.2 is a map of activities that undergird the practice of keeping a journal in your professional life. Organizational activities begin the journey while the more creative and expressive journal-writing activities lie at the other end. Of course, you can pick and choose what you consider to be the most helpful activities. As you engage in these, you are organizing, tracking activities, documenting experience, reflecting on experience, affirming your voice, and creating new connections between your ideas. You may even find a few surprises as you explore expressive writing activities, such as the focused free-write or dialogue from chapter 5.

Lists, Logs, and Records

A journal can contain lists, logs, and records. In its simplest form the journal can just be a place to keep your lists, to refer to as needed. I have a list in the back of my journal of my current doctoral students. Others have lists of books suggested by other faculty. A log is more of an expanded list that would add details about an event. Logs don't necessarily include reactions to the items on the log. Examples might include a log of the number of meetings you have had with a certain committee, a log of the

Figure 6.1 Example of a table of contents from a journal

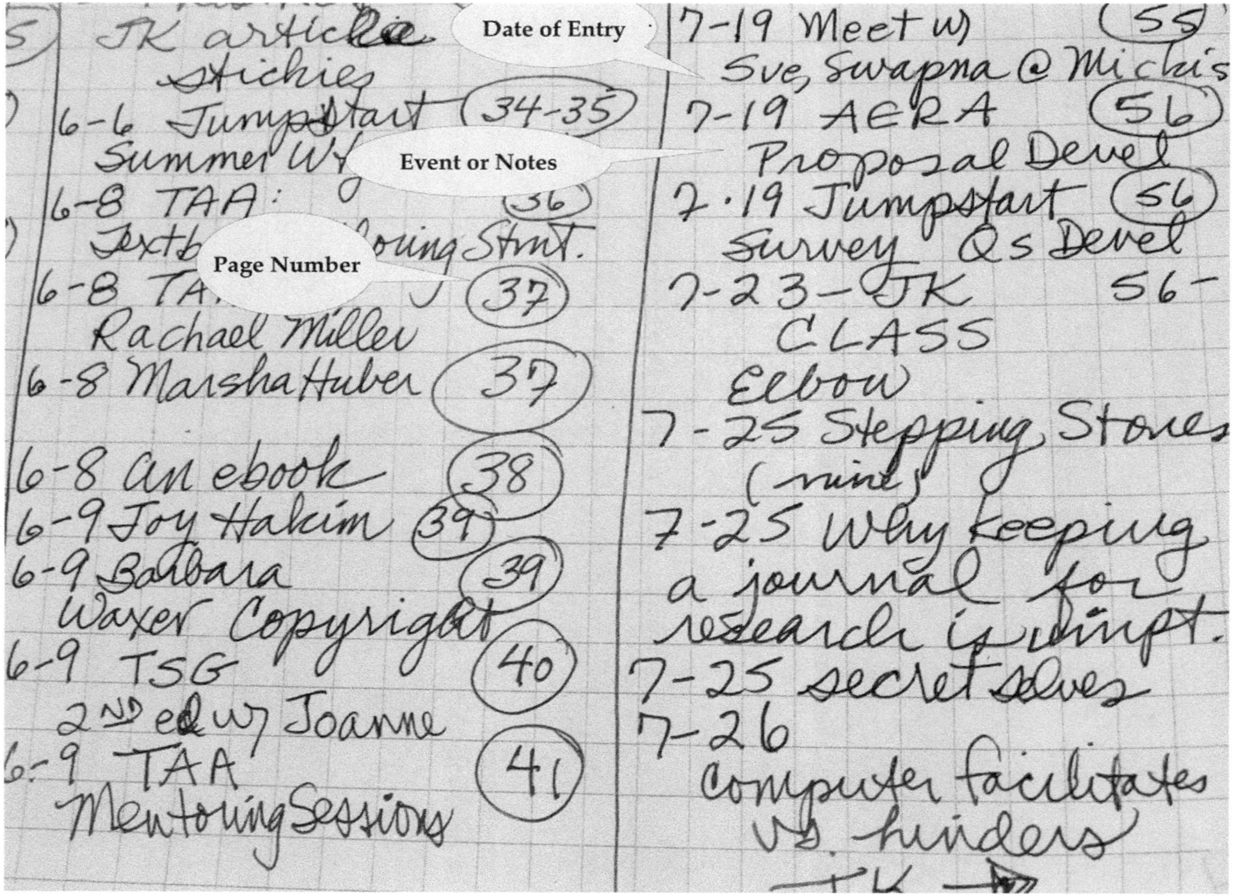

Figure 6.2 Map of journal-keeping activities

Map of journal-keeping activities

Explore
Create
• expressive writing
• drawing
• mapping
• dialogue

Make Lists
• resources
• people met
• "to do"

Reflect
• on teaching
• on research
• on writing
• on career

Keep a log of all activities
• Use Table of Contents
• Track meetings
• Make conference notes

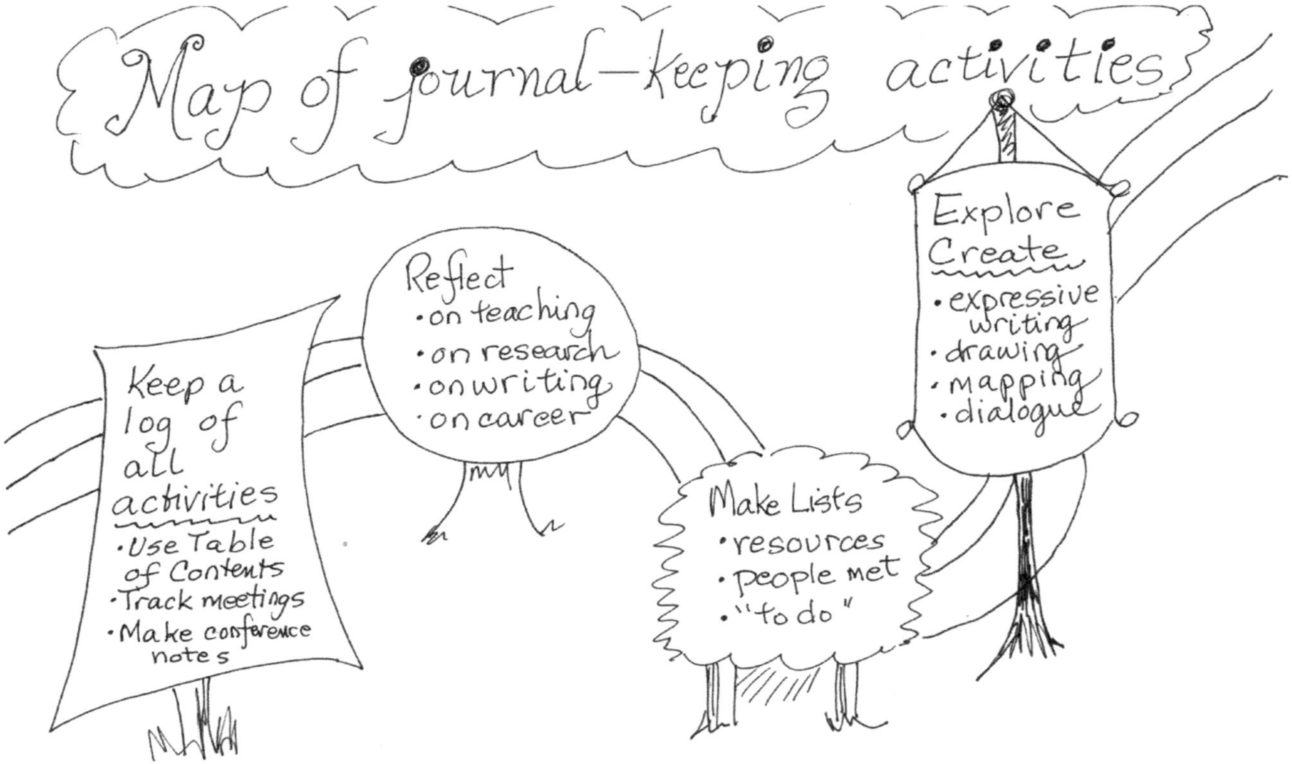

meeting agendas for department meetings, a log of activities related to your research project, or a log of articles proposed for conferences or journals. Because research requires such systematic attention to gathering data, analyzing data, and reflecting on results, a journal can be a good place to make entries along the path to better organization with your research.

Generative Writing Activities

As mentioned earlier, the journal can be a sketchbook for your ideas for current or future writing projects. By using Post-its to brainstorm initial thoughts for a writing project, as described in chapter 5 and here, you are laying the groundwork for future work. Brainstorming ideas in your journal may loosen up your current ideas and offer fresh connections.

Review and Reflect on Your Career

After you have completed the table of contents for your journal, you have a record of all the activities you have been involved in over a few months. By looking at the table of contents from several journals over the years, you have the evidence of your various contributions. You may have a list of manuscripts you have submitted and published. You may have a list of the conferences attended, as well as the number of committees you are on. As you reflect on all that you have done, you can begin to identify patterns that will be useful when you describe and defend your academic work as you write the narrative for promotion. All your work is right there in your journal—day by day, week by week, month by month, year by year. You do not have to retrieve it in your calendar nor do a frantic search in your files.

Conclusion

The main purpose of this chapter is to introduce you to keeping a journal in your professional life. Keeping this kind of journal is different from a diary of personal reflections. The journal in your professional life offers you a variety of benefits, from being more organized, reducing your stress, generating more ideas for your work, to reflecting on the direction that your overall career is taking. This chapter describes the benefits of keeping a journal, different ways to set up your journal, and a variety of activities that can be done in your journal. Whether you keep your journal on a computer or in a handwritten volume, you will have a place for ideas to incubate as well as have a significant archive of your professional life.

CHAPTER 7

Write Book Reviews

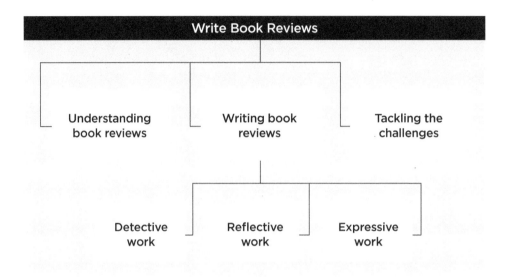

Writing a book review is a relatively fast way to get a line on your CV. For those of you unfamiliar with the term *CV*, I will explain. A CV, or curriculum vitae, is what academics call their résumé. A CV differs substantially from a resume because it is comprehensive and, thus, both longer and much more detailed. If you are relatively new to academe, a CV is a record of all your education, employment, publications, presentations, teaching, grants, awards, committee work, and contributions to professional organizations since you started graduate school. Increasing the number of publication lines on your CV means that you are presenting at conferences, receiving grants, and publishing your work. Committee work, teaching, and university service on search committees are important and expected. However, many promotion and tenure committees pay much closer attention to the number of publication lines on your CV. A published book review will add a line to your CV.

Understanding Book Reviews

What is an academic book review? A book review, in its simplest terms, is like a book report. You read a book and write a review about the book that is then published in a journal. In general, there are five basic questions that a book review answers:

1. Overall, what is this book about?
2. What are the specific contents of the chapters?
3. To whom would this book be useful?
4. What does it add to the literature on the topic?
5. What does the reviewer think about the book?

The first question is the most important one. The next three are also important because they flesh out the book contents. The last question is an evaluation. Because some journals just want the reviewer to describe the book, evaluating the book may or may not be part of the review. The purpose of this chapter is to make you more aware of what steps you can take to be relatively confident that the book review editor will publish your review.

There are two types of book reviews. The first and most common type of review is where the author writes a two- or four-paragraph review in the book review section of a peer-reviewed journal. The book review section is usually found at the back of the journal after the full-length research articles. This short review is usually more about what is in the book rather than a critique, although authors often include their evaluation of the audiences that would be interested in the book. In a book review, your job as author is to tell the reader about the contents and scope of the book. Boxes 7.1 and 7.2 are two of these shorter book reviews. Box 7.1 is from the *Magazine of Concrete Research* whereas Box 7.2 is from *Research on Social Work Practice*. Despite the disparate disciplines, you will see how the book reviews have

BOX 7.1

Analysis of text structures in a book review in *Magazine of Concrete Research*

Bertolini, B. Elsener, P. Pedeferri, E. Redaelli and Polder R. (2013). *Corrosion of Steel in Concrete—Prevention, Diagnosis, Repair,* (2nd ed.) Weinheim, Germany: Wiley-VCH Verlag, 414 pp. £115. ISBN 978-3-527-33146-8.

Review	Text structure elements
The corrosion of reinforcing steel in concrete structures has become a major concern of infrastructure owners and operators. Damage induced by steel corrosion can dramatically reduce the designed service life of the structure through strength reduction of corroding bars and loss of bond between steel and concrete. In order to design durable reinforced concrete structures it is necessary to understand why the reinforcing steel will corrode in concrete, but more importantly to know how the reinforcing steel corrosion can be prevented or controlled. The book *Corrosion of Steel in Concrete* provides a comprehensive and in-depth coverage of the science and technology of the corrosion of reinforcing steel in concrete.	Book overview and purpose

(Continues)

BOX 7.1 (*Continued*)

Review	Text structure elements
Different aspects of corrosion of steel in concrete are examined, starting from basic and essential mechanisms of the phenomenon and moving up to practical consequences for designers, contractors and owners—both for new and existing reinforced and pre-stressed concrete structures. The book comprises 20 chapters. They cover general aspects of cement and concrete materials (chapters 1 and 12), transport mechanisms of moisture and ionic species in concrete (chapter 2), degradation of concrete due to chemical attacks (chapter 3), corrosion of reinforcing steel due to concrete carbonation and chloride attack (chapters 4–6), electrochemical mechanisms of steel corrosion (chapters 7–9), hydrogen-induced stress corrosion cracking (chapter 10), concept and principle of design for durability (chapter 11), prevention of corrosion by using corrosion inhibitors, surface protection systems, and corrosion-resistant reinforcement (chapters 13–15); and chapters 16 through 20 deal with the practical aspects, which include inspection and assessment (chapter 16), monitoring (chapter 17), and methods for repair (chapters 18–20). Each chapter provides very detailed references.	Description of each chapter and its contribution to the overall topic
At the end of the book there is a well-defined subject index. The authors are five internationally well-known researchers who are experts in the fields of materials, structures, and electrochemistry. Compared to other books in the field, this book offers many useful features, such as its wide coverage of topics, emphasis on the aspect of electrochemical processes, updated contents with recent findings and new perspectives in the field and with attention to recent European standards, in-depth discussion on performance-based durability design approaches, and detailed description of the practical applications of technologies. This new edition provides valuable information for the understanding of reinforcing steel in concrete, as well as the knowledge, tools, and methods needed to prevent and/or control the deterioration of concrete structures induced by reinforcing steel corrosion. The book will provide an essential reference for students and materials scientists, who can learn from the explanations of corrosion and degradation mechanisms, as well as for practical engineers who work in the field of civil and construction engineering and are involved in the design, execution, and management of reinforced concrete structures. They will be able to concentrate on the parts of the book that deal with practical aspects of assessment, monitoring, prevention, and protection techniques.	The reviewer's evaluation of the book, the authors, and the content of the book in comparison to other texts. In addition, the reviewer describes how the book will be useful.
Long-Yuan Li, School of Engineering, University of Plymouth, Devon, United Kingdom	Who wrote this review

BOX 7.2
Analysis of text structures in a book review in *Research on Social Work Practice*

Gitlin, L. N., & Lyons, K. J. (2014). *Successful grant writing: Strategies for health and human service professionals* (4th ed.). New York, NY: Springer. 348 pp. $47.00. ISBN 978-0-8261-0090-0.

Review	Text structure elements
In an environment where budget cuts make external funding a challenge to obtain, *Successful Grant Writing: Strategies for Health and Human Services Professionals* serves as a comprehensive and strategic tool for completing competitive grants. With particular emphasis on federal grants, namely those from the National Institutes of Health (NIH), the strategies proposed within this essential resource for grant writing can also be applied to foundations. This fourth edition of the book builds off of previous versions and incorporates the significant changes NIH requires for proposal submissions, the electronic submissions of grants, and recent trends reflected in the funding priorities of human service agencies.	Book overview and purpose
The format of this book parallels previous versions, with 23 chapters subsumed under seven parts. Part 1 focuses on beginning the grant writing process by determining reasons to write a grant, gaining familiarity with funding sources, developing funding ideas, and using infrastructural support in the grant writing process. Part 2 outlines the process of grant writing itself, with detailed descriptions of specific proposal sections, writing strategies, grant writing pitfalls, as well as information on particular research proposals and supporting documentation. Part 3 covers budget preparation, and Part 4 provides models for proposal development, including varying project structures and collaboration agreements. Proposal submission intricacies are thoroughly covered in Part 5, and Part 6 affords insight about post-submission considerations, including the review process. Finally, Part 7 highlights post-award activities, such as managing the grant. The book ends with useful appendices complete with practical resources.	Description of each chapter and its contribution to the overall topic

(Continues)

BOX 7.2 (*Continued*)

Review	Text structure elements
Although this resource can be useful for any human service professional, it is specifically tailored to the novice researcher and professional seeking external funding. It provides a precise, practical, and tangible step-by-step guide for successful grantsmanship. This incremental approach makes the book useful both for writing a grant from start to finish and as a resource to write particular aspects of grant proposals. The authors also explicitly address how grant writing can be an integral component of a successful career trajectory across health and human services fields. 　　Gitlin and Lyons exemplified their grant-writing strategies by simultaneously writing in a strikingly concise and clear way and providing explicit instruction on each component of the grant writing process. For example, chapter objectives are clearly delineated. Information is conveniently summarized through the use of bullets and text boxes, with narratives covering this information in detail. This feature enables the book to be used as a reference and resource guide with information about specific components of the grant writing process being easily accessible. Furthermore, case studies provide practical application of the major tenets of the grant writing process. 　　The grant writing strategies were derived from the authors' extensive success in securing federally supported grants along with interviews with key insiders and key personnel in the grant review process. This resource provides novice professionals with credible instruction on successful grantsmanship, with particular emphasis on quantitative proposals and mixed methodologies. Although the vast majority of strategies apply to all researchers and professionals, those who tend toward more qualitative approaches may need supplemental instruction that explicitly delineates special considerations related to this methodology. 　　As a resource providing a comprehensive overview of the grant writing process, this book provides early-stage grant writers with the needed perspective to create a long-term career trajectory that includes successful grantsmanship in a highly competitive environment. The logical and consistent format of this book make it conducive for use by individual professionals and researchers, and it could easily be developed to guide a grant writing workshop or a course focusing on applying for NIH and other federal funding. This resource has direct relevancy to social work practice, as external funding becomes increasingly essential in an environment affected by tightening budgets. Therefore, successful grantsmanship is needed to develop and implement innovative and evidence-based social work interventions, training programs, and prevention programs.	The reviewer's evaluation of the book, the authors, and the content of the book in comparison to other texts. In addition, the reviewer describes how the book will be useful to particular audiences.
Catherine E. Burnette, Tulane University School of Social Work, New Orleans, Louisiana, USA	Who wrote this review?

similar text structures. Both start with an overview of the book and then march forward with a chapter-by-chapter content analysis. The last section of the review contains the reviewer's evaluation of the authors, the text itself, and the audiences who might appreciate the work.

The second type of book review is longer, approaching article length. I have seen these in several different formats. One format is an extended review where the reviewers provide paragraph-length details about each chapter (see Garcia-Laborda, 2009). Another common longer review is to compare three or four books on the same topic and critique the strengths and weaknesses of each (see Richert, 2007). In Richert's article-length review, she compares three books on the topic of teacher dispositions. Another approach for this longer review is to make a class research project out of the book review. Have your students read the book and gather data from them about the book and its usefulness. The article, then, is about their responses to the book. As with a short review, you still have to discuss the contents of the book, but the core purpose is comparing and contrasting several books or gathering responses from a sample of the book's intended audience. Many of these longer reviews are not found in the book review section of the journal but in the journal's research article section.

Not all journals publish book reviews. In addition, some journals may limit reviews to a specific issue of an annual volume. Although it varies from one journal to the next, often one faculty member is designated as book review editor and has no role in managing the manuscripts submitted for peer review for other sections of the journal. Because book reviews can be beneficial for sales, publishers usually send appropriate books speculatively to review editors. A book review editor manages the review process with prospective book review authors. If the editor has several books he or she wants reviewed, he or she will approach reviewers. These may be people who have published research articles on the topic in the journal or be members of his or her professional organization. Most short reviews are not sent out for blind peer review like a research article is. The final reviewer of the book review is the book review editor. Because the longer article-length book reviews are really more like journal articles, more than likely these will be sent out for blind peer review. Blind peer review means your article is read by the editor and other scholars, with your name removed from the manuscript.

The advantage of writing book reviews includes the fact that your writing is published. Having a published review indicates that you are getting your writing out for public scrutiny. If you might be reading this book anyway, writing the review may not be too demanding. Book reviews tend to follow a predictable text structure pattern. Short book reviews are just that, 500 to 800 words, that is, about 2 to 3 pages of double-spaced 12-point-font text. The long, article-length book reviews are 3,000 to 5,000 words, depending on the journal expectations. The longer reviews, obviously, are a bigger time commitment. In terms of your contribution to scholarship, you can argue that writing a book review is a service to your colleagues who might want to read about the book before they assign it to a class or use it in their research. This is truly a service that others value.

Book reviews are certainly appropriate at any stage of your career. If you are reading the book anyway, you might as well submit a review. However, the biggest disadvantage of writing book reviews is that as you go up in rank book reviews are less and less valued as evidence of your scholarly contribution, especially the short reviews. Before you embark on too many reviews, be sure to have a conversation with your department chair and dean as to the status of book reviews for your career track. When I have been on promotion and tenure committees, I have valued book reviews as evidence of scholarly and service contributions. But, others on the committee were skeptical of the real contribution of book reviews.

Writing Book Reviews

The section headings on detective work, reflective work, and expressive work recur in the remaining chapters related to writing specific kinds of manuscripts (chapters 8–11). One of the first steps in gaining a deeper understanding of writing different kinds of manuscripts, such as book reviews, conference proposals, journal articles, book proposals, and books, is doing some detective work. I scan the external environment looking for clues about how, where, and what other scholars have published the specific type of manuscript. What data I gather during the detective work will be fodder for reflective work, the internal work, in preparation for writing. After reflection, the expressive work is gathering my insights from the detective and reflective work to actually write the manuscript and send it off for publication. Table 7.1 identifies these three steps involved in the detective, reflective, and expressive work that you can do to write a publishable book review.

Detective Work: Scanning the External Environment

One of the biggest challenges in writing a book review is finding a journal that publishes book reviews. This is truly detective work because it is not obvious which journals publish reviews. One way to start is to look at your reference list for a manuscript or proposal that you are working on. Highlight the journals on that list. Those are the journals that are publishing work that is in your topic area. Go to the website for one of the journals. If the journal accepts book reviews, it is usually indicated in the "instructions to authors" section, and book reviews are one of the submission formats. Because you have cited an article from that specific journal in your work, it's a reasonable assumption that the journal will be interested in pertinent books you might want to review.

My librarian suggests that you do the following:

- Go to the *database* tab on your library website.
- Select search "by subject" to find your discipline.
- Select your discipline to find the collection of databases in your subject area.
- When you see the boxes in which to search for a review, write the words "book review," using quotes, in the search engine. By using the quotes, you are limiting the search to finding places where both of these words appear together.

TABLE 7.1
Writing book reviews

Detective work	Reflective work
Objective: To select a journal that publishes book reviews	**Objective:** To compare two book reviews from the same journal.
Method 1: Identify journals from your current reference list. Go online and check if they have book review submissions. Method 2: Use the library databases. In your discipline, put "book reviews," with quotes, in the search engine.	After you have filled in the second and third columns of the TSA for book reviews (Table 7.2) look across the two columns and fill in the last column to identify the text structure patterns across these two reviews. Ask what is the same and what is different across these two reviews. This column will help you structure the review for submission.
Objective: To analyze the text structures of two book reviews	
Print out two reviews from a journal in which you want to publish. Make sure they are within the last two years. Fill in Table 7.2 with details about each review.	

Expressive work

Objective: To write the review
Review the last column of the TSA where you have analyzed two book reviews. This column will guide you toward creating a review that matches the text structures of typical reviews for this specific journal. Write out organizing questions for each paragraph based on your TSA analysis of the review. For example, the first paragraph may answer the questions: Why should we care about this topic? What is the main idea of the book? Note how many sentences are typically devoted to this section and try to match that in your review.
Objective: To submit the review
Go to the journal's website and look for the "authors" section. More than likely you will not e-mail your submission to the editor but upload it to the online system. Because you have written to the editor and the editor is expecting the review, it is also helpful to e-mail him or her and tell him or her you have submitted the review and assure him or her you are open to any feedback that he or she might want to give you. Smile, take a breath, and be pleased that you are on the way to adding a line to your CV!

- Scan the list that resulted from this search. These are the journals that have book reviews. NOTE: Journals may not have reviews in every issue during the year.

You will get some citations that are strictly book reviews as well as a variety of articles whose titles contain the words "book review." My goal in this process is to identify journals that publish reviews. I also usually look for the number of pages in this citation. A short book review is usually one to two pages. This gets you started in identifying journals that publish book reviews in your discipline. Make a list of these journals for now and future reference. For the journal keepers among you, write that list into your digital or handwritten journal.

Journals vary a lot in their procedures for accepting, soliciting, and publishing book reviews. As a reviewer, once you have identified a journal, one option—which I generally don't recommend as it may not be a book the journal wants reviewed or the editor may have assigned the book to another reviewer—is to complete and send in an unsolicited review, just like sending in a journal article.

As an example of why this may be problematic, I went through the *JSTOR* database, put in the descriptor "book reviews" in the search engine, and located the journal *African Studies Review*. Its website includes the statement "The *African Studies Review* accepts neither unsolicited book reviews nor requests by potential reviewers to review specific books."

Other journals are very receptive to reviewers offering to write a review. The best approach is to e-mail the book review editor with a message that is along these lines:

> I would like to write a book review for your journal. Here is my CV, so you can see I have background related to your journal's focus. I am qualified to write a review. Here is also a list of three current books I would consider reviewing for you. Are you interested in a review of any of these? Or, do you have other suggestions?

The worst thing the book review editor can do is not respond. The second worst thing is say "no." However, you have a list of journals, so just move on to the next one. At best, some will respond and will be delighted that you would like to write a review. The caveat is that there is no guarantee of publication. That said, I have, however, found that it is rare for a journal to not accept a review, especially if you do the detective, reflective, and expressive work outlined here.

As evidence, for many years I have required (not suggested) my doctoral students to write a review and begin by contacting at least two or three book review editors. They have all expressed nervousness about writing the book review editor. In identifying a suitable book to review, some have drawn from the recommended readings for class, others have identified books in the reference list of articles they are reading, and others have undertaken an Amazon search on a topic to make a selection. The book should be very current—published in the last two years. I then guide them through the detective, reflective, and expressive work to submit a review.

They have approached book review editors using my suggested language and including the suggested information. While some editors reply that they do not accept reviews from doctoral students, others are enthusiastic, with some even sending my doctoral students the book that they want reviewed, and a few, after accepting one review, asking students if they would be willing to review a second book. Over 85% of my students proudly tell me that they have their first line on their CV, so I can vouch for the value of undertaking book reviews.

After identifying the book to review and after the journal accepts that book to review, the next step is the detective work: Find at least two reviews from a recent issue of that specific journal in which you want to publish. Journals may have unique expectations. The TSA in Table 7.2 helps you identify the typical text structures used by book review writers. When completing the TSA, note that the various criteria for the analysis are in the left column. As you read each review, jot down brief notes about that particular review in the appropriate column. Completion of a TSA is not about the actual content of the book review. You are looking for typical text structure patterns across several reviews to help you write your review.

Reflective Work: Working From the External to the Internal

Looking at both reviews that you have analyzed on the TSA for book reviews, begin to compare the two and note any consistent patterns. Beginning with how the review references the title of the book reviewed and the name of the reviewer, you look at the structures. Some reviews use subheads; some don't. Some go into great detail about each chapter; some skim the chapters very quickly. Some journals just want you to summarize the book's content and objectives without your evaluation of the book. Filling in the TSA will give you the answer to these questions: What are the common patterns across these two reviews? Should I critique the book? And, if so, how much? By filling in the TSA, you can also identify how much of your own voice and opinion are acceptable in this review. When faculty members fill in this TSA, some have found inconsistencies in the text structure of reviews within the same journal. Some include reviewer critique and some do not. If you come across any such inconsistencies, I suggest you e-mail the book review editor for an opinion.

Expressive Work: Writing and Submitting the Review

Given the TSA for book reviews' information and your reflection on the typical patterns in book reviews in the journal, you are ready to do the expressive work of writing the review. Remember that the basic questions to address are, Overall, what is this book about? What are the contents of the chapters? Who is the audience for the book?

Completion of the TSA for book reviews will more than likely affirm that a typical text structure for a short book review has an introductory paragraph that crystallizes the problem and the central thesis of the book. It would answer the question, What is this book about? Then, the next paragraph or two might march through each chapter,

TABLE 7.2

TSA: Book reviews

Title of Journal _____ Volume # _____ Issue # _____ Date(s) of analysis _____

Text structural characteristic	Book Review #1: Date: Reviewer: Short title of book reviewed:	Book Review #2: Date: Reviewer: Short title of book reviewed:	Patterns noticed across these two book reviews
1. Introduction to the review: Citation format			
2. Find sentences that answer the question "Overall, what is this book about?" Number of sentences: ___ In first paragraph: yes/no	How does the author set the book in a larger context?	How does the author set the book in a larger context?	
3. Approximate total words in review: ___ Any subheads?			
4. Total number of paragraphs: ___			
5. Find sentences that answer the question "What are the specific contents of the chapters?" Number of sentences: ___	Are there one or more sentences devoted to each chapter?	Are there one or more sentences devoted to each chapter?	
6. Find sentences that answer the question "To whom would this book be useful?" Number of sentences: ___	Who is the audience? How are they described?	Who is the audience? How are they described?	

(Continues)

TABLE 7.2 (Continued)

Text structural characteristic	Book Review #1: Date: Reviewer: Short title of book reviewed:	Book Review #2: Date: Reviewer: Short title of book reviewed:	Patterns noticed across these two book reviews
7. Find sentences that answer the question "**What does it add to the literature on the topic?**" Number of sentences: _____	How did the reviewer cite other literature? How many citations?	How did the reviewer cite other literature? How many citations?	
8. Find sentences that answer the question "**What does the reviewer think of the book?**" Number of sentences: _____	Notes on sentence patterns:		
9. Other noteworthy items: surprises, charts, references			

Items 7, 8, and 9 may nor appear in the book review, and that is good to note as well.

devoting a sentence to summarizing the content of each. Finally, the last paragraph answers the questions, Who is the audience for the book? How would they benefit from reading the book? The audience could be fellow academics, practitioners, or students. As you write the review, if the TSA you completed shows that the selected book reviews deviate from these patterns, it is very important to make sure your submission matches the common patterns for that particular journal.

The longer, article-length reviews will vary considerably in their text structures. I suggest reading chapter 9 on writing journal articles to assist you in completing a longer book review.

Today, our submissions to journals are digital. Therefore, once you have written and saved the review, go to the journal's website and follow the instructions. I suggest you have all the pieces (headings, paragraphs, citation formatting) in a .doc file format before you go to the website so that it is easy to quickly cut and paste the pieces into the book review section of the website. If you cannot easily find the submissions page, I would e-mail the book review editor for guidance. Remember, book review editors need reviewers nearly as much as you want to add a line on your CV. I have found them to be very helpful.

Tackling the Challenges

The four major challenges in writing book reviews are finding an appropriate journal, contacting the editor, settling on a book to review, and understanding the specific book review expectations submission process. By doing the detective, reflective, and expressive work in this chapter, you can surmount these challenges. Once you figure out how to write your first review, it becomes easier and easier to write subsequent ones. You can keep the list of journals that accept reviews handy for future reference. Depending on what stage of your career you are in, decide if a book review is worth the time and energy.

Conclusion

Book reviews do not require heavy lifting. Writing the review will be relatively easy after you have done some initial work communicating with the book review editor and used the detective, reflective, and expressive work guidelines offered in this chapter. Most important, recognize that a book review is an excellent first step into the world of academic writing and publishing. For many early career professionals, a book review is a perfect entry point into the world of academic publishing. A book review is a relatively undemanding exercise to get one more line, or your first line, on your CV.

CHAPTER 8

Prepare Conference Proposals and Presentations

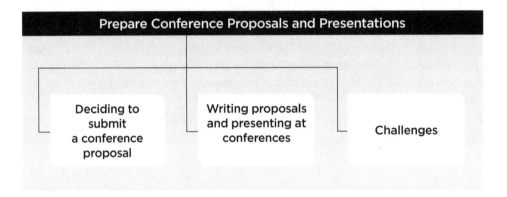

Scene: 7:30 a.m. It is your first national conference. You are standing in line for coffee and notice the name on the badge of the person in front of you.

Alex: Well, hello, Dr. Extraordinary, I just noticed your name on your badge. I want to tell you that I used at least five of your articles in my dissertation.

Dr. E: Great! I am pleased that my work was helpful.

Alex: Indeed it was. I like the way you combine theory and practice and make it accessible and understandable. Would you have a few minutes now to chat about your work with me?

Dr. E: Say, I was just getting a cup of coffee. Let's see, I can manage 10 minutes.

A conference is a perfect venue to engage in conversation with others about your work. The venue can be formal, that is, at your presentation; or informal, at a reception; or even more informal, chatting while standing in line to get your morning coffee. Even before the conference, your engagement starts with writing and submitting the proposal. When you write, you imagine the audience. When you receive feedback from reviewers before and during the conference, you see how a few select peers respond to your work.

The reviews of your submissions, conversations, and audience feedback to your presentations are the seeds for improving your work in the future. Therefore, writing conference proposals moves you further along the path to learning how others respond to your work and to writing a journal article. The ideas can germinate, develop even further at successive conferences, and willfully flower in the journal article submission.

Most faculty have many more conference presentations on their CV than publications, partly because the bar for acceptance of conference proposals tends to be lower than for the publication of a journal article. Conference proposals are typically shorter than journal articles and are usually not as polished as the journal article submission must be.

Importantly, conference proposals are another line on your CV. When promotion and tenure committees look at your CV, they will note your conference presentations. Seeing the titles and locations of these conference presentations, the committee can see the pattern of your work and the breadth of exposure of your ideas at local, regional, national, and international conferences. If you have attended two or three conferences a year fairly consistently, it will be obvious that you are willing to get your work out for public scrutiny. In addition, universities appreciate that you are also getting their name out as well. They are thinking, "Here is one of our faculty members making a national or international contribution."

Deciding to Submit a Conference Proposal

One way to make the decision to submit a conference proposal is to consider the advantages and disadvantages. Understanding these will help you make an informed decision about whether this is an appropriate time in your career to allocate your effort to submitting, attending, and presenting your work at a conference.

Advantages

The advantages of submitting a conference proposal are largely focused on refining your ideas for public presentation that can ultimately be used for a journal article or book.

You Can Try Out Different Formats for Presenting Your Work
Most conferences offer you several different formats for presenting your work. You can try out a roundtable, or, at another time, you can present a poster on a single-authored paper or one that is coauthored with others. These formats are slightly different and allow you to broaden your vocabulary of ways to describe your work. In reshaping your work to meet the expectations of different formats, you might find a new way to connect your ideas as well.

A Conference Is an Opportunity to Test-Drive Your Ideas With Peers
A conference is a wonderful place to test-drive your nascent ideas. You are not necessarily committed to writing a long journal article, and yet you can get feedback. Do your ideas make sense? What questions might people have about the topic that you

have not thought about? At a conference, the answers will be in real time, not months after you have sent in the journal article. It is a good idea to have your journal handy to jot down people's responses and questions as well as their contact information should you want to follow up on the connections you make at a conference.

You Get Acquainted With Proposal Guidelines That Are Similar to the Structure of Journal Articles

Some of the proposal guidelines contain the elements you will need to include in a final journal article. Local, state, and regional conferences have fewer guidelines and structures. Table 8.1 illustrates two sample conference proposal guidelines: the first at the state level, the second at a national/international level. One of the biggest differences between these two conference proposal guidelines is the word limit. For the Oregon Science Teachers Association (OSTA), the word limit is 100, whereas for the American Educational Research Association (AERA) the word limit is 2,000. OSTA will accept work in progress and hands-on activities, whereas AERA accepts only completed research.

As Table 8.1 illustrates, the format for conference proposal submissions and the rating scale for acceptance vary greatly. In addition, the expectations vary depending on the discipline. In the sciences and social sciences, national and international conference proposal guidelines typically expect you to use a similar text structure as you would for journal articles. The applied linguists among us call this the IMRAD model: the text structure follows the format of I, introduction; M, methods; R, results; A, analysis; and D, discussion. By following the guidelines while writing your proposal, you are familiarizing yourself with the structures often found in a journal article. The humanists among us are not generally collecting data and following the IMRAD model. Humanists depend on the scholar taking a fresh perspective on a topic. Be sure to carefully read the guidelines for the conference you are attending. I would consult senior scholars in your department or field to get a better sense of the expectations for conference proposals in any field.

You Have a Deadline

Conference proposals have deadlines. Deadlines push us to get our work out, sometimes before we think it is ready. Journal article submissions typically do not have deadlines unless you are submitting your work for a topic-driven special issue of the journal.

You Receive Feedback

The feedback on the proposal and at the conference can be encouraging. Exposing your ideas to public scrutiny is a solid way to get feedback at the early stages in the development of your final paper. First of all, you get feedback from the reviewers who decide whether your work is an example of rigorous and sound scholarship that is acceptable for conference presentation. Second, at the conference itself, you will get feedback from the discussant as well as those who attend your presentation.

TABLE 8.1

Conference proposal guidelines: Example of state- and national- level guidelines

State Conference: OSTA: Proposal Guidelines
Please include the following sheet in your proposal for the conference.
Session title: _____
Brief description: This description will appear in the final program. Please limit to 100 words.
Type of session: Choose one of the following:
1. Hands-on session that actively engages a limited number of participants in a hands-on experience with materials
2. Presentation to share an innovative teaching idea, results of research, or to discuss a topic of general or specific interest
3. Networking opportunity
Science area: Choose one:
Physical, life, earth and space, engineering and technology, general science, education research
Intended audience: Choose one:
Grade level; general; supervisors/administrators
Evaluation
All proposals will be evaluated based on the extent to which they
• adhere to the science area description and intent,
• align with one or more science area goals,
• are based on current and available research, and
• involve participants through activities and/or discussion.

(*Continues*)

TABLE 8.1 (*Continued*)

National/International Conference: AERA Guidelines

2018 AERA Annual Meeting Call for Submissions

Theme: "The dreams, possibilities, and necessity of public education"

Paper requirements: A paper submission is an individual paper with one or more co-authors, to be presented in a paper, poster, or roundtable session.

- Papers must be in the form of a complete narrative paper, whether these papers are still in progress or are the final versions for presentation. PowerPoint slides, summary tables, abstracts, or proposals to write a paper will not be considered.

- Word limits: 15 words or fewer for paper title; 120 words or fewer for abstract; 2,000 words or fewer for paper upload containing no author identification. References, tables, charts, graphs, images, and figures should be added to the end of the document and are not included in the word count. Submissions will be removed from consideration if the paper exceeds the word limit or includes author identification.

- Paper must address and will be reviewed on the following six elements:

1. Objectives or purposes

2. Perspective(s) or theoretical framework

3. Methods, techniques, or modes of inquiry

4. Data sources, evidence, objects, or materials

5. Results and/or substantiated conclusions or warrants for arguments/point of view

6. Scientific or scholarly significance of the study or work

For Some Conferences, the Process Pushes You to Create a Solid Draft
After proposal acceptance for paper presentations and some roundtables, some conferences require you to submit and upload a full paper, three to four weeks before the conference, for another review by the person who critiques your work at the conference (the designated discussant). Many faculty develop their paper well enough at this stage so that, with some slight polishing, they are ready to submit the paper to a journal after the conference. Because you are close to the work and have received some feedback on it, it is a good practice to get it out into the stream of ideas as soon as possible. However, when we return from the conference, it is hard to achieve this practice because we may have to catch up with the rest of our work as teachers and community members.

You Can Network With Like-Minded Peers
You can find "your people" at a conference, that is, colleagues from other colleges and universities who are thinking about, working on, and engaged in the topics in which you are interested. Some people find collaborators for research projects. Some connect with peers whose work can inform their work. Others attend conference professional development workshops and meet experts in the field, as well as meet other participants who share common interests. Some faculty use the conference to meet international colleagues as well. The large national and international conferences often foster subcommunities interested in specific topic areas often called SIGs, or special interest groups. These groups tend to be much smaller and welcome new members. If you attend an SIG meeting, volunteer to help with a committee or even run for office so that you get to know others who are doing work similar to yours. These networking opportunities are invaluable for your future.

Disadvantages

The disadvantages of preparing conference proposals focus on how the proposal fits in with your overall career plans because of the amount of time and money it takes to prepare and attend a conference.

Many Promotion Committees Do Not Highly Value Conference Presentations
In general, conference proposals are not as highly valued as blind, peer-reviewed journal articles. While for many of the larger national and international conferences your papers have been blind peer-reviewed, the review may not have been as thorough as the one for a journal submission. Therefore, some colleagues on these committees will not put much value on conference presentations.

The Feedback on the Proposal and Presentation Itself Can Vary Greatly
The written feedback on your proposal will contain some helpful information about how others view your work. You will get two to three reviews, often rated on a numerical scale. Yet, the quality of the reviews can vary considerably. Conference organizers put out a call for faculty to volunteer to review. Usually there is not much

monitoring of who gets to do the reviews. The chairperson of the subcommittee or the conference organizers (if it is a small conference) monitor the consistency and quality of the reviews. Chairpersons are usually well established in the organization and are published scholars. Yet, generally all they do is put out a call for reviewers and accept all who show up. If they find a reviewer who is consistently out of sync with other reviewers, they have the power to disregard the reviews.

Paper and Roundtable Presentations Have Set and Often Short Time Limits
Often, when you present a paper at a paper session or a roundtable, you are with 3 to 4 other presenters. You may have 8 minutes or 12 minutes to present. You will have to learn how to distill your topic and research into a very short time frame. When I do this, I am continually asking myself, "What would the audience really want to know about this topic?"

Conferences Are Expensive
Another significant disadvantage is the expense of attending a conference. From the flight to the hotel room to the meals to conference registration fees, conferences are expensive. Why would it be important to bear this expense?

One of my campus colleagues said she would go to conferences only if her department paid for it. She decided that it was best for her to stay on campus and write, rather than spend all that time and money. Indeed, it is a real question for each of us: "Is it worth it to spend our own funds attending conferences?"

I have found it is best to take my career in my own hands, even if I have to pay for it myself. I suggest you weigh this decision carefully. Early in your career, especially, it might be better to attend conferences. Where else can you listen to how others are thinking about the same things you care about? Where else can you make connections with others who might be collaborators on a project? Where else might you find external reviewers for your promotion and tenure files? Where else can you hear examples of what it takes to create a successful conference proposal? Even if you are not presenting, you can attend sessions where others are presenting in your topic area. You can approach scholars after the presentation to discuss their work. Attending conferences has created invaluable opportunities in my career. I made international connections. I found collaborators for research projects. It was through a conference that I sought out co-authors for my first book, an edited volume that I published with Joanne Cooper, *Tenure in the Sacred Grove: Issues and Strategies for Women and Minorities* (Cooper & Stevens, 2002). Those connections would not have happened had I not been involved in an SIG that met at the national conference.

There may be some sources on campus for travel funds that are not well advertised. You may have to investigate this yourself. I recommend you ask your department chair. I urge you to pull out all the stops to attend and present at conferences. Some universities and colleges have special budgets for travel, especially international travel. Often, to get these funds, you have to write a short proposal to the university travel committee.

The long-term investment in sharing your ideas, the networking with others with similar ideas, and the range of feedback you may gain are essential in developing your work and clarifying your career path. And, by the way, you are traveling to cities that you may not have been to before. Travel itself can be energizing, fulfilling, and a much-needed break from campus routines and, dare I say it, department politics.

Writing Proposals and Presenting at Conferences: Detective, Reflective, and Expressive Work

To write and present conference proposals, I use three approaches: detective work, reflective work, and expressive work. These three approaches do not have to be done in order. However, being cognizant of these approaches will ultimately strengthen your submission. Detective work includes a scan of the external environment: What are conference proposals? Where are conferences? The reflective work involves taking what you have learned from the external environment and scanning and reflecting on it to decide on an appropriate conference and shape your proposal to fulfill the criteria. The expressive work is writing and submitting the proposal as well as presenting your work at the conference. Table 8.2 summarizes the objectives and activities that you can do when writing proposals and presenting at conferences. The details of the detective, reflective, and expressive work follow.

Detective Work

Detective work focuses on a careful analysis of the characteristics of the external environment. What are the different kinds of conferences? What kind of proposal do I write? What does a successful submission look like? Gathering information on the range of conferences available, the type of conference presentations, and the formats of submissions will help you decide how to approach writing a conference proposal, given your discipline, interests, and career trajectory. I suggest you keep all of this valuable information in a computer file or paper file for future reference.

Become Aware of the Different Kinds of Conferences
Typically, conferences vary in size and scope as well as submission requirements. For most disciplines there are local, regional, national, and international conferences. Sometimes there are more general conferences across disciplines, such as the teaching and learning conferences that address the issue of teaching and student learning in all disciplines (Kennesaw State University, n.d.a).

Conferences differ considerably in the requirements for proposal submissions, as noted in Table 8.1. Typically, for local, state, district, and regional conferences, the bar for acceptance is lower. Local and regional conferences may require only a title and a paragraph description of 100 to 250 words. Some may allow you to present a work in progress rather than completed research.

At national and international conferences the bar for acceptance is higher. Usually national and international conferences are highly competitive and may require a

TABLE 8.2

Writing and presenting conference proposals: Summary of detective, reflective, and expressive work

Detective work	Reflective work
Objective: To become aware of different conferences	**Objective:** To shape your work to the conference theme
Learn about the different types of conferences available at local, regional, national, and international level	Consider the title of your paper to see if you can incorporate the conference theme into the title Frame the rest of your proposal to include the conference theme
Objective: To learn about the conference	**Objective:** To decide on the best presentation format
Talk to colleagues about different local, regional, national, and international conferences Go to the conference to check out the different formats Attend sessions thinking like a presenter rather than an audience member Volunteer to be a reviewer	Read the conference call for proposals on presentation formats and decide which might be the best for your work
Objective: To analyze evaluation criteria	
Carefully analyze the current conference call for proposals, including the presentation guidelines and evaluation criteria for proposal acceptance	

Expressive work

Objective: To write the proposal

Follow the exact guidelines from the call for proposals.
Use the headings offered for organizing your proposal.
Include the conference theme in your title, abstract, and body of the paper.
Write the paper in .docx format for easy uploading into the online system for submission.

Objective: To attend the conference

Attend different sessions not only for the content but also for the presentation style to learn about effective and ineffective presentations.
Find SIGs in your topic area.

Objective: To make a powerful and persuasive presentation

Recognize that different types of presentations require different types of preparation.
Practice your presentation ahead of time, especially if you have a short time frame for presentation.
Use the conference to get feedback on your work. Take notes and reflect on what captures people's interest and what doesn't.

submission of up to 2,500 words, reference lists, and completion of the corresponding research. Promotion and tenure committees value your presenting at national and international conferences more than presentations at local and regional conferences. However, if your work is in an embryonic stage and you would like to have feedback, local and regional conferences are quite appropriate. Presenting at the smaller, less competitive venues indicates to others that you are interested in getting feedback on your work. Your peers will value your efforts, especially if you are in the early stages of your career.

Where do you find out about these conferences? Some may have become acquainted with the regional, national, and international conferences during graduate school. Others may join their discipline's professional organization and find out that it organizes conferences. One way to find out about conferences is to ask the senior colleagues in your department to see which conferences they recommend that you attend. Librarians are also aware of conferences in the disciplines.

Know Formats for Conference Presentations
Typically, there are three different formats for conference presentations. When you submit your proposal for the conference, you select one or more formats for presenting your work. Roundtables, posters, and paper presentations are the common formats. Each has its own advantages and disadvantages and requires different kinds of preparation after the proposal has been submitted. Table 8.3 defines each type and summarizes the preparation needed to use this format.

Roundtables are a small gathering of three to four presenters and a usually small audience all seated around, you guessed it, a round table. Sometimes there is also a discussant who might have read your paper ahead of time. Alternatively, there may be a chair who establishes the order of presentations and has the role of timekeeper, making sure everyone has the opportunity to share their work and that there is time for questions.

The greatest advantage of roundtables is the conversation with the 8 to 12 colleagues gathered around the table. The roundtable setting is more intimate than the other two formats, posters and paper presentations, and you will hear a wider range of responses to your work. Conference organizers may not have as high a level of review for roundtable submissions. The main disadvantage of roundtables is that they may not be as highly valued by your promotion and tenure committee. Some conference organizers view roundtables as a way to present work in progress, not work completed. Other organizers hold roundtables to the same level of completed work as paper presentations and expect the submitter to have all the research done and analyzed for the submission. This expectation should be evident in the conference proposal guidelines. If it is not, try to find out who the program chair for the conference is and send him or her an e-mail.

Poster presentations are just what the title indicates. You prepare your work in such a way that it can be displayed on a large bulletin board (usually 4' by 6' or 1.2 meters by 1.8 meters). Poster sessions are usually laid out in aisles of bulletin boards, so you will have close neighbors who also have posters. Conference attendees will scan

TABLE 8.3

Three basic types of conference presentations: Roundtable, poster, and paper presentation

Type	Definition	Preparation
Roundtable	A small gathering of three or four presenters and a seated audience around a table. Offers an opportunity for an exchange of ideas with peers in an informal setting.	Depends on conference how finalized work needs to be for a roundtable. Some conferences view roundtables as a way to share work in progress; others insist roundtables are for sharing completed work.
Poster	A large bulletin-type board (4' by 6') for displaying the work. Large poster that summarizes work. Stand by the poster and be available to answer questions. No discussant.	Most successful format: Summarizes work using several eye-catching visuals and succinct text. Least successful format: Text-dominated poster with no visual appeal from the layout.
Paper presentation	Set time frame for presenting the work. Shared "stage" with others (usually presenting on related topics). Strict time limits. Discussant who publicly shares comments on the work.	Paper sent to discussant ahead of time. Preparation is much like that for a journal article. Most successful: PowerPoints that summarize the work. Least successful: Reading of paper to the audience.

posters as they walk the aisles to see what topics attract them (so succinct titles and engaging layouts are important). Poster sessions are usually 45 to 60 minutes long. The posters may also be divided up in sections by preidentified topics of interest. As a poster presenter, you generally can talk to only one person at a time. Some poster presenters have handouts for people who summarize the key points of the work or are a smaller version of the larger poster.

The poster session audience needs to understand the big picture of your work quickly, and striking visuals help immensely. The poster should invite the passers-by to engage in conversation. The least successful posters are in small print without accompanying visuals: photos, diagrams, or maps that summarize the topic. The text dominates the poster and requires a close reading to even begin to understand what is important about the work. Table 8.4 is a poster evaluation rubric that includes only the highest level of performance. However, it gives a clear picture of the many parts of a poster that make it a "visual abstract" of your work, as the rubric notes. Following these criteria can help you produce a better poster.

TABLE 8.4
Poster evaluation rubric

Category	*Highest level of performance*
Overall appearance Rule: Use a light background color, solid nongradient fill pattern; two or three font colors (dark text on light background works best).	**Very pleasing** to look at. **Particularly nice** colors and graphics. Winner: An effective visual display of data, an "illustrated abstract."
White space Rule: Don't create large, monolithic blocks of text. Do not give impression of solid mass of text and graphics.	**Lots.** Plenty of room to rest the eyes. Lots of separation.
Text/graphics balance Rule: Use graphics (pie, bar, line) when possible to present data but don't force audience to guess the point of the graphic.	**Balanced.** Text and graphics are evenly dispersed in the poster. **Enough text used to explain the graphics.**
Text size and accuracy Rule: Use 16-point font at the bare minimum, preferably sans serif. Must run spell check and check spelling of medical and research terminology.	**Very easy to read.** Fonts large enough to read from two meters away and fonts must be consistent. **All words and terms spelled correctly.**
Organization and flow Rule: Use headings in contrasting color; use three- or four-column format for flow.	**Explicit** numbering used or **columns** used to indicate logical flow (top to bottom, then left to right)

(Continues)

TABLE 8.4 (*Continued*)

Category	Highest level of performance
Author identification Rule: Identify authors and affiliations. Drop the dot in PhD, RN, and after first initials; use comma to separate names.	**Complete.** All names listed with affiliations. Enough information to contact author by mail, phone, or e-mail.
Research objective Rule: Tell readers why your work matters	**Explicit.** This includes headings of "Objectives," "Aims," "Goals," and so on
Research method/main points Rule: Tell reader about the design, sample, and main variables relevant to the research objectives/aims.	**Complete.** This includes research design; eligibility criteria; overall number for the sample; predictor; outcome; and confounding variables, if they apply.
Results Rule: Share just the main results relevant to the research objectives/aims.	**Explicitly labeled.** Uses heading (e.g., "Main Points," "Conclusions," "Results")
Discussion/Conclusion/Recommendation Rule: Interpret findings, summarize, and recommend what's next	**Explicitly labeled.** "Discussion," "Conclusions," and "Implications" headings are used and stand out.

Adapted from Hess, G. R., Tosney, K. W., & Liegel, L. H (n.d.). 60-second evaluation. *Creating Effective Poster Presentations*. Available from www.ncsu.edu/project/posters

Paper presentations at national and international conferences are generally regarded as meeting the most rigorous review criteria. Using a list of established criteria, other faculty from your discipline review your proposal. This is a blind review, which means that your name is not on the paper they evaluate. Once your proposal is accepted, you will need to write a paper that fully describes your work, which is sent in to the discussant a few weeks before the conference. The discussant, having received all the papers, is expected to prepare comments on your paper and the other papers accepted for this paper session. During the paper presentation session itself, the three or four paper presenters typically must distill their work into a short time frame (10 to 20 minutes), often using a PowerPoint to highlight key ideas from the paper. The discussant has some time at the end of the session to comment publicly on your work. Time can also be set aside for audience questions. The most successful paper presentations crisply summarize their work using succinct and appealing slides. The least successful paper presentations are where the presenter reads the paper to the audience and ignores time limits. Given that many of us have little training in creating an effective PowerPoint, you might want to access resources such as the eLearning Brothers site (https://elearningbrothers.com/6-tips-creating-effective-powerpoint-presentation/).

Analyze Guidelines for Writing Your Proposal
The last bit of detective work that you can undertake is to read the conference call for proposals very carefully. Typically, conferences have a title and a description of the focus of the conference for a particular year. Whether you are doing a roundtable, poster, or paper presentation, typically the guidelines are the same. By analyzing these guidelines and then reflecting on the conference description, you can begin to think how your work contributes to the ongoing themes of the conference itself.

Reflective Work

Reflective work begins as you gather information about conferences and proposals during the detective work stage. You will need to make decisions about which conference is best for you, as well as what type of format you might want to choose.

Decide on a Conference
After you have become aware of the local, regional, national, or international conferences in your discipline, your next job is to decide what kind of conference is appropriate for your work at this time and at this stage of your career. The local and regional conferences are valuable for networking within your region. In addition, because it is not as difficult to write 100 words versus a 2,500-word document, you might want to consider local and regional conferences early in your career. The accepted presentation becomes another line on your CV, after all. However, the more valuable lines come from presenting at national and international conferences where your work is reviewed more rigorously. Another reason to consider the national and international conferences is that this is an opportunity to network with like-minded individuals across the world.

Select a Presentation Format
The next bit of reflective work is to decide what format you would like to use: poster, roundtable, or paper presentation. For many conferences, the proposal is the same for all three and you can select one, two, or all three alternatives as presentation formats. When I was a conference program chair, I gathered all the reviews of the papers and compared the scores for the different proposals based on the predetermined criteria. I was given a certain number of program time slots to fill. Generally, I had more roundtable and poster slots and fewer paper presentation time slots. Some authors often selected only one format. That choice limited my options for allocating slots, given the reviewers' scoring. If you submit only for a paper presentation, your paper may be rejected on the grounds its overall score isn't high enough for a paper presentation. Yet, your score may be high enough to be included as a roundtable or poster presentation. I suggest that you do not close your options and lose the opportunity for public input on your work. It's advisable to select as many different formats as possible.

One criterion for your choice of format might be the amount and type of feedback you would like on your work. Roundtables are designed for face-to-face discussion in an informal question-and-answer format. Other scholars will also be presenting their work, so the full time period has to be divided up among the presenters, and the opportunities for interaction are good. Even as a full professor now, I often rank roundtables as my first choice, largely because roundtables give me the most opportunity to talk casually with others about my work. The input is not limited to just one person, the discussant, as is often the case with paper presentations, where general Q&A time may be limited. Posters are another opportunity for informal conversations with those attracted to your work. Of course, they will not have read your paper, but they can comment on the key points that you have on the poster.

Paper presentations are formal opportunities to receive public feedback from the discussant who has heard you present your paper as well as read it. The only one who will have read your full paper is the discussant. Discussants tend to be respected scholars who have a broad view of the field. A helpful discussant will often compare all the papers presented in the paper presentation session and offer suggestions for strengthening and clarifying your work. All these options are opportunities to take notes of the comments and questions your research has generated and use this feedback in your next iteration of your work.

The feedback you get from these various audiences is critical in the development of your work. I pay attention to the questions that people ask as well as the comments that people make. Some questions, such as "What do you mean by reflection on your teaching practice?," reveal the need for greater clarity. Others, such as "I was wondering if your doctoral program was in the United States or England," indicate the need to provide context. Context is essential for an increasingly international audience. I write down the questions and comments in my journal to be able to reflect on them when I start to revise the work.

Expressive Work

The expressive work you will do next refers to writing and submitting the proposal, as well as attending and presenting at the conference.

Write the Proposal

From the detective and reflective work, you have enough information to write a proposal. Make sure to closely follow the guidelines in the call for proposals for the conference. If the guidelines list the sections of the proposal that will be reviewed, I typically use those exact words as boldfaced headings for my sections of the proposal. Reviewers are going down the list of these criteria and checking off the quality of the work in reference to the criteria. I figure, why not help them out and label my sections to match their review categories? Go back to Table 8.1 for the AERA conference proposal guidelines. I would divide up my paper into the six elements listed and use those elements as my headings. The first one would be "Objectives or Purposes."

Most conferences have themes. The organizers are interested in engaging the community in a deeper and substantive conversation on the conference theme. Usually the theme is the result of the conference organizers deciding that this topic is timely and germane to the discipline and deserves a closer examination by scholars. Your inclusion of the conference theme often is one of the review criteria. Where should you include the conference theme? I start with the title. For the 2017 Professional and Organizational Development Conference, the theme was "Defining What Matters." The title of our presentation was "A Community of Practice That Matters: Developing a Faculty Academic Writing Program." Including the theme in the title and abstract of your work indicates you are excited and ready to join the conversation around this theme.

Write the proposal in Microsoft Word format and include all the headings from the guide for proposals. Proposals today are submitted online. You will have a field for the title, then move on to another field for the abstract; then on to another field for the body of the paper. You may have a different field for the references. If I have the proposal in Word format, I can cut and paste all the pieces into the right fields as I move through the online submission process.

Attend the Conference
How you spend your time at the conference can improve the quality of your future submissions and enhance your career. Go to roundtables. Walk around the poster sessions. Attend paper presentations. Besides attending these sessions for the content, I suggest you think like a presenter and glean insight into giving presentations themselves. Which presentation styles appeal to you? What is the presenter doing that engages the audience? What is the presenter doing that confuses the audience? What can you learn from his or her presentation style about what you can do in the future?

Make a Powerful and Persuasive Presentation
The last step in working on conference proposals is to make the presentation at the conference. Given that there are typically three different kinds of presentations at conferences, preparation for each one is different.

Table 8.5 summarizes the key ideas for preparing for each type of conference presentation before, during, and after the presentation. Even after you make your presentation, to glean as much from the feedback as possible, recall the questions that people had during your presentation. Often their questions can point you to areas where your work can be strengthened. In this way, you are "mining" the feedback. The attendees of your session are your audience, the audience you will be writing for in the future. Therefore, their responses, from questions to casual conversations, provide gems of wisdom about what aspect of your work others are interested in. You can imagine this audience as you write. Your work will communicate more clearly to this audience, and you will meet audience and reader needs because of these insights.

Challenges

Given all the preparative work you have done up to now, you will be able to submit a strong proposal. However, there are some significant challenges with writing

TABLE 8.5

Comparison of preparation for presentation before, during, and after the roundtable, poster, or paper presentation

Type of presentation	Before presentation	During presentation	After presentation
Roundtables	Copies of your paper for you; two to three to give away. Write on front: "Draft copy, please contact me before this paper is distributed to anyone." Make sure your e-mail and contact information are on the front of the paper.	Clarify how much time you have to present. Some people prepare a short PowerPoint and show it on their iPad or computer as they present. Others simply present the paper.	Recall questions audience asked. Write down questions for future modifications of your paper or have a peer write them down during the roundtable.
Posters	Make a mock-up of your poster in PowerPoint. Get poster printed professionally.	Stand by your poster. Have business cards or a small version of your poster ready.	Write down any questions people asked as soon as you can during and after the poster session.
Paper presentations	Make a PowerPoint of key parts of your presentation. Practice your presentation to stay within time limit.	Get to the room ahead of time to set up. Clarify how much time you have to present with the discussant. Try not to read your PowerPoint with your back to the audience.	Write down any comments or questions from the discussant and the audience. Stay for a few minutes after the end of the session. Some audience members prefer one-on-one conversations.

and submitting conference proposals. First, it is very difficult to find examples of successful conference proposals on which to model your proposal. Second, variability among reviewers may be confusing and, yet, it is part of the proposal submission process. Third, making a financial commitment to attend and present at conferences is an important step in your career. Let us look at these in turn.

Finding Examples

I am not sure why there are not examples of successful proposals to review. In my experience, conferences don't give you examples of typically successful proposals; therefore, make it your job to find some examples, or to make a collection of proposals from your work or from that of your peers. One way to improve on your conference proposals is to keep a file of your accepted and rejected proposals as well as the reviews of these proposals. Another way to find out about writing a successful proposal is to ask senior colleagues and other faculty for examples of their successful conference proposals. Making a collection of successful proposals and analyzing their components as detective work can help you hone your next conference proposal.

Coping With Reviewer Variability

Proposal reviews are often uneven; that is, there can be wide variances in the ratings among reviewers. Newer and sometimes inexperienced faculty might be the reviewers for conference proposals. Generally, there is no training for reviewers, and the use of inexperienced reviewers can result in wide variance among the review scores. I suppose the assumption is that if you can write a proposal and you are a member of the discipline, you qualify as a competent reviewer of conference proposals. That is not always the case. Don't let yourself be discouraged or devastated by a highly critical review. If there are stark differences among the reviewers on one proposal, sometimes the program chair will send the proposal out for review by another faculty member. Note that the person who finally settles the differences among the scores is the program chair.

Making a Financial Commitment to Attend Conferences

Finally, as noted previously, attending national and international conferences is expensive. I urge you to pull out all the stops to attend and present at conferences. The long-term investment in sharing your ideas, networking with others with similar ideas, and obtaining the widest range of feedback possible is essential in a faculty career.

Conclusion

Proposing, attending, and presenting at local, regional, national, and international conferences has great benefits for your long-term career trajectory. Even though conference presentations are usually not the most valued type of manuscript for promotion and tenure committees, they play an important role in helping you engage with others about your work and laying the groundwork for a journal article. This engagement can be as a presenter, a reviewer of conference proposals, or simply as an attendee. You can network with those who share your common interests and build up a community outside of your own university or college with those whom you converse about your ideas. You can learn from others and they can learn from you. You can see which of your ideas seem to have the most appeal. You can see also which ones might need to be clarified. Your promotion and tenure committee can see that you are seeking feedback outside the narrow confines of your own university by submitting and presenting at conferences. Writing and presenting conference proposals is a winning choice in an academic career.

Presenting at conferences may also be an important step in developing and refining eventual journal articles. As noted in the introduction to this chapter, there is a continuum of activities as an academic that set you up for success. Think about your CV as your academic life curriculum, which you have designed. No one will tell you to write a book review, conference proposal, journal article, or book. You will need to reflect on where this type of manuscript fits into your career plan as well as what you can gain from doing it. Hence, you are creating your own education, your own curriculum, for studying and advancing your work.

Write and Submit Journal Articles

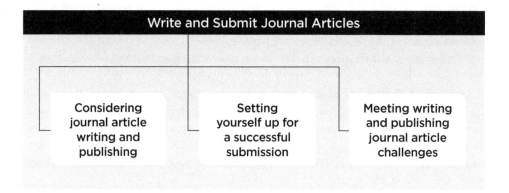

This chapter is about the why and how of writing for and publishing in peer-reviewed journals. When people think of the adage "Publish or perish," the publishing part usually refers to publishing blind, peer-reviewed journal articles. For some faculty positions, if you do not publish, you will "perish" and not receive the tenure. If you are not on the tenure-track system, publishing may or may not be important. For non-tenure-track faculty, while publishing may not be expected, institutions may acknowledge your contribution positively. Indeed, there are many publishing opportunities that are not necessarily blind reviewed that can add to your career trajectory. Yet, today it seems more and more difficult to get articles published (Weaver, Robbie, & Radloff, 2014). Dickson and colleagues (2009) have noted that there is an overall journal article rejection rate of 65%. The career stakes, plus high rejection rates, coupled with increasing pressure to publish become a recipe for anxiety, frustration, and stress. The purpose of this chapter is to offer you the knowledge, strategies, and insights to publish journal articles and meet the challenges with persistence, confidence, and awareness.

The aforementioned journal article rejection rate suggests there are many ways to go wrong when you submit your work to a journal. Belcher (2009b) argues that the basic reason that journal articles are rejected is that they contain no argument. Although very important, lack of argument is not the only reason. When I ask faculty why journal articles are rejected, most say it is because the article fails to convey one of two key ideas: It does not communicate anything of significance or it lacks depth in covering the literature. As managing editor of all the education journals for Routledge, Hobbs (personal communication, April 15, 2013) surveyed his editors and created a list of the top 10 reasons why journal articles are rejected (Table 9.1).

The list of reasons why journal articles are rejected includes different ways the writer can go wrong. What faculty find startling about the list is that the majority of items have nothing to do with lacking significance or depth. Six items out of 10 (items 1, 3, 4, 5, 7, and 9) have to do with journal selection, formatting, and attention to detail.

The good news is that attention to detail, monitoring the length of text, sending it to the right journal, using proper grammar, and so on are easier to fix than attention to the theoretical framework or significance. You will increase your chances of publication by taking care of these details while working on the more complex issues such as identifying the theoretical framework; making sure it is a "proper journal article," to use Hobbs's phrase; and crafting an argument. The right-hand column in Table 9.1 refers to what actions you can take to avoid this reason for rejection. In the next section, I step back from these details to consider the overall context of journal article writing and publishing through describing its advantages and disadvantages.

Considering Journal Article Writing and Publishing

One obvious reason to publish journal articles is that your institution has linked promotion, even tenure, to the number and quality of your publications. Your university expects you to publish, or does it? You need as definitive an answer as possible from your institution. Ask the person who explained your work responsibilities when you were hired. This may be your department chair, your dean, or other supervisor. If you have a faculty committee that contributes to promotion decisions, you can check with the chair of that committee. These administrators and peers might be able to tell you exactly what is expected—the number and type of contributions. More than likely their answer will be vague. Because each faculty member's contributions can be so very different, he or she doesn't want to be held to a commitment. Yet, it is still wise to get as much information as you can about the institutional expectations for publishing in peer-reviewed journals.

Some of you may be at teaching colleges and universities whose missions are to serve students through teaching and there is no expectation that you publish. Yet, even in a teaching university or college, and, as you plan your career path, the answer to the question of whether publishing in peer-reviewed journals contributes to your advancement is very important. As you approach journal article writing and publishing, it is worth considering the advantages, disadvantages, and some cautionary tales.

Advantages

In most academic career paths the advantages of writing journal articles are significant.

TABLE 9.1

Top 10 reasons journal articles are rejected and what to do about each

Reason for rejection	How to address this reason for rejection
1. Sent to the wrong journal; doesn't fit aims and/or scope; fails to engage issues addressed by journal	Detective work
2. Not a proper journal article (too journalistic, clearly a consultancy project such as a grant or report)	Reflective work
3. Too long (ignores journal limits) or too short	Expressive work
4. Poor regard to journal conventions or academic writing conventions	Expressive work
5. Bad style, grammar, punctuation, poor English (not corrected by native speaker)	Find peer reader or hire an editor
6. Fails to say anything of significance or states the obvious at tedious length	Reflective work
7. Not properly contextualized (e.g., concentrates on parochial interests and ignores needs of international or generally wider readership)	Reflective work
8. Poor theoretical framework (including references to relevant literature)	Reflective work
9. Scrappily presented and clearly not proofread	Hire an editor
10. Libelous, unethical, rude	Share document with others to modify tone

Hobbs, G. (April 15, 2013). Publishing in academic journals: Tips to help you succeed. (PowerPoint, personal communication).

You Will Get Your Ideas Out for Review

Even if publishing journal articles is not a requirement at your university, sending your work out for publication means you are sharing your ideas with others. You are subjecting your work to public review. When you write a journal article, you are entering the conversation with others who are interested in this topic. The readers will not only be the relatively small group that attends a conference but also constitute a potentially larger audience with national and even international reach.

You Will Clarify Your Thinking Through Writing

I recall a cartoon where a person had a swirl of ideas in her head, a pen in hand with her arm arched ready to write, but hesitated as she realized, "I had it all figured out in my head. What happened? Writing is nature's way of telling me how sloppy my thinking is." As noted earlier, writing is thinking. Writing is sometimes done after you have spent some time thinking, for sure. Some people believe that their work has to be finished in their heads before they put pen to paper or fingers to the keyboard. For very few of us, this is true. For the majority of us, when we first put words on the page for a new manuscript, we realize that the ideas were not as clear as we first thought. However, writing itself actually is a process whereby, as you write, you start articulating, thinking, and connecting ideas and making sense of your experience through the written word.

Why is writing as thinking important in terms of writing articles for publication? Writing a journal article depends on the development of personal, professional, and scholarly traits. All of these are threaded through the needle of your real-time writing experience as you sit down to write. Adopt the idea that your first draft will be a "sloppy copy" and accept it, knowing that the draft will improve as you write, rewrite, edit, and rewrite. Your thinking will get progressively clearer and clearer. A journal article requires you to hone your writing in certain ways—to limit the number of words, to follow a text structure, and to be rigorous in your research methodology, to name a few key rhetorical moves. As you proceed, your thoughts become more refined, specific, and clear. An additional benefit comes after you write about a topic; your words are woven into the tapestry of your oral expression so that you speak more clearly about the topic.

You Are Contributing to the Academic Community

Remember what we are doing in writing journal articles is making a contribution, sharing our discoveries and perspectives. If you don't write what you know and believe, it will not get communicated. Who will then communicate these ideas? You. You have a unique contribution to make to your discipline and to your audience. Your writing may not be as perfect as you want it to be, but, over time, your writing will get better and better with practice. You will begin to reap the benefits of being an active, scholarly community member who contributes his or her own ideas and fresh perspectives to those you serve and care about.

When Politics Get Squirrely, You Have Something Positive to Do: Just Close Your Office Door and Write

In my many years in the academy, I have seen my share of politics and even fell victim to them as well. By allocating time to writing, I have kept myself balanced. I knew that in the long run my overall work would be judged on the number and quality of my published contributions—grants, journal articles, and books. Connecting with my "people" in other departments on campus and at national and international conferences, as well as getting my work published, kept me excited and energized. The challenging department politics paled in the light of these valuable professional connections with esteemed peers who cared about me and my work.

You Are More Than Likely to Advance in Your Academic Career

For over six years, I served as member and chair of my department's promotion and tenure committee at PSU, an urban comprehensive university. Over my 20 years at PSU for evaluating both tenure-line faculty and contingent faculty (no tenure guarantee, fixed terms of service), my advice to faculty was to demonstrate a pattern of consistent publication across a variety of writing types, from book reviews to conference presentations and journal articles. As chair, I voted favorably for the faculty member who was willing to do the hard work of writing and take the risks of having others review his or her work for publication. Therefore, from my experience and that of others, given a pattern of performance over time, it is more likely you will advance in your career.

Disadvantages

Considering the disadvantages will help you decide whether or not writing journal articles fits in your career trajectory.

Writing Is Not Easy

Writing takes time. You need motivation and momentum to keep at it. If you find that writing is not easy and that it seems to gobble up your time with little immediate evidence of its benefit, then you understand a fundamental notion about writing. It is not necessarily easy, and the returns are not immediately obvious. No one will tell you when to write, what to write, how to write, or even the best strategies to get it done. However, as you become a student of academic writing and begin to collect and internalize the strategies that keep you motivated and engaged, your understanding of and patience with the writing and publication process will grow.

The Feedback Is Not Immediate

One basic problem with writing journal articles is the time it takes to get feedback on your manuscript. Those who have studied the effects of feedback (Hattie & Timperley, 2007) remind us that one of the best ways to foster responsiveness to feedback is to give immediate feedback. The closer the feedback is to the production of the work, the more likely the writer will be able to incorporate the feedback.

However, peer reviews of faculty manuscripts are far from immediate. It can take three to six months or more to get a response from journal reviewers. The only time you get a quicker response is usually when the editor rejects the submission outright and does not send it out to reviewers. You will then get your manuscript back in a couple of weeks. Sigh. (But, move on to the next journal on your list!)

Peer Reviews Can Be Demoralizing
Faculty review of journal articles can be helpful. They also can be demoralizing. Some reviewers have a tendency to be highly critical, not only of the work but also the writer himself or herself. On the positive side, I've encountered very helpful reviews that have helped me clarify my work. Chapter 11 goes into much greater detail on how to respond to a review and not be discouraged and demoralized.

Journal Article Text Structures and Expectations May Feel Constraining
Academic writing is not creative writing, although, as I argue in chapters 5, there are many creative elements. Yet, for some of us, one downside can be the structures that constrain your thinking. Using the IMRAD (introduction, methods, results, analysis, and discussion) structure over and over again can feel formulaic and even boring.

It Is Difficult to Decipher Expectations
Even within these somewhat predictable structures for journal articles, there are often so many choices to make when approaching writing a journal article that it can be difficult to know what is the best choice. Which journal is the best choice? What kind of argument should I make? What is the best title for the work? What should I put in the abstract? For social scientists and the physical scientists, the choices may be different: How do I present results? What kind of tables should I include for quantitative results? How do I manage the qualitative results? Where do I put the intervention I used, in the methods or in the introduction? In the humanities, the choices might also be different: How much time do I spend acknowledging prior thinking on this topic before I get to my ideas? When is a draft really done? These are critical decisions. With so many decisions to be made, it is difficult to feel confident that you are making the best decisions. Many of the strategies in this chapter and others offer you some insight into how to meet the often not-so-obvious expectations and make more informed decisions.

In summary, when considering the advantages and disadvantages of journal article publishing, I suggest, as I have earlier, that becoming a student of academic writing will give you the strategies as well as the confidence to benefit from the advantages and to diminish the effect of the disadvantages of journal article publishing.

I have worked with the faculty at PSU as the faculty in residence for academic writing for five years. In this role, faculty members have applied many of the strategies to their various manuscripts in different disciplines. In addition, I have had the opportunity to share these strategies at workshops and in international settings. In the remainder of this chapter I share what I've learned from faculty through identifying the external expectations (detective work) and the internal choices (reflective work) and writing activities (expressive work) that will lessen your frustration and stress related to meeting journal article writing and publishing expectations. I hope these strategies and insights will ultimately foster the knowledge and confidence that lead to increased productivity, deeper satisfaction, and much less stress with the journal article writing process.

Setting Yourself Up for a Successful Submission: Detective, Reflective, and Expressive Work

Detective work, reflective work, and expressive work are three approaches for writing a journal article that lead to the creation of a manuscript that meets the tacit expectations of a selected journal. During detective work, you scan the external environment—finding a journal that is a good match for your work and mining the expectations of that journal. The next approach is reflective work, where you are more internally focused, reflecting on what you have learned during the detective work as well as what you already know about journal article writing and publishing. You might ask yourself, "How can I modify my manuscript to match that journal's expectations and thereby increase the likelihood that my work will be accepted?" Building on the foundation from the detective work and reflective work, the last approach, expressive work, weaves together your insights to structure, write, and submit your manuscript. These three approaches are just a framework to consider and do not have to be completed in any particular order.

Detective Work

The focus of detective work is to become very familiar with the journals in your field. Ultimately, you want to find journals that share your interest and are engaged in the academic conversation about your topic. Once you have identified appropriate journals, then you can "mine" them for a deeper understanding of the journals themselves. Because the turnaround time for feedback on journal articles is so long (three to six months) and the publication time is at least one year from initial submission, figuring out which journals will be the best match for your work is critical. In the long run, time invested at this part of the process will pay large dividends in time and in more of your work will be published.

Finding Journals

Early on in your career, because there are so many journals available, finding an appropriate journal may seem like a daunting task. There is not one simple strategy for doing so. To begin, what you are looking for is a journal where others are writing about what you are writing about. By the end of detective work, and depending on your discipline, you should have a list of 10 to 15 journals that are potential outlets for your work.

Where do you start? Remember, you are not looking for the specific content of a single journal article per se; you are interested in the name of the journal itself. Here is a list of several places to start your search using journal articles and manuscripts:

- One of the first places to look for journals related to your topic is in the *reference list of an article on your topic*. This is probably an article where you have taken many notes.
- If you have already published or are in the later stages of writing an article, look for journals *in the reference list of the manuscript that you are crafting*. Because you have cited the work, it is likely that that specific journal will be interested in more manuscripts on this topic.
- If your topic is related to your dissertation, *the reference list in your dissertation can certainly provide a wealth of potential journals*. After all, the people you are citing are having the "conversation" about this topic and, when you submit your work, you can join that conversation.

Highlight all the journals on each of these reference lists. Then, move this list either to your own handwritten or online journal, or to a spreadsheet that ultimately will include vital information such as title, link to website, acceptance rate, journal scope, and topics covered.

The next place to identify potential outlets for your work is in library databases that focus only on journals for publishing academic work. For a large set of journals, these particular databases link to submission guidelines and note acceptance rates, reviewer policies, and so on. Cabell's Directories and Ulrichs International Publication Directory are common ones. You can use these lists to enlarge your list of potential outlets for your work as well as dig deeper into the journals themselves. You can get journal lists for certain categories such as education or communication. Once you get the list of journals, there are pages for individual journals that include some very useful information, such as the acceptance rate. Another link found on Cabell's Directories for each specific journal is a hot link to the journal's website where you can find the topics the journal covers, as well as the author submission guidelines. In our library, Cabell's Directories is listed online under the section titled "Databases and articles," which, when clicked, takes me to an alphabetical list of databases and articles where Cabell's Directories is listed under "C," along with all the other databases.

Alternatively, you can access databases such as EBSCO Host, JSTOR, or Web of Science. Do a search for articles using the key words you commonly use or use the key words from articles that you have read. The key words of articles are often included at the end of the abstract. Enter several of those words into the search engine boxes and, instead of looking at the articles, note the journals that come up in your database search. These are obviously journals that are publishing articles in your topic area. Take note of these to investigate them further to check their acceptance rate, their scope, and their review process.

Yet another way to add to your repertoire of journals is to ask your experienced and well-published peers what journals they might suggest. Many will be reviewing for journals already. Others may even be journal editors. If your peers are journal editors, they might be able to give you specific insight into making a submission as well.

Finally, if you are using a citation management system (CMS) such as Zotero, Mendeley, EndNote, or others, your references are probably in a file within that system. By sorting your list of references in the CMS by publication, you will see that some journals appear more often than others. These could also be potential outlets for your work. For more detailed information about how to use Zotero, the CMS I prefer and know very well, see appendix D.

Mining Journals

After you have identified some potential journals, start to mine those journals to understand how they are alike and different, and how you can use what you have learned to inform your choice of a journal for submission.

How are journals alike? Journals are alike in their publishing model. Journals are also called *serials,* as librarians call them, because they are published in a series. If you look at the bibliographic citation for a journal article, you can see how serials are numbered. In both APA and Chicago's author-date formatting of the reference list, the volume number, issue, and pages appear after the title of the journal. The volume number ties the journal to a year. See the following examples:

APA formatting:
Cameron, J., Nairn, K., & Higgins, J. (2009). Demystifying academic writing: Reflections on emotions, know-how and academic identity. *Journal of Geography in Higher Education, 33*(2), 269–284.

Chicago formatting:
Cameron, Jenny, Karen Nairn, and Jane Higgins. 2009. "Demystifying Academic Writing: Reflections on Emotions, Know-How and Academic Identity." *Journal of Geography in Higher Education* 33(2): 269–84.

Using this article as an example, the volume is 33, the issue is number 2, and the page range is from 269 to 284. The characteristic of journals or serials is that they are published multiple times per year, ranging from four to six issues with pages numbered consecutively across all issues throughout the year. At the end of the year the issues are "bound" into one volume. If you go to the library for the physical copy of the journal and the journal is not on the shelf, often there will be a sign that reads, "Out to be bound." The actual title of the volume is *Journal of Geography in Higher Education.*

How do journals differ from each other? Journals vary in several ways that are important to pay attention to so that, once again, you find the best match for submission of your manuscript.

Journals vary by rigor and acceptance rate. When you assess your journal list, I suggest putting them into three categories: *stretch, within reach,* and *fallback.* Table 9.2 gives the differences among these categories and will help you identify certain key characteristics that distinguish these journals.

TABLE 9.2
Three typical types of journals: Stretch, within reach, and fallback

Journal type	Description	Acceptance rate	Review type	Audience, format
Stretch	Most rigorous, most competitive	5%–10%	Blind, peer reviewed	Scholars
Within reach	Moderately competitive	10%–75%	Blind, peer reviewed	Scholars, scholarly practitioners
Fallback	Can generally be assured of publication	40%–90%	Editorial review, sometimes peer reviewed	Practitioners; has photos, sidebars, few references, and sometimes advertising

First, journals vary on their acceptance rate, which is based on how many submissions are received and how many articles are accepted each year. *Stretch* journals are the most competitive, most rigorous, and often called the "top-tier" journals in your discipline, and they have the lowest acceptance rates, such as 7%. For U.S. education, the *American Educational Research Journal* easily fits the stretch category with a 7% acceptance rate. A 7% acceptance rate means 7 out of every 100 articles submitted are published. *Within-reach* journals will include peer-reviewed research journals, but their acceptance rate might be well above 40%. For some disciplines, *within-reach* articles may not be articles presenting original research but articles that introduce research results for practitioners, such as *School Science and Mathematics* for teachers. The final category, *fallback* journals or even magazine format publications, such as *Citizenship Teaching and Learning,* are those with a generally high range of acceptance rates, from 40% to 90%. You can be relatively confident that your work will be accepted. Several of these fallback journals follow a magazine format and do not require much, if any, literature review; might not have citations within the article; and might have very few citations at the end.

Second, journals will fall into one of these three categories based on how the editors and reviewers handle submissions. Typically, the stretch and within-reach type of journals undertake blind peer reviews. When reviews are blind, the author's name does not appear on the manuscript. For some journals, when the author refers to some of his or her prior work, he or she is also renamed as "author 1" in the reference list. Peer reviewed means reviewed by peers, that is, the journal's editor(s) and two or three scholars who are experts in the field. The database Cabell's Directories reports on the number of reviewers for your manuscript in each specific journal. Some of the fallback journals are not reviewed by peers but by a well-informed editorial board that is seeking current thinking on a topic written for a practitioner audience.

Which category is the best to publish in: stretch, within reach, or fallback? One answer to this question has to do with your institution and its expectations. You need to ascertain if your promotion committee expects publications in the top-tier stretch journals. If your institution does not require you to publish in top-tier stretch-type journals, then, with your career clock ticking, it might be wise to consider the within reach and even fallback journals. Because these journals tend to be less competitive, their turnaround time may be shorter and you will get feedback quicker, thereby ending up with more publications in the long run.

This typology of journals is not an exact science. Journals do not always meet all the characteristics found in these categories. In fact, the categories are not hard and fast and, as you classify journals, you may find disagreement among your colleagues about which journals belong in which category. However, many journals will fall into these categories of stretch, within reach, and fallback. These are broad-sweep categories that begin to help you sort journals to make decisions based on your career goals. With the advent of online journals and open-access journals, the field has gotten more complicated and, in some ways, more accessible for writers. Some journals today do not meet the standards of rigor expected; some require the author to pay a substantial fee to be published. Promotion committees in the social sciences are quite wary of journals that charge the author for publication. However, in the sciences, sometimes the authors are charged for figures and photos that may be paid for by a grant. Cabell's Directories has identified some of the questionable journals on "the blacklist" of deceptive and predatory academic journals that will publish your work for a fee and with little or no review. Your librarian is an excellent resource for identifying both online and suspect journals.

Journals vary by discipline and focus. The journal's website will describe the focus and scope of the journal. New journals are launched over time, and some evolve by responding to the needs of the academic communities. A recent example is the uptick in journals devoted to teaching different disciplines. Some of these journals have been published for many years, such as the *Journal of Chemical Education*. Some are new. Most are discipline specific. Nursing education journals, such as *Nurse Education Today*, focus on articles about how to educate nurses. The *Journal of Engineering Education* is one for engineering faculty. In fact, within the last 10 years, all disciplines seem to have education or teaching journals that include articles by faculty about teaching methods they have used in their classes. Further examples include the *Journal of Public Administration Education* and *Teaching Sociology*. Some journals use SOTL, the scholarship of teaching and learning, as a marker and are cross-disciplinary. The best website to search for and identify these teaching journals by discipline or across disciplines is at Kennesaw State University (n.d.b).

Articles within journals vary by type and purpose. Within the journal itself, typical types of journal articles can be classified as *reflective practice, point in time, change over time,* and *literature review*. Table 9.3 lays out the basic characteristics of these types of articles and cites a few references that illustrate the type. Note that journals can be solely devoted to one type, such as only including articles that are literature reviews (e.g., *The Review of Educational Research*). Other journals may include several of these formats. As you look at the type of manuscript you are creating, be sure to note if the journal you have identified actually publishes your kind of manuscript, for example, reflective practice manuscripts. If it is not obvious, you can always check out the journal's website and even e-mail the editor with this question: "Do you publish reflective practice articles?"

The characteristic of a *reflective piece* is that the author has reflected on his or her work and, in contrast to the other types, has not gathered data from others. Shepherd (2006) exemplifies this where he analyzed his own personal journal entries when he took a new job as a manager. Another example is Belcher's (2009a) article where she writes about her work with faculty and students on academic writing.

A *point-in-time* piece generally gathers data to describe a situation at one point in time, not over time. Often, these journal articles include the results of surveys, case studies, or other qualitative research. Some refer to this as descriptive research. As you can see from Table 9.3, point-in-time articles all focus on an issue or a problem. However, one subtype gathers and compares data from the same participants but using different data sources, whereas the second subtype gathers data from different participants about the same topic. Our article in *College Teaching* (Reynolds et al., 2013) exemplifies the point-in-time category because we gathered survey data and artifacts from students at the end of the term.

The *change-over-time* study seeks to gather data about the impact of some intervention or experiment at two or more different and distinct points in time, sometimes called pre-post research. These articles are called "experimental design" and often use quantitative data to test a hypothesis.

Another example of journal article type is a *literature review*, where the author does not analyze data but compares and contrasts a group of journal articles about a certain topic. The data for a literature review are from the articles collected that are then analyzed to identify and summarize themes. Some journals are entirely devoted to literature reviews, such as *Review of Educational Research*. Sinclair, Barnacle, and Cuthbert's (2014) purpose statement describes their literature review from the journal *Studies in Higher Education*: "This article investigates 15 existing studies for evidence of what factors in the doctoral experience may contribute to the formation of an active researcher with a capacity for later research productivity" (p. 1972).

How does all this variance among and within journals help you? The fact that journals vary by acceptance rate, by discipline and focus, and by the purpose of articles within them signals the importance of spending some time learning about journals in your field. Some faculty have found it helpful to make an annotated list in Excel or Google Sheets of all significant journals in their field (or have your students create one that you both can use!). Here is an example of what a spreadsheet might look like where you log the list of journals in which you might want to publish:

Journal title	Website link	Scope: mission, vision, audience	Acceptance rate	Type of journal: stretch, within reach, fallback	Notes: How often published?

In addition to having a system for organizing your journals, here are a few final tips in finding and mining journals: Always be on the lookout for learning more

TABLE 9.3
**Different types of articles found in journals: Reflection, point
in time, change over time, and literature review**

REFLECTIVE PRACTICE	*POINT IN TIME*
Characteristics: Author reflects on his or her own practice to share challenges and insights. No data are gathered from others. Sources might be the author's journal.	Characteristics: Author systematically gathers, analyzes, and presents data from research participants in reference to a particular issue or problem. There may be several data sources from one group or several groups of people describing the issue at one point in time.
Belcher, W. (2009a). Reflections on ten years of teaching writing for publication to graduate students and junior faculty. *Journal of Scholarly Publishing, 40*(2), 184–200. Shepherd, M. (2006). Using a learning journal to improve professional practice: A journey of personal and professional self-discovery. *Reflective Practice, 7*(3), 333–348.	Monaghan, C. H. (2010). Communities of practice: A learning strategy for management education. *Journal of Management Education, 35*(3), 428–453. Reynolds, C., Stevens, D. D. & West, E. (2013). "I'm in a professional school! Why are you making me do this?" A cross-disciplinary study of the use of creative classroom projects on student learning. *College Teaching, 61*(2), 51–59.

(Continues)

TABLE 9.3 (*Continued*)

CHANGE OVER TIME	LITERATURE REVIEW
Characteristics: Authors systematically gather, analyze, and present data from research participants over two or more points in time with the ides of comparing effects over time. The author is seeking to understand how an "intervention" (teaching method) affects certain outcomes.	Characteristics: Authors gather many recent research articles on one topic. They compare and contrast the findings from these articles to identify and summarize themes. The data are the research articles themselves.
Harris, G. L., & Stevens, D. D. (2013, Summer). The value of midterm student feedback in cross-disciplinary graduate programs. *Journal of Public Administration Education, 19*(3), 537–565. Pololi, L., Knight, S., & Dunn, K. (2004). Facilitating scholarly writing in academic medicine. *Journal of General Internal Medicine, 19*(1), 64–68.	Sinclair, J., Barnacle, R., & Cuthbert, D. (2014). How the doctorate contributes to the formation of active researchers: What the research tells us. *Studies in Higher Education, 39*(10), 1972–1986. Parsons, S. A., Vaughn, M., Scales, R. Q., Gallagher, M. A., Parsons, A. W., Davis, S. G., . . . & Allen, M. (2018). Teachers' instructional adaptations: A research synthesis. *Review of Educational Research, 88*(2), 205–242. doi:10.3102/0034654317743198

about the journals. As an excellent way to get a "feel" for the journal, consider sub-scribing to it. If the journal is handy at home or in your workspace, you will peruse it more frequently. I recognize this is not a realistic option for scientists because of the price of subscriptions. For those who do not want to subscribe, you can also work with your librarian to receive online the table of contents from specific journals every time they have a new issue. Another way to learn more is to collect free copies of journals from publishers' conference exhibits. Check out the journal's web page as well; sometimes they will offer to send you a free copy.

Reflective Work

After you have scanned the external environment through the detective work, you are ready to do the reflective work where you apply what you have learned to your own manuscript. Specifically, during reflective work your job is to determine and connect to your audience, to pay close attention to the tacit infrastructure of journal articles that you are reading, and to collect the scholarship relevant to your manuscript.

Connecting to Your Audience

You need readers. Connecting to your audience is essential if you expect your work to be read and used. If you do not pay attention to what the readers expect, your work might languish. This section offers some strategies to help you become more aware of your audience expectations and address these expectations so that your work gets read, published, and cited.

Identifying structural patterns to connect with audience, the reviewers, first. Who is the audience for your journal article submission? Your first external audience is the journal editor and reviewers. The editor is the gatekeeper and will decide initially if your work fits the scope and rigor of the journal. If it does not, you will get the article back forthwith. If your work meets the initial publication criteria, most editors will send your manuscript to two or three reviewers who should have experience in your topic. This process can take three to six months. Reviewers will be looking for articles that follow a similar structure as other articles in the journal.

To be more confident about meeting audience needs, pay attention to the obvi-ous expectations as well as the not-so-obvious ones. At the very least, when you submit your work, refer to an obvious resource—the author guidelines found on the journal website. These are specific and often very detailed. Table 2.1 compares the purposes of typical author guidelines with those of a TSA to show you how complet-ing a TSA can refine your manuscript to align with the expectations of a particular journal's editors. If you have a question about the submission expectations, e-mail the editor before you submit. To become more aware of and responsive to a journal's not-so-obvious expectations, there is one particularly valuable strategy, a TSA that illuminates some of the text structures and patterns across three articles from the same journal. I detailed the process of doing a TSA in chapter 2 and have included a blank TSA for journal articles in appendix A.

Here are a few reminders of what you will need to gather to complete a TSA: Find three articles published within the last year from your selected journal. These do not have to be in your topic area. The TSA is a fine-grained structural analysis. Your analysis is not about content; it is about identifying the structures and patterns typically found in the articles published in this one journal. Table 9.4 is the completed TSA template from the *Journal of Engineering Education.*

Note that in the last column on the right are the patterns discerned from completing the TSA template. As you read across the three articles collected for the TSA template, you can use the patterns to structure your submission, such as creating the title and writing the abstract. One outcome of doing a TSA template is that you may realize that this journal is not a good match for your work. If so, select another journal, find three articles, and do another TSA template.

Contacting the editor. After completing the TSA and identifying a journal that seems like a good match, contact the journal editor. The journal editor is your first reader. You can connect with him or her even before you submit your manuscript. In a brief e-mail you can describe the topic, describe the work you have done, and state why it is significant. The e-mail we sent to the editor of *College Teaching* was as follows:

> Dear Editor,
>
> Giving students the opportunity to respond in creative ways to class assignments seems to be one way to build students' creative capacity. Yet, two of my colleagues and I wondered if our creative activities actually impacted student learning as well. We conducted a study in three different classes in our three different disciplines and compared results. We would like to share the results of a student survey and examination of classroom artifacts regarding the impact of creative activities on student learning on our subject matter goals. We were wondering if this is a topic that your journal might be interested in. Thank you for your consideration.

By sending an e-mail like this, the worst thing that could happen is that you get no response. The best thing is that the editor responds and informs you that the work is a good fit for the journal or that it is not a good fit, which is also very helpful. An even better response is that the editor tells you they have a special journal issue on your particular topic coming up in six months, and they would certainly like to see this manuscript very soon. As a side note, it is easier to get your work into special issues than the general issues. Don't be shy about writing this e-mail. Journal editors need submissions almost as much as scholars need to be published. Some editors and reviewers see their job as mentoring early career faculty, and the review process helps them do this.

Branching out from narrow to broad focus. Another way to connect with the audience, your readers, is to think more broadly about how to engage the audiences that might be interested in your work. I call this "branching out" from your topic. Your research may be narrow and specific in one certain context. In the introduction of the article, you can place your work in a broader context to get more readers.

TABLE 9.4

TSA: *Journal of Engineering Education*

TSA: Journal articles: Compare three recent articles from the same journal for the following text structures. In the final column on the right, look for patterns across these three journal articles.

Title of journal: *Journal of Engineering Education* (JEE) Date of review: January 15, 2016

Text structure and possible descriptors: author, year	*Article #1 Menekse et al., 2017*	*Article #2 Hess et al., 2017*	*Article #3 Guzey & Aranda, 2017*	*Patterns across articles*
1. Brief 10-word gist of article. Not sentences. Big ideas, participants, themes, content	Robotics, team collaboration X team performance	Empathetic-perspective-taking in engineering ethics course	Student participation in engineering practice	Title should be simple, clear, and direct
2. Title: Friendly, formal, long, colon, tone, inviting, academic; number of words:	14 words: straight description	10 words: clear description	11 words: clear description	Title should be simple, clear, and direct; under 10 words
3. Abstract length, content	Very structured, like a typical research paper (260 words)	Very structured, like a typical research paper (198 words)	Very structured, like a typical research paper (280 words)	Follow pattern set-up by journal; not over 300 words
4. Purpose of research, where stated—What is it?	Last paragraph of theory	Last paragraph of theory	First paragraph of methods	Put at end of theory right before methods
5. Research questions included?	Yes, two at end of introduction.	Yes, two at end of introduction.	Yes, two at end of introduction.	Include research questions in intro
6. Number of headings in article—levels, sub-heads?	22 headings 5 major headings	38 headings 6 major headings	17 headings 6 major headings	Use typical headings and many subheads
7. Paragraphs devoted to introduction, literature review/ background, method, results, discussion/conclusion	Introduction: 5 Literature/Background: 15 Methods: 14 Results: 11 Discussion/Conclusion: 9	5 10 26 23 12	4 16 12 13 6	Elaborate methods; include results

8. Number of figures/tables; content of figures/tables	3 tables 1 figure	5 tables 1 figure	8 tables	Tables and figures are helpful
9. Research methods: type (survey, etc.), participants	Robotic team score rubric: collaboration	Critical incident interview	Discourse analysis	Variety of research methods
10. Overall tone of article: first person (I, we), third person	"We" but used infrequently	"We" but used infrequently	Third person: "the researcher"	Keep a bit of distance
11. References—number, age, type (journals [J], book [B], book chapters [BC], report [R], conference presentation [CP], other [O], number of references from this journal [JEE]	Total = 68 J = 55 B = 5 BC = 4 R = 0 CP = 2 O = newspaper JEE = 7	Total = 77 J = 47 B = 17 BC = 8 R = 0 CP = 4 O = 1 JEE = 9	Total = 50 J = 32 B = 4 BC = 10 R = 3 CP = 1 O = 0 JEE = 6	Many references, dominated by research articles with books as support
12. Other noteworthy items: international focus, audience different research methods	Can use rubric, included	Interview questions included	Eighth-grade students	

An example can be drawn from some consulting work I did with a faculty member at a university in Bogota, Colombia. As a sociologist, he was writing about the social structure in rural villages in Venezuela. He was frustrated that he could not get his work published. I wondered how he started his manuscript. He said with the rural villages in Venezuela. I suggested he might start at a different place. I drew a box at the bottom of the white board and put his topic in the box. I then asked him about other broader audiences who might be interested in this work. He realized that he could enlarge his audience by writing about rural villages in general before he got to his specific topic. And, before that he could even write about different social structures. His work would then become an example of social structures in a rural context. He could capture those interested in rural life and even those looking for examples of different social structures, thus enlarging his readership.

Connecting with your audience, therefore, involves two sets of audiences: the journal editors and reviewers, as well as the readers. Through completion of the TSA and revision of your manuscript to match the patterns you found, you are demonstrating to journal editors and reviewers that you have worked hard to meet their expectations. In addition, by contacting the journal editor ahead of time and learning that your work is a good match for that journal, you are saving time by sending the manuscript to the right journal in the first place. Finally, by thinking of branching out from your specific topic to broader audiences and using that information in the introduction, your manuscript will connect with more readers.

Attending to the Infrastructure Elements to Add Coherence
What is infrastructure? The definitions of *infrastructure* are

1. an underlying base or foundation for an organization or system; and
2. basic facilities, services, and installations needed for the functioning of a community or society (www.thefreedictionary.com).

When applied to typical journal articles, the infrastructure would be all the textual signposts that are consistently used throughout a single article and across the genre of academic writing that support the smooth delivery of content and contribute to its cohesion and readability. Completion of a TSA will acquaint you with the broader infrastructure elements, such as the number of paragraphs in each section, across three articles in one journal. In this section, we dig deeper into specific elements within a journal article that also strengthen its infrastructure, add coherence, and increase readability.

Making key word links across the title, rationale, and purpose. The first way to strengthen the infrastructure in your work is through repetition of key words in the title, rationale, and purpose. Let us look at an example first (Table 9.5).

Notice how the key words "undergraduate Medical Imaging students" identify the study participants in the title, rationale, and purpose. In addition, the authors were interested in reflective processes, so the word "reflective" appears in the title, rationale, and purpose. This paper was sent to the journal *Reflective Practice.* No

TABLE 9.5
Example of how the title, rationale, and purpose are linked with key words

Title	Rationale for study	Purpose	Key words
Title: A peek into oneself: Reflective writing amongst undergraduate Medical Imaging students. Fernandez, S. C., Chelliah, K. K., & Halim, L. (2015). *Reflective Practice, 16*(1), 109–122.	". . . reflection is quintessential in healthcare education. . . . Research is ongoing on the benefits of **reflective writing** in practice globally and locally in many disciplines, namely nursing (Chong, 2009, Hong & Chew, 2008), medical education (Nalliah & Chinniah, 2012) English education (Faizah, 2008; Maarof, 2007) and law (Krishnaiyer, Mushahar & Ahmad, 2012) to name a few. Since **reflective learning** is essential, it was introduced to **Medical Imaging undergraduates.**" (pp. 110–111)	"The aim of this study is to report on how a group of Medical Imaging students perceived reflective practice." (p. 111)	Undergraduate Medical Imaging students Reflective practice Reflective learning Reflective writing

doubt the editor quickly discovered that the work was appropriate for the journal. In chapter 2, Table 2.3 has several other examples of how authors have strengthened their manuscript's infrastructure through the repetition of key words across the title, rationale, and purpose statements.

Clarifying and defining your purpose. The second element in infrastructure is the purpose statement (also called the "aim" of the paper). The purpose statement tells the reader exactly what you are writing about. And, as a writer, clarifying your purpose early on in manuscript preparation also helps keep your writing and research focused (Goodson, 2017). In chapter 2, I introduced a writing exercise (Exercise 2.1) to help you improve your purpose statement. Whatever the purpose statement is, it has or implies the following structure:

The purpose of _____ A _____ is to _____ B (infinitive) _____.

"A" is what kind of manuscript it is. Is it a study, commentary, case study, or review? "B" is a verb. The manuscript is to do something—examine, report, describe and explain, demonstrate, compare and contrast, or explore. Let us look at some purpose (or aim) statements in the literature. I have set the infinitives in bold font.

1. The aim of this study is **to report** on how a group of Medical Imaging students perceived reflective practice. (Fernandez et al., 2015, p. 111)
2. This study has three purposes: (1) **to determine** the definition of and criteria for nutrition education among allied health professionals, (2) **to identify** commonalities across health professions for nutrition education definitions and training requirements, and (3) **to determine** if there are criteria for nutrition education and training for health educators. (Ettienne-Gittens et al., 2012, p. 288)
3. The purpose of this study is **to examine** the role of self-monitoring (SM) support for writing skill improvement in a reciprocal peer review of writing system called scaffolded writing and revision in the disciplines (SWoRD). (Cho, Cho, & Hacker, 2010, p. 101)
4. The aim of this paper is therefore **to review** published literature that reports the effectiveness of measures designed to promote publication: *(So that)* It is hoped that this may identify strategies that can be used by university departments and their staff to meet their publication targets. (McGrail et al., 2006, p. 21)

The last purpose statement includes a sentence that is the larger objective of the paper. You can easily identify the "so that" in your own purpose statement by adding this phrase to the end of the opening purpose statement and completing it by defining the larger goals of your work. Purpose statement 4 is also from an article that is a literature review; thus, the infinitive is "to review," a clear signal to the reader just what the paper is about.

Understanding text structures in the journal article abstract. The third infra-structure element is the structure of the abstract. Typically, the abstract is a very brief version of the complete paper. Some journals have helped authors and readers by providing a framework for the abstract, the bold headings for the author to fill in. Here is an example from *Nurse Education Today* (Gopee & Deane, 2013):

> ***Background:*** Students develop better academic writing skills as they progress through their higher education programme, but despite recent continuing monitoring of student satisfaction with their education in the [United Kingdom], there has been relatively little research into students' perceptions of the active support that they need and receive to succeed as academic writers.
>
> ***Aim of the study:*** To examine the strategies that university students in health or social care courses utilise to develop as writers in the face of many pressures and demands from different sources.
>
> ***Research method used:*** Qualitative research conducted at a British University into undergraduates' writing practices in the field of healthcare. Ten participants took part in semi-structured interviews, half of whom were international students. The data was analysed by the researchers from the field of writing development using thematic analysis.
>
> ***Results:*** The main findings are that certain students struggle as academic writers if they do not receive tutoring on appropriate and effective academic writing through institutional provisions, or through non-institutional strategies, that can promote success with the writing process. There is also uncertainty over the extent to which nurse educators are expected to teach academic writing skills, alongside their discipline-specific subject areas.
>
> ***Conclusions:*** Both institutional provisions for academic writing development, such as a dedicated writing support department, and non-institutional factors such as peer-collaboration should be fully recognised, supported and resourced in tertiary education at a time when students' satisfaction and performance are high on the agenda. (p. 1624)

This journal article's framework is an excellent example of what is typically expected in an abstract. You may notice that the abstract follows the basic format of many social science, science, and education journal articles themselves: **b**ackground (introduction), **a**im of the study, **m**ethods, **r**esults, and conclusion (**d**iscussion). In the abstract example, the *background* gives the rationale for the study and identifies the gap that the study will fill (i.e., there is "relatively little research" on this topic). The *aim* is the purpose statement. The *research method used* identifies where the study was conducted, with whom and how many participants, what kind of data were collected, and how they were analyzed. The *results* describe two major findings, one for students and the other for nurse educators. The *conclusions* identify the key stakeholders who would benefit from knowing the results of the study. Actually, this is quite a feat because this abstract only runs to 240 words and succinctly covers all those topics! Most journals expect the abstract to cover this range of information because their readers want to know right away, "Do I want to read this article for my research?" A clear and concise abstract will answer that question. In addition, you will notice there are no references in the abstract. Why waste valuable words on citations? Leave those to the manuscript. When you complete the TSA, check each of the sentences in the abstracts to see the typical pattern in the journal you want to submit to. Once you identify those typical infrastructure patterns, you can use them when you create your own abstract for that particular journal.

Completing a methods structure analysis (MSA). The final infrastructure element I want to draw your attention to is found in the methods and results sections. Because there seem to be no easily accessible models of how to present the study methods and results, figuring out the best way to describe the methods and present the results of your study can be a daunting task. One way to do it is to analyze at least two articles from your selected journal that have used the same methods you used in your study using an MSA.

Completing the MSA is similar to the way you completed a TSA, except you are now focusing on how the authors have structured the methods and results sections of the articles. Again, this analysis is not about content, but about structure, that is, how the authors wrote about their participants, procedures, data, data collection methods, and results.

Table 9.6 is an MSA of two journal articles that report the results from using the research method of a semistructured interview. As you look across the analysis of both articles, you may see some patterns. Both groups of authors had one page of short descriptions of the participants and procedures. In submitting your article to this journal, you should try to distill these descriptions to one page, just as the articles in the MSA. Based on the analysis of the qualitative data, both had found four or five themes and each had selected just a few quotes to illustrate each theme. In both articles, the results were the longest sections. The journal *Studies in Higher Education* did not seem to care about the consistency of the purpose statements. By completing the MSA, you are enlarging your "vocabulary" of different ways to present your results. Appendix C includes a blank MSA that can be copied and used for an analysis of how two articles structured their methods and results sections.

In this reflective work section, so far I have highlighted the importance of connecting to your audience as well as identifying the infrastructure components found in typical journal articles. Finally, I turn to the foundation of your work, the place where you gather and include the voices of other scholars who have been working in your topic area through analysis and synthesis of the research literature.

Establishing Your Scholarly Contribution

As an academic, you are a scholar. Just what does that mean? It means that you do not stand alone in the field of your ideas. It means you respect others who have done work in your topic area. In fact, it means you seek to cite their work in your manuscript to acknowledge what they have done and how their work informs yours. The purpose of this section is to highlight where and how to include those scholarly connections.

TABLE 9.6
MSA

Methods structure analysis (MSA): What text structures are used when writing about this method?

Name of journal: *Studies in Higher Education*

Method used in articles: Semistructured interview   Date of Analysis: _____

Criteria: Author: ____ Year: ____	Journal article #1 Walsh et al. (2013)	Journal article #2 MacLeod et al. (2012)	Patterns, comparisons, notes, observations
1. Title: Write out. Underline key words.	Reclaiming creativity in the era of impact: Exploring ideas about creative research in science and engineering	Time is not enough: Promoting strategic engagement with writing for publication	Both titles have colons; after colon, gerund with specifics about the study
2. Purpose (aim): Write out. Key words? Where in the manuscript is the purpose in relation to introduction of methods section?	The objective was to explore STEM doctoral and post-doctoral researchers' views of creativity and how conceptualized its role is in their work.	"We set out to establish the extent to which attending a writing retreat enabled participants to overcome barriers to writing on return to work settings" (then, listed three research objectives)	Did not use the wording "The purpose or aim of the study was to . . ." Did have an action verb in each: "to explore" and "to establish"
3. Research questions?	No	No	Not needed
4. Overall # of paragraphs in paper	Total: 46 Use this # in items 8 and 9	Total: 54 Use this # in items 8 and 9	
5. Theoretical frame: Yes/no; # of paragraphs	Yes; introduction, definition of *creativity*; 11 paragraphs	Yes; 7 paragraphs on writing retreats; 13 paragraphs on containment theory	Strong theoretical frame in each article
6. Method: Qualitative, quantitative, or mixed methods	Qualitative	Qualitative	Qualitative only

(Continues)

TABLE 9.6 (*Continued*)

Criteria: *Author:_____ Year:_____*	*Journal article #1* *Walsh et al. (2013)*	*Journal article #2* *MacLeod et al. (2012)*	*Patterns, comparisons, notes, observations*
7. Intervention: Yes/no; What was it? Brief description	No	Study: Faculty responses to writing retreat over several years	One had no intervention. The other did but only briefly described it.
8. Data sources: Survey, semi-structured interview, focus groups, # of participants	Semistructured interviews 12 doctoral 12 postdoctoral 10 supervisors, investigators	Semistructured interviews with 27 faculty	Over 25 interviews at one point
9. Paragraphs devoted to description of methods:	Description of participants: 2 Procedures (data collection): 1 Data analysis: 1 Overall–paragraphs/Methods: 6	Description of participants: 2 Procedures (data collection): 1 Data analysis: 2 Overall # paragraphs/Methods: 4	Short, one page, devoted to participants, data collection and analysis Very few paragraphs devoted to methods
10. Paragraphs devoted to results: Qualitative, [QL], quantitative [QT], mixed methods	QL # of paragraphs: 22 QT # of paragraphs: Number of themes: 5 Number of quotes: 2 to 4 per theme Overall # of paragraphs in the paper: 46 Percent devoted to results: 47% Notes: Used open coding. No predetermined themes from theory or literature.	QL # of paragraphs: 17 QT # of paragraphs: Number of themes: 4 Number of quotes: 11, one to two per theme Overall # of paragraphs in the paper: 54 Percent devoted to results: 31% Notes: Used coding system, narratives for codes from containment theory	Results were at least one-third of the paper in paper #2; almost half of paper #1. Both used quotes to illustrate themes identified from the data.

11. Tables/figures	Number of tables: None Number of figures: None	0 tables 0 figures	No tables or figures
12. References: Check reference list and text for methodological researchers used.	**Total Number: 46** Number from journal itself: Number of methodological references: 2	**Total number: 35** Number from journal itself: 6 Number of methodological references: 1	Thirty-five to 45 references. Only one to two references to support methods used.
13. Noteworthy and unique presentation of methods and results (unique data collected).	**Limitations included at the end of the methods section before the results. Interview questions not included.**	Interview questions not included. No limitations included.	Do not have to include the interview questions. May include limitations.

Including the scholarship of others across your manuscript. The first way to make a scholarly connection to others is through the use of the literature in different sections of your manuscript. Table 9.7 lists four main sections of the manuscript where authors typically refer to the scholarly literature: the introduction and background, the theoretical framework, the methods, and the discussion or conclusion. The results were not included here because, typically, the discussion and conclusion sections refer to relevant literature that helps to explain the results.

Given the number of ways you can use the literature, reading and writing a scholarly manuscript requires a deep familiarity with the various ways that you can use the research literature. As noted in Table 9.7, the literature in each of the four sections in a journal article (introduction, theoretical framework, methods, and discussion or conclusion) is designed to accomplish certain different purposes. Knowing that the literature should accomplish different purposes can affect what you are looking for as you read the literature and to what use you can put those ideas in your own manuscript.

As a reader of the scholarship of others, you are sometimes looking at the study only for the results. Yet, to find some models of how others have used the literature, you can read like a writer and see how other scholars have handled the literature in

TABLE 9.7
Uses for the research literature in journal articles

In what section of the manuscript is the literature typically found?	*What purpose do the citations from the literature serve in this section?*
Introduction and background	To include broader audiences interested in the work To acknowledge the research that others have done on this topic To make a persuasive case that the work is important in relation to other work that has been done in the past
Theoretical framework*	To define key terms within the theories To show how these theories apply to this study
Methods	To identify methodological scholars who have investigated ways to conduct the methods used in the study To describe the limitations and strengths of the methods chosen for the manuscript based on the work of methodological scholars
Discussion/ conclusion	To show how the results of this study have contributed to, elaborated on, or extended the work already done on the topic To indicate how the work has "filled a gap" in the literature

*Not all papers will have a theoretical framework.

their work. Sometimes, you might want to see how other authors used a theoretical framework to justify their research. Or, as the MSA indicates, you may want to see how others have described a certain research method. Or, in the discussion, you may want to see how others have looped back to the research cited in the introduction to show how their results now inform this earlier work.

Crafting your argument. The second way to make a scholarly connection in the introduction and background section is to cite other scholars' work and to weave those citations together in such a way as to make a persuasive case. Essentially you are making an argument that is designed to show how your work fits in, extends, and/ or addresses the work of others. Argument is a complex area of study. I acknowledge that there is much more to this topic than what I present here (Heinrichs, 2013). Yet, without going into all the nuances of argument, I have found that the argument templates of rhetoricians Graff and Birkenstein (2010) work in distilling arguments in academic writing into several rhetorical moves. In chapter 2, I elaborated on the steps in designing your own argument. I suggest that by using a template you can identify the relevant literature, establish your contribution to the literature, and persuade the reader of the significance of your work. Box 9.1 illustrates three different kinds of templates you can use to make an argument:

1. Focus on a *controversy*.
2. Show *agreement* and contrast how your work is different.
3. Offer different solutions to an enduring problem (*problem-solution*).

Following each template is an example from the literature.

To understand how the authors have used the structures in Box 9.1, I suggest that you read one of the arguments from the journal articles (controversy, agreement, or problem-solution) without paying any attention to the bold, italicized words. Then, read the template at the top of that section with the blanks for the argument. Finally, go back and reread the argument with the bold, italized words to see how the structure of the argument works. Note how the examples in Box 9.1 do not use the words from the template but that the writing follows the path set out by the template (i.e., some people say this/others respond this way).

As noted in chapter 2, I suggest you try out these templates with your own topic to get a "feel" for writing about your topic and making an argument to support it. If you use the argument template in the early stages of your work, you may discover that you do not have all the literature in one part of the argument to make the persuasive case. However, by completing the argument template, you now know you need to gather those articles to complete the argument. Using the template and identifying the key components of your argument saves you from doing a more random, exhaustive search of the literature. Following this analysis of your argument, your search of the databases will be more focused and fruitful.

Considering a CMS. The third and final way to establish your connection to scholarship is developing a way to organize and access the literature effectively and efficiently. Working with the research literature today is very different from working

BOX 9.1

Argument templates: Three approaches—controversy, agreement, and problem-solution

I. **Controversy: Find the controversy and offer a solution.**
In discussions of _____(your topic)_____, one controversial issue has been _____a.____.
Some _____1_____ contend _____2b.____. Others _____3_____ argue _____4c.____.
Still others _____5_____maintain _____6d.____.
The purpose of my study is to _____ so that_____.
1, 3, 5 = scholars; 2, 4, 6 = their work on the issue; a, b, c, d = bodies of literature to include in your argument

Example from the *Journal of Creative Behavior* on the benefits of brainstorming:

(***In discussions of . . .***) Brainstorming is a popular method for generating original ideas. (***One controversial issue has been the presumption that . . .***) One of the basic presumptions of brainstorming is that a focus on generating a large number of ideas enhances both the number of ideas generated and the number of good ideas (original and useful). (***Some contend . . . Others argue . . .***) Prior research* has not clearly demonstrated the utility of such a quantity focus in comparison to a condition in which quantity is not emphasized. (***Still others maintain . . .***) There have been some comparisons of the impact of quantity and quality focus on the number and quality of ideas, but the results of these comparisons have been mixed. (***The purpose of the study is . . .***) The present study examined brainstorming with four different types of instructions: no specific focus, a quantity goal, a quality goal, or a joint quantity and quality goal. (Paulus, Kohn, & Arditti, 2011, p. 38)

*These references are laid out specifically in the longer introduction.

II. **Agreement: Indicate general agreement but different approaches.**
When it comes to _____(your topic)_____, most would agree that _____a.____.
Where this agreement ends is _____b.____.
Whereas some _____1_____say____2c.___,
Others _____3_____approach it _____4d.____. Even some _____5_____ suggest _____6e.____.
The aim of my paper is to _____so that_____.

Example from the journal *Nurse Education Today* on academic writing for nurses:

(***When it comes to academic publication . . .***) Academic publication rates are used internationally as an indicator of both individual and institutional perfor-

(*Continues*)

BOX 9.1 (*Continued*)

mance, and there are promotional and financial imperatives to publish (Creamer, 1998; Emden, 1998; Ramsden, 1994). . . . (***Most would agree that . . .***) Despite widespread acceptance of the need to increase academic publication . . . , (***where this agreement ends is . . .***) little is known about the effectiveness of practical strategies to support academic writing rates. (***Whereas some have said that . . .***) Publication has been reported to be inhibited by many factors. (***Others have approached the problem . . .***) A recent review by McGrail and colleagues (2006) critiqued reported interventions designed to increase publication rates. (***Even some have suggested . . .***) Although the literature review described suggests that a writing course, writing support group, or writing coach increases publication rates, it is not known which aspects of these programs are most facilitative. (***The aim of this paper is to explore . . .***) The aim of this project was to explore the experiential aspects and the effectiveness of a combined approach—structured writing course plus writing support group—on academic publication rates. (Rickard et al., 2009, pp. 516–517)

III. **Problem-solution: Identify a problem and show different solutions.**

When it comes to _____(your topic)_____, the problem is that
_____.
_____1_____ approached it from this way ___2a.____ ____3____worked on this idea,_____4b._____.
_____5_____ offered another idea, _____6c._____.
What they have not considered is _____(your contribution)_____. The purpose of my study is to _____(so that)_____.

Example from a PSU faculty member in urban planning:

Most scholars agree that direct market farms bring positive economic, social, and environmental benefits (***topic***). (***The problem . . .***) Where there is less certainty, however, is the future of direct market farming (***Some have worked on . . .***) In recent years, there has been growing attention to the difficulties other categories of farmers, such as beginning farmers and historically disadvantaged farmers, face in accessing land (Becket & Galt, Balvanz). (***What has not been considered . . .***) But there has been little research about direct market farmers on the issue of land access. We suspect that direct market farmers face significant land access challenges that are exacerbated by their locational needs and low incomes. (***The purpose of the paper is to examine . . .***) In this paper we examine the experiences of direct market farmers in accessing land in the north Willamette Valley region of Oregon (***so that***) so that we better understand their challenges and can design interventions to strengthen the future of direct market farming. (Personal Communication, Megan Horst, April 21, 2017)

Items I and II adapted from the work of Graff & Birkenstein, 2010, pp. 222–223.

with it years ago when, as a graduate student, I had to find the physical journal in the dusty library stacks of Michigan State and then find a place to copy the article. Today, library databases can call up thousands of articles on any broad topic based on the key word search. When I use subdatabases such as ERIC and Academic Search Premier in the larger database of articles in EBSCO Host, the key words "academic writing" offer me 13,597 articles. After narrowing my search to add "faculty" with "academic writing," I get 1,255 articles. By adding one other key phrase, "writing programs," I get 115 articles. Still, 115 articles is a lot of reading.

Because it is so easy to find references in the online databases, the problem is not finding the research literature, but facilitating easy access to the riches within the references once they are identified. Some people print them and put them in stacks or files. Others use matrices in a Google or Excel spreadsheet. Goodson (2017) uses the table feature in Microsoft Word. I have found that a CMS, Zotero, offers remarkable and considerable benefits.

The differences among CMSs are like the differences between a Toyota and a Mercedes. When driving, the cars operate the same way; they have very similar features; the locations of features such as the car heater might be found in different places. Some CMSs may seem more intuitive for you. Most librarians can explain the differences among the CMSs. Later, I will explain the one feature in Zotero that the other CMSs do not have that makes it particularly valuable for academic writers.

If you wish to get started using a CMS such as Zotero, I have identified five different levels of interaction that move from initial use as a storage spot for your references to a relatively sophisticated way to quickly pull out quotations with page references from your references. To demonstrate the power of using Zotero in particular, I have created a series of YouTube videos that can guide you along through the different levels of interaction. I suggest that you put the videos on a device such as a phone or iPad next to your laptop or computer. Then, open Zotero on your computer and follow my steps, turning the video off and on as needed.

To show you the beauty and efficiency of using a CMS such as Zotero, I provide three quotes from three different articles in Zotero. In addition to cutting and pasting the quotations, I tagged (labeled) that individual note to identify and retrieve later. I tagged all three of these as "lack of research on the emotions of doctoral students." When I searched for that tag, Zotero produced these three articles because they had notes that were tagged as "lack of . . ." Then, as I looked at the notes in the articles, I found the specific note that had the quotation about the lack of research.

1. Although a number of valuable articles on writing have been published over the last 20 years (e.g., Aitchison and Lee, 2006; Bharuthram and McKenna, 2006; Lea and Street, 1998), relatively few have addressed the affective domain and the personal difficulties that students and other writers perceive and experience in writing. (Wellington, 2010, p. 136–137)

2. We suggest that adopting a broader approach to academic writing, one which acknowledges the commonality of all writing activity and sees all writers, whatever their style or genre, as sharing similar concerns and experiences, is the key to developing more satisfactory support for academic writing. (Antoniou & Moriarty, 2008, p. 159)

3. Emotion is perceived by many dominant stakeholders as soft, subjective, and an impediment to acquiring objective knowledge. The importance of emotion is under recognized. (Aitchison and Mowbray, 2013, p. 859)

All three of these references point to the lack of research on the emotions that doctoral students experience and the need for further research. When I am writing an article based on data gathered about doctoral student emotions, I can use these references to argue that there is a lack of research in this area according to Aitchison and Mowbray (2013), Antoniou and Moriarty (2008), and Wellington (2010), and that my research on doctoral student emotions begins to address their concerns. Because I have the original quotation with the citation and page number, I can also use the actual words to make my argument. Appendix D details the different levels of use as well as provides links to YouTube videos that explain the steps to take to use Zotero at these different levels.

Before we turn to expressive work, I would like to conclude this section by pulling together all the ideas from reflective work through a metaphor. Figure 9.1, a tree, illustrates three different reflective components of writing a journal article. The leaves, flowing and responding to the breezes that pass, show how important it is to be responsive to your environment, that is, to pay attention to your audience. A tree responds to the environment through its leaves and branches and gets its nourishment through its leaves. The tree trunk—sturdy, and thick—stands for those aspects of your article that connect ideas, the infrastructure. The tree needs the trunk to connect the leaves to the roots. No tree can survive without its roots. The roots reach out for the deep connections to the scholarly literature. Prior scholarship provides a foundation for your work today. When you put all three elements together, you have a lovely, sturdy tree. When you make sure you have these three elements in your manuscript, you have addressed the audience expectations, drawn nourishment from other scholars through a sturdy structure.

Expressive Work

After completing the detective and reflective work in preparation for writing and submitting your manuscript, you are ready to begin to put the pieces together into a whole document.

Assembling Your Manuscript

Up to this point in this chapter and the book, you have been introduced to a set of strategies designed to support the development of your manuscript. Table 9.8 is a summary of many of those strategies applied to writing and assembling your journal article.

Figure 9.1 Summary of reflective work: Tree metaphor

TABLE 9.8

A strategic approach to writing a journal article

Section of manuscript	Strategy	How to use the strategy	Specific application to my manuscript
1. Title	TSA	Check for any patterns across the titles of the journal articles used in the TSA. Modify your title accordingly.	Number of words in title: _____ Colon: Yes/No
2. Abstract	Abstract template	Check typical length on TSA. Write at least one sentence for each element: introduction/ background, methods, results, discussion.	Number of words in abstract: _____ Number of sentences for introduction_____; methods _____; results _____; discussion _____.
3. Introduction/ background	TSA	How many paragraphs for the introduction/background?	Number of paragraphs in the introduction: _____
	Argument template	Write out your argument using the template. Make sure you have literature to support your argument.	Which argument are you making?
	Purpose or aim	Complete the purpose statement activity (Exercise 2.1) to clarify your purpose.	The purpose of my study is to _____.
4. Methods	TSA	Check the typical number of paragraphs for methods on the TSA.	Number of paragraphs in methods section: _____
	MSA	Find at least two articles that use your method. Check number of paragraphs and methodological literature cited.	Methodological literature cited:
5. Results	TSA	What is the typical number of paragraphs in the results section?	Number of paragraphs in results section: _____
	MSA	Review different ways to organize your results based on what others have done. What tables or figures were used, if any?	How will you organize your results?
6. Discussion/ conclusion	TSA	What is the typical number of paragraphs in the discussion/ conclusion?	Number of paragraphs in discussion/conclusion _____.
7. References	CMS	Put your references in a CMS	

TSA: text structure analysis; chapters 2 and 9.

MSA: methods structure analysis; chapter 9.

The first column is the section of the manuscript that can be developed using the suggested strategy. The second column is the name of the strategy. The third column is a description of how the strategy contributes to the development of that section of the manuscript. The fourth column is the application of the strategy to your manuscript.

Let us look at two similar strategies that offer insight into several sections of your manuscript, the TSA and the MSA. From these two strategies, you are gaining a picture of the infrastructure, the consistent patterns, of the articles in that one journal. As you identify these patterns, remember what you are looking for is the typical range of acceptable length for each section. Other text features to note from the TSA are the use of tables and figures. Chapter 2 details other text features to pay attention to in the TSA as you craft your manuscript.

The good news is now that you may have a somewhat rough, but written, manuscript in hand, you can use the strategies from chapter 3 for allocating time to write your manuscript. In addition, chapter 4 may help you create or seek out a writing group to support and acknowledge your progress. If you get stuck or need some motivation at some point or want to add some creative pieces to your work, chapter 5 suggests some writing exercises to try out.

Doing a Reverse Outline

One final strategy in polishing your manuscript for submission is to check for the flow of the ideas across the manuscript. When you have a solid draft, a quick way to check for flow is to pull out the headers and the key sentences from each and every paragraph in the manuscript. This is called a "reverse outline," an outline done after the fact. Read the sentences aloud and see if they flow from paragraph to paragraph. If they don't, put on your editor's hat and start rearranging, cutting, and rewriting to get back to the flow.

Submitting Your Manuscript

It is a pleasure to know that you have arrived at the final phase of journal article writing and publishing, the submission of your work to the journal. The submission guidelines will be on the journal's website. If you are a perfectionist or you know one, this is when he or she needs to get to work on the section formatting, the citation formats, the layout of the tables, and so on. Recall the list at the beginning of the chapter about why journal articles are rejected. Many of the reasons were not meeting the kinds of expectations found in the author guidelines. Check and double-check all the expectations, several times. You do not want all your hard work to be rejected because you did not format your tables correctly or your citations were sloppy.

It is also time to prepare for the long time line between submission, feedback, and publication. This is typical. So, at three months out, e-mail the editor and ask a simple question: "What is the status of my manuscript, #_____?" I often put my name in capital letters in the subject line as well as the manuscript number and a few words about the topic: "STEVENS MS #34216, Writing groups." This shows that you value the editor's time and makes it so much easier for the editor to find your work quickly.

To not lose your writing practice and momentum, it is best to have two or three writing projects in process at different stages. Some people keep track of these on a spreadsheet, noting at what stage they are in. Try out different systems to keep track.

If you get a rejection, prepare for that by having an alternative list of journals. Some faculty members polish the article slightly with the feedback from the first reviewers and send it out quickly to another journal. Chapter 11 offers some ways to respond to feedback in the form of a rejection or an R & R request. There is always hope.

A quick career tip: When your manuscript is published, celebrate. In addition, make two hard copies of the published manuscript. I put "FYI" on the top of the first page of the hard copy and then drop it in my department chair's and dean's mailboxes. No shouting from the rooftop, just a subtle notification that I have a publication. Sometimes my administrators congratulate me; other times they do not. However, with this publication, I have added a line on my CV.

Meeting Writing and Publishing Journal Article Challenges

Writing and publishing journal articles is hard work. The advantages and disadvantages are real. How do you meet the challenges of writing and publishing journal articles? Admit it is a challenge and recognize it is not easy for anyone. Yet, like any challenge, it benefits from careful attention. There is a lot to learn about journal article writing and publishing.

There are several dispositions that will support your work and help you accomplish your goals. A disposition does not mean that you will always act in a particular way; however, it means you will have a tendency to move in a certain direction. I suggest that the primary disposition is to be mindful about your work. That means paying attention to the environment, gathering data, and shuttling back and forth from external expectations found in the detective work and internal processes in the reflective work. It is this shuttling back and forth that will help you glean riches from the environment to apply to your work. The second disposition is to cultivate curiosity, always asking, "Well, how does this work? How are these journals different? How do others do this work?" Curiosity is not judgmental but is open to experience to see what you can learn. Mindfulness and curiosity give you a reservoir of choices and a strength that comes from analysis and reflection. Why would all of this be important? Knowing more about the process, the expectations, and your own responses to the environment increases your sense of control over the outcomes. This, in turn, will lead to less stress and more confidence. By being mindful and curious about how things work, you will meet the challenges of writing and publishing journal articles.

Conclusion

The purpose of this chapter is to alert you to the broader considerations around publishing in journals, as well as give you some strategies for tackling this complex process. Through the detective, reflective, and expressive work you became aware of how the world of journal publishing functions, how to connect to your various audiences in your writing, how to recognize and respond to the tacit infrastructure of journal articles, as well as how to make scholarly contributions.

As an academic, writing and publishing journal articles tend to be a career advancement insurance policy. Yet, much more than sitting down to write, managing the journal-writing process takes organization, time, and attention. This chapter was written to provide you with the background knowledge about journals, the strategies you can employ to connect to your audiences, the awareness of the tacit infrastructure of the articles themselves, and the need to establish your scholarly connections so that you can enjoy the satisfaction of publishing your work, ideas, and insights with other scholars and broader audiences.

CHAPTER 10

Write a Book

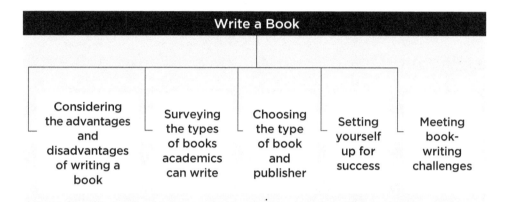

In the trajectory of academic life, book writing typically comes after you have established your career. Yet, in some colleges and universities, having a published book is one of the criteria for promotion. More specifically, in some disciplines, such as history, having a single-authored book is essential for promotion and advancement within the field. A history colleague tells me that most history search committees expect to see either a book or several articles based on the dissertation in job applicant materials. Other disciplines, such as mathematics and most sciences, usually do not expect that faculty have written a book to be hired. On your career path, asking your department chair or dean about the role of book publishing is a very good idea. You might ask the following questions: "How much do books count toward promotion? Are there certain kinds of books that count more than others? Is there a time in my career when books are more important on my career path?"

Clearly the decision of whether and when to write a book is complicated. For many of us, having a track record of published blind peer-reviewed articles is the best insurance policy for job security. Writing and publishing journal articles may be the most important writing we do. I still publish journal articles. However, with five books to my name, I have found that book publishing is a rewarding and satisfying professional activity. The purpose of this chapter is to give you some ideas about the world of academic book publishing as well as offer some concrete steps in developing your book proposal and managing the book-writing process.

As with journal articles, the choices are many and the time lines long, so if you decide to write a book, it is absolutely essential that you understand the world of book publishing. Once you know more about what writing a book entails, you'll be in a better position to decide if you want to make a commitment to write a book.

Considering the Advantages and Disadvantages of Writing a Book

An understanding of the advantages and disadvantages in your career offers you a framework by which to make your first decision if you want to write a book at all. Once you have decided to write a book, what type of book do you want to write? From textbooks to edited volumes, to professional books to discipline-specific books, to self-published books and trade books, the field is wide.

Advantages

When you write a book, you have more choices than when you write a journal article. What kind of academic book do you want to write? Closely aligned with the type of book is the audience for whom you want to write. How will it be organized and formatted? What are the key features? Choices, choices, choices. The fact that there are so many choices may feel exhilarating (or, perhaps, daunting). Yet, one upside is the fact that in book writing you have much more room to create the kind of text that you want than in the typical journal article.

Writing a Book Is an Opportunity to Demonstrate and Disseminate Your Accumulated Experience, Research, and Wisdom on the Topic

Because of the granular nature of journal articles—shorter, more focused, limited audience—you may begin to feel frustrated by the limited scope. You may feel ready to present a more comprehensive, more integrated view of your field. Writing a book is your opportunity to jump higher into the balcony and look down on your years of work to share your broader insights and understandings with others.

You Can Become Known as an Expert in Your Field

With the help of your publishing partners, your work may reach a larger audience than single-conference presentations and journal articles. You'll need to select a publisher who has a reputation in your field, whose program is respected for its quality and contribution, and that actively markets to your audience.

Don't be seduced by the fact that there are over 22,000 universities in the world including over 4,000 in the United States (Sarino, 2014). That seems like a huge market. Yet, who buys the books? On one hand, libraries buy books. However, libraries' budgets for books and "monographs" are very tight because of the high cost of maintaining their journal (serials) subscriptions. U.S. academic library sales for a book may be as low as 50 to 200 books. Some publishers specialize in selling monographs to the world library audience, with the expectation of selling no more than 250 to 350 copies worldwide at very high prices. On the other hand, a textbook publisher will have expectations of selling multiple thousands of copies. Beyond textbooks and monographs, scholarly and professional book publishers will have print runs within a spectrum from library sales to textbooks. Writing a book can potentially spread your good work to a larger audience, but you'll need to do your homework to match what kind of book you want to write and who might be the best publisher for that book.

Disadvantages

The disadvantages of writing a book are mostly related to the amount of time it takes to complete the project as well as the new set of skills it demands.

Writing a Book Is a Long Project

By its very nature, book writing can disrupt your teaching and personal life. Your students, peers, friends, and even your family may not understand the time it takes to write a book. Because most know little about the writing process, they may wonder why it takes so long to see a real product. They may be curious and even impatient with you about why this book is taking so many hours away from other commitments and it is still not done. The reactions from those around you can be discouraging, even embarrassing, as you may begin to ask those same questions of your writing.

You Cannot Always Depend on the Publisher to Market Your Book

You will have to develop some knowledge about marketing and selling your ideas. When you entered the academy, you may have thought that scholarship is about debating ideas and that dissemination of your ideas would take care of itself. Committing to writing a book assumes you have identified your audience, have reflected on how to shape your ideas to appeal broadly to that audience, and are interested in meeting its needs to achieve the widest possible sales. Therefore, you will need to know more about your audience and the market for your book than perhaps you had expected.

Typically, the Financial Return Is Not Great

For most academic books, the financial return is not great. Royalties over the life of a monograph are likely to be modest, frequently below $750.00. While "trade" (general interest, novels, etc.) publishers often offer advances, scholarly publishers generally offer no advances.

Scholarly books, however, can offer other financial incentives beyond royalties. The hidden benefits of book publication are that your book may identify you as an expert and give rise to invitations to present keynotes or give workshops at campuses around the country or world. Invitations like these will result in honoraria, a set fee with travel expenses included.

In summary, the advantages and disadvantages illustrate that writing a book involves several considerations—professional advancement and financial and marketing details—that you may not have anticipated. In the next section, I survey the five different types of books that you can publish: textbooks, edited books, professional books, scholarly monographs, and self-published books.

Surveying the Types of Books Academics Can Write

One of the first decisions you have to make is what type of book to write. There are a small variety of books that can be written. Faculty members typically write five different types of academic books: textbooks, edited books, professional books, scholarly monographs, and self-published books. Table 10.1 defines and summarizes the advantages and disadvantages of each.

Textbooks

Most faculty members write textbooks because of a felt need. The motivation may be that current textbook offerings are not meeting the learning needs of their students. As faculty create supplemental course materials, they may begin to realize that a new text is needed. The seed is planted: "Maybe I can write that textbook?" When it germinates, the seed will grow into a project that will engage them not just for months, but potentially for years.

Writing a textbook for large, undergraduate introductory courses in the major disciplines such as chemistry, sociology, and psychology is a huge undertaking. If you choose to write one and your proposal is accepted, managing the life of the textbook can consume your time for many years, largely because these books need to be updated frequently. You have to stay on top of your field, and you have to be ready to make the needed and expected revisions. Textbook publishers will not only let you know when new editions are needed but also stipulate their timing and frequency in your book contract. Faculty textbook authors tell me that they are always in revision mode, finding new materials, keeping up with current research, and getting ready for the next edition. Royalties for popular textbooks can be substantial and continue for many years as well. Some faculty members have quit their full-time academic jobs to devote time only to their textbook and its supplements, such as podcasts, websites, and student workbooks. Join the Textbook & Academic Authors Association (TAA; TAAonline.net) and attend its annual conference to keep informed about textbook authoring issues such as contracts, copyright, and even managing the writing project itself.

On many campuses, textbook writing is not valued as a worthwhile activity on a career path, especially for those on a tenure line contract (Hayes & Sternberg, 2017). In an American Association of University Professors (AAUP) online article, Hayes and Sternberg (2017) argue that textbook writing is a worthwhile endeavor:

> Writing a textbook is a special form of teaching. Instead of teaching just a few score or a few hundred students, a textbook author can reach thousands of students. Through textbooks, we reach more people than we ever could teach on a personal level. One of the authors of this article has received communications from complete strangers who used her textbooks as students, demonstrating that a textbook can do more than simply assist people with their studies. It can transform their understanding, inspire them, and even help them directly in their everyday lives and work. If we care about teaching, as the academic rhetoric claims we do, then we should care about textbooks too. (para. 4)

TABLE 10.1

Types of books written by academics: Advantages and disadvantages

Type of book	Advantages	Disadvantages
Textbook	Meets your needs for material customized to your teaching and experience Pushes you to keep current on overall content in your field Can be financially lucrative, especially for introductory textbooks in high-demand fields (e.g., chemistry, sociology)	Requires a high level of organization, particularly for intro texts If successful, it can be daunting to keep up with the various revisions expected by publisher May not count for promotion and tenure in your institution
Edited volume	Gathers together people with different perspectives and contributions on one topic May require less writing than other books	Requires a high level of organization to make sure contributors get their work in to you on time Needs editing skills to ensure contributions meet your criteria Low royalties
Professional book	Helps you crystallize your own practice Can establish you as an expert in your field May generate consulting opportunities If it becomes a standard reference can generate steady royalties	May not be highly regarded by your disciplinary colleagues Development of text may require conducting unpaid workshops at conferences to better understand audience needs
Monograph: Scholarly investigation	Encourages opportunity to research a topic in depth Tends to guarantee advancement in the discipline (history, English, philosophy) May generate consulting and lecture opportunities	Requires highly developed research skills Usually takes a long time to write (5 to 10 years) May not generate many royalties
Self-published book	Offers full control over writing, review, editing, production, distribution and marketing May be produced more quickly than those that proceed through publishing houses May generate more income	Requires an initial investment to get the book published Requires knowledge of production, distribution and marketing May suffer from lack of editorial feedback

Textbook writing is teaching and, as Hayes and Sternberg (2017) argue, if institutions value teaching, then they should reevaluate their stance toward textbook writing. Textbook authors influence more students than those sitting in front of them in the classroom.

Faculty may write textbooks for lower or upper division students. Lower division texts (for freshmen and sophomores) offer foundational knowledge in a discipline. These seem to require frequent revision and attention to keep the work updated. Upper division (for junior-, senior-, or graduate-level courses) texts don't require the same degree of organization or frequency of revision and generally don't generate significant royalties because sales are lower, often being recommended rather than required reading.

Edited Books

Edited books are volumes that contain separate chapters by different contributors. The people who bring faculty together to write these chapters are called the editors. For most edited volumes, the audience is other faculty. Sometimes the editors themselves add their own chapters. The focus is one topic selected by the editors. Some edited books may gather together the latest research on a topic or may aim to crystallize a new concept that's gaining traction in a field. Some are used as textbooks in upper division and graduate classes. Others may present alternative perspectives to an issue with which faculty might be dealing, such as managing large classes, fostering classroom discussion, or advancing in one's career.

My first coauthored book, *Tenure in the Sacred Grove: Issues and Strategies for Women and Minorities* (Cooper & Stevens, 2002), was a volume coedited with my colleague and friend Joanne Cooper. Like my other books, this book grew out of what I was doing at the time. In 1998, as a member of the committee on the role and status of women at AERA, the largest national and international educational organization and convention for faculty, I and a group of colleagues conducted a workshop on the variety of strategies for success on the route to tenure, especially focusing on the needs of women and minorities. Responding to the overflow crowd and the workshop evaluations, I suggested to my workshop presenters, "You know I think this material seems to be so helpful. No one is writing about it. I want to plant a seed, or, rather, a tree. Why don't we write a book, an edited volume?" Four years later the State University of New York (SUNY) Press published the book, which included chapters by the presenters at the conference workshop. Just like textbook writing that works well when it grows out of your classroom teaching, edited volumes work best when they grow out of the day-to-day work you are doing at the time.

One of the challenges of edited volumes is finding chapter contributors. As we did with *Tenure in the Sacred Grove*, you can solicit colleagues that you already know. Alternatively, you can put out a call for chapter proposals through electronic mailing lists or your professional organization's website. As a potential author, you may notice these requests for chapter contributions in a broadcast e-mail from your professional organization, or you may see hard copy flyers that invite chapter proposal submissions on a table near registration at conferences. Editors may make an announcement at special interest group meetings at larger conferences. Some post the idea on social media such as Facebook or LinkedIn. If you are thinking about doing an edited volume, make a collection of these "calls for chapter submissions" to see how others are soliciting contributions.

Soliciting contributions from scholars whose work you already know is more likely to result in a cohesive volume of predictable quality. Broadcast calls for contributions may involve sorting through and evaluating numerous submissions.

If you are the editor, you are responsible for selecting and finalizing the list of chapter contributors and developing a table of contents. You develop the criteria for accepting and reviewing the chapter submissions and make the final decision about suitability of the chapter for your edited volume. From the abstracts for submissions, you decide on a table of contents that indicates how each chapter contributes to the whole book. Once that is done, you then write the book proposal to be sent to a publisher. Later on in this chapter, I will guide you through the book proposal development process. For now, it is important to know that the editors will need to submit a proposal for the publisher to review.

An advantage of putting together an edited volume with scholars you know is that—with conditional commitments from them in hand—you can approach a publisher before chapters are written to determine the degree of interest ahead of time, and even get some feedback on your proposal.

When the proposal is accepted, as editor, you are responsible for the organization and coordination of contributors who might be at different universities, even in different countries. A well-developed table of contents that clearly shows the purpose and contribution of each chapter will remind the contributors about how their work contributes to the document as a whole. However, the challenge is getting faculty to adhere to a schedule, keep to their topic, and turn in their chapters on time.

The level of royalties depends to a great extent on the distribution networks and efforts of your publisher. Big university presses such as Chicago, Oxford, Princeton, and Harvard have extensive distribution channels, so they may sell more books. The smaller university presses often focus on specific disciplines and concentrate their marketing accordingly. While *Tenure in the Sacred Grove* generated no income for us editors, as the contract stipulated no royalties would be paid on the first 1,000 copies, the volume impressed my promotion and tenure committee and, along with my other work, earned me tenure.

Professional Books

This book that you hold in your hand or that you are reading on an e-reader fits into the category of a professional book. Professional books are designed either to assist faculty in their various roles as teachers, researchers, and faculty members, or to provide advice and guidance to administrators or other practitioners in their work, such as laboratory practices, medical procedures, or research methods. University presses, such as Teachers College Press, Johns Hopkins University Press, and SUNY, and higher education presses, such as Routledge, Stylus Publishing, SAGE, and Information Age, publish most of the professional books in education and educational research. CRC Press publishes several handbooks and dictionaries in the sciences. Guilford Press publishes professional books in psychology, psychiatry, and the behavioral sciences. By attending the book exhibits at your national and international conferences, you probably have a good sense of the professional publishers in your discipline.

Writing professional books is an affirmation of your values, experience, and practice. You are writing about what is familiar to you on a topic that you care deeply about for an audience you know well. My writing is informed by my many years as a graduate student and teacher at four universities, from two research I institutions (Michigan State and University of Utah) to a small liberal arts college (Whitman College) to an urban comprehensive university (PSU). Given that these institutions have different students and cultures, when I am writing, I can easily visualize a broad audience that might benefit from my work. For several years during graduate school, I earned extra income by being a part-time corporate trainer for Arthur Anderson, an accounting firm, where I taught courses such as "Effective Presentations" and "Effective Business Writing" to young professionals, another audience that at times appears in my university classroom. In addition, my degree in educational psychology gave me the research skills to use the literature to inform my writing and to develop research projects to learn about the impact of my work. Finally, when I write professional-type books, I can include more of the breadth and depth of my teaching, education, and life experiences to engage the reader.

In relation to your career trajectory and promotion, the downside of professional books is that your institution may not regard them as "scholarly enough." If the book is outside of your disciplinary focus, the promotion committees may wonder why you are not writing books that contribute to your discipline. In particular for some promotion committees, if you are not also publishing journal articles, writing professional books may cast a shadow on your attempts to advance in your career. Again, you can explore the professional book–writing climate at your institution by checking in with your department chair or dean.

Most professional books will not generate the level of royalties generated by textbooks, but they can be rewarding in other ways. Apart from *Tenure in the Sacred Grove*, which generated no royalties, my next two coauthored books fall under the category of professional books: *Introduction to Rubrics: An Assessment Tool to Save Grading Time, Convey Effective Feedback and Promote Student Learning* (Stevens & Levi, 2005, first edition and 2013, second edition) and *Journal Keeping: How to Use Reflective Writing for Teaching, Learning, Professional Insight and Positive Change* (Stevens & Cooper, 2009). Both command continuing audiences and generate regular sales and royalty payments. What is particularly satisfying about my books is that they have led to many national and international consulting opportunities.

Scholarly Monographs

Across the disciplines, but most especially in the humanities such as English, history, and philosophy, faculty write monographs that are in-depth scholarly investigations on a topic. The positive side of writing these narratives is that they are an opportunity to research and write about a topic near and dear to your core academic skills and discipline. In some disciplines, you are expected to write such a book to guarantee advancement along your career path. A well-crafted volume may generate consulting and lecture opportunities as well.

The disadvantages of scholarly investigations are that they tend to take a long time to write and require highly developed research and organizational skills. Most scholarly monographs do not generate many, if any, royalties. Because libraries are buying fewer and fewer monographs, university presses are looking for books on broader topics that may attract a wider range of buyers. As already noted, those scholarly publishers that do still focus on the library market, expecting small sales, will price the book high. Yet, a monograph can ensure advancement on a career path, and certainly that is a financial reward in itself.

Dissertation advisers often urge graduate students to turn their dissertation into a book. You put a lot of time and energy into the dissertation. After all, it looks like a book, with a table of contents, chapters, and references. However, there are many, many challenges associated with converting your dissertation into a publishable book. One issue is that you wrote your dissertation for a small, expert audience and probably followed a format determined by your discipline that showcased your new scholarly skills but didn't encourage using a structure or writing style that would appeal more widely. Making your dissertation into a book will require you to recraft the work you have done for a broader audience. Because converting a dissertation into a book is such a comprehensive task, I will not cover the process here. I suggest consulting other resources about how to make the conversion. Germano (2013) offers some excellent ways to do this.

Self-Published Books

A more recent phenomenon is the self-published book. You write the book and pay someone to publish it, or do so for free on a platform like Amazon. The upside of self-published books is that you have total control of the product. You design it. You do not have to go through external review of any sort. And, after you pay your production costs, you make all the money on it. That can be a substantial sum for some authors.

One disadvantage is the potentially questionable status of a self-published book in your department, discipline, and university. Another disadvantage is that you will have to take the time to market the book. In addition, the culture of academia tends to look down on self-published books and will not count them toward career advancement, largely because they are not peer reviewed. Dadkhah, Borchardt, and Maliszewski (2017) warn medical faculty about fraud in academic publishing when unscrupulous publishers approach faculty to publish their work for a fee. It is important, if you are writing as a scholar, to establish the quality, integrity, and rigor of the publisher. Your librarian can help here. Another significant downside of self-published works is that you will be responsible for editing and design and will generally—unless you publish through an entity like Amazon—have to take care of sales and distribution through a myriad of channels such as wholesalers, online vendors, bookstores, and direct mail. When an established publisher produces your book, it is responsible for all these functions. Ideally, the publisher's representatives attend conferences, mail out catalogs, maintain a website, and have a comprehensive contact database to spread the news about your work. Managing this distribution effort is difficult for faculty authors who have many other teaching, community, and research obligations.

Trade Books

I have not singled out trade books as a typical academic book for faculty. Yet, it is a book category that you might be interested in. The audience for trade books is the general public. Trade books include novels, children's literature, travel logs, mysteries, memoirs, and how-to books, among other genres. The publishers are not the same as those that publish the typical academic books such as textbooks, edited books, professional books, and scholarly monographs. The upside of this kind of writing is that there is a potential for wider distribution of your work and, hence, a greater source of income. There's also potential for the sale of movie, audio, and other subsidiary rights.

The disadvantage of trade books is that promotion committees may not recognize these books because they may not use the scholarly literature. In addition, writing a novel can take an inordinate amount of time and focus that can pull a faculty member away from his or her teaching and service responsibilities.

Choosing the Type of Book and Publisher

While leading workshops on writing a book proposal, faculty have asked me a number of questions that I will address next:

- *How is the type of book I choose regarded in my promotion process?* Because you will be putting so much effort into writing a book, it is wise to seek insight from your department chair and the dean as well as published faculty in your department about how they regard certain kinds of books. In addition, you can ask if this is a good time in your career to write a book. You may want to write the book anyway, but you will need to weigh the decision carefully.
- *Am I limited to one type once I start with that type?* You are not limited to one type of book once you have written a single book. However, having an existing relationship with a publisher and having experience with a particular type may reduce start-up time on your next book.
- *What is the review process for each type?* Textbooks are reviewed "in-house" first, which means that the acquisitions editor or the publications board reviews the proposal. University presses have faculty editorial boards that require evidence of peer review when they consider projects for approval. The publisher will set up the peer reviews. Publishers of professional books may rely more heavily on their internal evaluation processes and may not always seek formal peer review, relying on more informal advice. All publishers are

concerned with market need, contribution to the field, the coherence of the project, the author's scholarly credentials, length (as it impacts pricing), timing (particularly important in a fast-moving field), and existing competition (which, these days, may encompass resources beyond printed media). Since every commitment entails risk and investment, the publisher will review these considerations carefully in deciding whether to take on a book or reject it.

A final piece of advice: If you need to indicate that you have a book under review for your department's promotion committee, let your potential publisher know. Even if it's a project for which the publisher doesn't feel that formal peer review is required, he or she will probably accommodate you with an assessment of the book and its potential impact in the field.

- *What is the publisher's role versus mine as author of the book?* Getting to contract may entail considerable correspondence on refining the table of contents and taking into account peer review comments. Once you have a contract, the publisher usually pays close attention to the writing of the book and will generally provide you with manuscript submission guidelines that will cover issues such as formatting headings, reference style, formats for figures, and permissions for extensive quotations. Because you typically send in a proposal with only sample draft chapters, and, particularly if you are a first-time book author, you will probably want some support and guidance as you start writing in earnest.

  Ideally, you will build a relationship with the editor, who will support you, encourage you, and assist you in meeting deadlines. However, it is generally up to you to be proactive and ask questions about the process and reach out to your acquisitions editor for help in determining whether your developing text meets expectations. It is also up to you to understand the stages of publishing. Most acquisitions editors have time to shepherd only 1 or 2 books in detail through development, given that they may be handling 20 to 30 projects through production that year, let alone having discussions with new authors about prospective projects. The larger presses may hire a "developmental editor" to assist you with the writing and structuring of your book. You might alternatively want to invest in hiring your own editor or writing coach. There are several fine organizations and individuals who offer coaching (Academic Coaching and Writing, Meggin McIntosh, Academic Ladder).

- *What is the issue of copyrights?* The issue of copyright ownership is complex. You can—as I have—ask your librarian for advice. Typically, you assign the copyright to the publisher in the contract, but not all publishers insist on that. The key factor for the publisher is control of the publishing rights to ensure that it can protect its investment as the sole publisher of the work. TAA (www.taaonline.net) has a list of lawyers who can help you negotiate contract terms as well.

- *What about formatting, editing, and indexing?* Once you sign the contract and establish a relationship with the editor, you will learn more about how this publisher works. It is a great idea to ask questions about how it perceives its role and what support it will give you. My publisher employs copyeditors, typographers, and designers. It also gives me feedback on my writing. I create my own indexes. While most contracts for scholarly books require authors to supply the index, publishers generally offer to undertake that on the author's behalf, recharging the cost against royalty earnings.

When publishers receive the final manuscript, most publishers will routinely put your manuscript through a copyediting process that entails providing advice about phrasing, consistency, and clarity of expression; querying ambiguous statements; checking spelling and grammar; and ensuring references are complete and correct, among other concerns.

- *Where do e-books fit in?* When e-books first came out, publishers were concerned about whether they would replace print books and, indeed, in the early years, e-book sales grew by vast percentages, admittedly from a low base. In scholarly publishing, e-books have not displaced print copies in any significant way. They may represent about 15% of sales. Where there is a shift to e-books is in textbook publishing. Students, on the one hand, appreciate the lower e-book prices, or being able to have time-limited access to a text for a semester. On the other hand, they forfeit being able to resell their used textbooks. This is a constantly developing area, and you, as a teacher, may have a better handle on trends among your students and the textbook market today. That said, all publishers today issue e-books simultaneously with print copies.
- *What are the financial incentives?* As stated before, textbooks can be the most lucrative. Typically with scholarly presses you will not make much money, largely because of the changing nature of the book market for monographs. However, a well-received book—particularly if it receives positive reviews in journals—can be a positive addition in your career path that would include salary increases with promotion.

Setting Yourself Up for Success: Detective, Reflective, and Expressive Work to Produce a Book Proposal

After considering what type of book you might want to write, the next essential task is doing the background work for developing the book proposal. A book proposal in academe is different from a commercial (trade book) book proposal. You may have heard that authors need agents who go out and sell the idea of your book to publishers. This is not true for the academic books. Academic book publishers do not expect you to have an agent. You "get to" do the work of finding a publisher and doing some promotion of your book. Beginning with the strategies in the detective, reflective, and expressive work described next and in Table 10.2, you are laying the groundwork for selling your book to the publisher through writing the book proposal.

We are the entrepreneurs for our work. Nowhere is that more evident than in conceptualizing and testing your ideas and then writing a book proposal. Some faculty may bristle at the idea that we need to be entrepreneurs. Yet, if you think about the argument you need to make in a journal article, you are first persuading the journal editor and then the reader that you have done the background work, you know the literature, and your work is worthwhile. You are "selling" your ideas. In general, a book proposal, then, is a document that describes the main idea for the book as well as persuades the publisher that you know the audience and there is a need for the book, and that your ideas are sufficiently worthwhile so others will pay to read about them.

To write a book proposal you will have to be confident about your topic and be knowledgeable about the audience and the potential impact of the book on this audience. To build confidence takes time. Before you submit your proposal, you need to "field test" your ideas and be open to how the audience responds to those ideas and then modify your work to meet audience needs and expectations. You will need to continually ask yourself, "Who is my audience for this work? Students? Peers? What do they really need? How will my book meet their needs?" The detective and reflective work that follows focuses on key goals to be accomplished as you move toward writing that well-informed and persuasive book proposal. Table 10.2 summarizes the detective, reflective, and expressive work to be done to write a book proposal.

Detective Work

As with the other types of manuscripts, doing the research to know the external context of book publishing will help you decide if you want to write a book.

Immerse Yourself in Your Topic, Determine Need, and Identify Audience
The objectives of the detective work are to determine how you can demonstrate your knowledge and expertise and identify why your project will appeal to or fill a need for the audience you have defined. Writing a book begins not one month, but years, before you submit the proposal. You begin with a small seed of an idea about a topic that you know very well and you really care about. Developing the idea; nurturing it; trying it out in different venues, such as in your classroom, or at conferences with posters, roundtables, or paper sessions, takes time. In this process, before you write the proposal you are finding out about the audience and the potential market for the book.

I strongly suggest that you teach the topic, either as a small one- or two-week unit in the middle of a course or as a special topics class. In the latter case, you can approach your department chair with an idea for a special class you want to teach. My coauthored book about journal keeping grew out of a special topics class called "Journal Keeping in Professional Life" and my use of reflective writing activities in all my classes. My co-authored rubrics book was launched following a series of workshops with educators when I saw how powerful rubrics were for shaping and getting feedback on instruction. This book has grown out of my continuing work with faculty in an academic writing program at PSU through our faculty teaching and learning center (chapter 12 describes that program and how to set up one on your campus). I continually say to faculty, "Write about what you do. That way you are immersed in the topic and know the nuances, roadblocks, and opportunities within the topic. And, as you record and reflect on feedback, you will begin to know very well how your audience responds to these ideas."

TABLE 10.2

Writing book proposals: Detective, reflective, and expressive work

Writing Book Proposals	
Detective work	*Reflective work*
Objective: To know your topic, determine need, and clearly define audience	**Objective: To organize ideas, organize references, and find models**
Teach the topic as an experimental class or as sections within one class.	Create an accessible system for collecting references.
Test your ideas through conference proposals, workshops, and journal articles.	Use Zotero tags (CMS—see chapter 9).
Gather responses from audiences at conferences.	Create a binder for the book with dividers for each chapter, or start a new Word file for each chapter.
Reflect in your journal on how students and others respond to your ideas.	Make a chart with all competing texts (Table 10.3).
	Analyze what is missing in those texts and how your book will distinguish itself.
	Look for successful models of similar books.
	Pay attention to text features you might use, such as a glossary, epigraphs at the beginning of the chapters, or case studies.
Objective: To identify potential publishers and competing texts	**Objective: To identify the text features you will use**
Visit publisher booths at conferences.	After review of the text features, decide which ones will add coherence to the text.
Talk to the acquisitions editor.	
Collect books on same or similar topic.	
Join TAA (www.taaonline.net).	

Expressive work

Objective: To write the proposal

Make a chart of different publishers' proposal guideline headers.
Be prepared to send off your proposal to at least three publishers.
Write your proposal using those headers.
Make a chart with each chapter that includes its title and a sentence such as, "The purpose of this chapter is . . ."

Know the Market
A book publisher will offer you a book contract only if it believes that it can sell the book. Some scholarly presses are closing up their shops because funds are tight and their universities can no longer justify subsidizing these monographs. The bottom line is the book must sell.

Begin the Conversation With Potential Publishers
You should begin at the book exhibition hall at one of your large national or international conferences because the larger publishers will be there. The first thing is to check out which publishers are publishing the type of book you want to write and addressing the audience you want to reach. Typically at four-day national or international conferences, I spend at least half a day at the book exhibits; in my early years, I would spend an entire day. Are there books on my topic being published? How many? Who is the publisher? I order books that could be competitors to my book, or check them out at my institutional library. I begin to build a library of my competition. This knowledge will come in very handy when I write my book proposal and have to describe the competitors in my field.

Your next very important step is to seek out the acquisitions or commissioning editor (titles vary by company) who is employed by the publisher to acquire books. Acquisitions editors often specialize in particular disciplines and have a good handle on their market, its needs, and its expectations. They attend their larger disciplinary conferences looking for authors. When potential authors approach them, they welcome conversations about potential submissions. In addition, they will often provide immediate advice and opinions, and, if they pursue your project, will navigate the process, from getting peer reviews to seeking approval by their editorial board, issuing the contract, attending to manuscript development, and moving your project into production. Their job is to acquire books that contribute profitably to the publisher's "list" or portfolio of titles. The sales people at the publishers' booths are often not acquisitions editors, but I have found that, if you ask, they will certainly direct you to the right person. After you have identified the acquisitions editor, you may see him or her having coffee with other faculty. Just keep thinking, "Soon I will be that person having coffee with the acquisitions editor and I will be talking about my book!" Well, maybe not this year but certainly in the next few years.

When do you approach an acquisitions editor? At what stage? What do you say? When you have just an idea for a book, even years before you write the proposal, you might approach him or her and say something such as, "My name is Dannelle Stevens, and I'm from Portland State. I am thinking of writing a book on a classroom assessment tool, rubrics." The typical response might be, "Tell me more about your idea." After chatting a bit, you might mention that he or she could attend a session at the conference where you are presenting some of the material you'll include in the book.

With these simple actions you are beginning a relationship with this editor, a key step to your eventual success in publishing a book. However, it's important to realize that you may begin the relationship with the editor three or four years ahead of even writing a proposal. Because the relationship with the acquisitions editor is so important, if the editor moves to another publishing house, you may want to follow that person. If not, you now know how to start a new relationship with another acquisitions editor.

Beyond attending book exhibits, I research the topic online. On Amazon and/or Barnes & Noble, I put in key words related to my topic and, first, note which books appear and, second, who is the publisher. In addition, I go to Google Scholar and put in my topic, followed by the word "books," and "academic writing books." Then, I get a list of book citations. You can do this same process with the online databases in your library catalog. Again, as with all detective work, you are scanning the external environment to get to know the field. After you identify the publisher online, you will need to go to the website to find the name and contact information for the acquisitions editor. Write an e-mail saying you are thinking of writing a book about . . . and you should get a response. When I have done this, I've often been asked which conferences I attend, opening the possibility of a face-to-face meeting. Identifying several publishers is a beginning step in writing a book proposal.

Reflective Work

After gathering data from the external sources during your detective work, you can move on to reflective work, making decisions about your workspace and the essential features in your book.

Decide How to Organize Your Workspace and to Create Systems to Gather Your Materials

The objectives for reflective work are to reflect on and organize your physical environment for efficient work. Think about what your workspace is like now. Are you free from interruptions? Can you get to your materials easily? Are your materials organized for efficient access?

Because of the size and length of the project, most faculty book writers have a dedicated space for writing at home or at work. Setting up a space at your institution is a bit risky because of the potential for interruptions that can derail your focus and attention. Also, if you work both at home and at your institution, you will have to move materials back and forth. A dedicated space at home visibly demonstrates your commitment to the project. Textbook authors often have two or even three computer screens so that they can have the text in front of them and view photo inserts or sidebars or other chapter features on the other screen. I find two screens are also invaluable. I can put Zotero, a CMS, and notes on my references on one screen and have the text on the screen in front of me. It is easier for me to weave in those references when I have two screens.

Organizing the materials that you will use in the book requires a solid, easily accessible system as well. The materials might include journal articles related to your topic, handouts you have used in class, and PowerPoints or posters that you have created about this topic. Over the years I have found several ways that facilitate organization:

- Use a physical, hard copy binder. I use numbered binder dividers. Number 1 becomes chapter 1, where I put current drafts of the chapter. Also, in the early stages, when I come across a reference or a conference handout that is particularly relevant to that chapter, it gets copied, printed, and tucked away in that chapter section of the binder. Having a binder with chapters also makes it feel more like a book. When I am ready to write the chapter, I already have some seeds to further my thinking. You can equally do this digitally, creating a separate file for each chapter (most publishers prefer receiving manuscripts in chapter chunks), and adding PDFs, notes, and scanned images for related material you are collecting.
- If you use a handwritten journal, take your journal to conferences (chapter 6) along with a glue stick. Cut out the handouts from presentations that contribute to ideas in your book. Glue the handouts into your journal. This ensures that the handout will not get buried in the stack of papers that that you took to the conference. If you use a digital journal, you can ask for the PowerPoints or photograph the significant points from the presentation.
- Have a consistent document-naming system for each chapter. Each day I open the text to write, I start a new file with that day's date in the file name. For example, today's file name is "Ch10Books9Aug2017." Yesterday's file was "Ch10Books8Aug2017." The only thing that changed was the date.
- If I am writing with a coauthor, I also put my initials at the end of the file name because I was the last person to touch this text. All of these documents end up in a file folder "Ch10BooksCurrentText." The other files that contain documents in the Chapter 10 folder are "Ch10BooksArchivalTexts." When there are too many revisions in the current manuscript, I move them to the archival file. Plus, I have these files: "Ch10Tables," "Ch10Figures," and "Ch10Misc." In the miscellaneous file, I put references or other materials related to the chapter that I might want to use later.

Other faculty have found that a digital "filing" system works well for them. Scrivner is a powerful system that keeps track of chapters, references, and sections of the book in an online environment. Whatever method you choose, you need to spend some time reflecting on and finding a system that works for you for collecting, organizing, and saving all your materials for easy access.

Analyze Your Competition and Decide Essential Features of Your Book
I have combined detective and reflective work in Table 10.2 because the two processes are interwoven when you develop and analyze a chart of competitor texts. On the detective side, you are placing key elements of competitors' books into a matrix, and on the reflective side, you are using those ideas to inform the development of your book. After all, these books have been published, so there

is generally something about the work that persuaded a publisher the book was a worthwhile investment.

The book competitor chart (Table 10.3) will help immensely in making decisions about your own book's features and structure. Your competitor analysis means you are reading like a writer, not like a reader. You are scanning the book environment to see what works for others and to then decide what shape you want for your book. One decision is what features your book will have. The book features add coherence or consistency across the chapters. An example of a book feature in this book is the concept map I have at the beginning of each chapter. In addition, the first five chapters are principles one to five. Each of the chapters on writing book reviews, conference proposals, journal articles, and book proposals are framed with the ideas of detective, reflective, and expressive work.

Besides gathering details on what features competitor texts have, other details on the competitor chart help me in writing the book proposal. By writing down the number of pages, I can begin to gauge how long my book might be. I note the number of chapters and sometimes I type out the table of contents from competitors to see the breadth and depth of the work others have done.

All this analysis of competitors feeds my creative process in making decisions about my book. I ask, "How is my book different from the others? What might make it unique? What features, if any, do I want to include?" When you share the chart with the publisher, you are telling the publisher that you know the competition. As noted later, publishers expect you to know and critique your competitors. I included this chart with my book proposal submission. Again, publishers appreciate this attention to detail and to your identifying the niche where your book fits in. Most importantly, you will need to tell the publisher what is missing from the other books and what you bring to the table.

Expressive Work

From your detective and reflective work you know your topic, you know the audience, you have some ideas about making contact with the acquisitions editor, you have set up your workspace, and you have some ideas about the features of your book. Given all of that, you are ready for writing and submitting the book proposal, the expressive work.

Write the Book Proposal

One good thing about book proposals versus journal articles is that you can send out several proposals at the same time. I suggest that you submit your proposal to three publishers. This is not like journal article publishing, where it is unethical to send an article out to more than one journal. If you do, you should reveal that fact in your proposal. It might speed up the publisher's response time or give it pause about investing time and money on peer review. If you have had preliminary discussions with a particular publisher while developing your idea, I would recommend starting by making a single submission to the editor concerned.

TABLE 10.3

Academic writing books: Competitor chart

	Author	Title	Publication information	Pages	Price	Table of contents	Features	Other
1	Silvia, P. J.	*How to Write a Lot: A Practical Guide to Productive Academic Writing*	2007, American Psychological Association	141 to index	$14.95	Small format. Eight chapters.	Handy, faculty like the length and the clear strategies presented.	He debunks reasons that faculty give for not writing. He writes with wit and whimsy.
2	Belcher, W.	*How to Write a Journal Article in 12 Weeks: A Guide to Academic Publishing Success*	2009, SAGE	340 to index	$80.50	Each chapter has one week of activities ending with sending the article in to the journal.	Full of timely advice. You can tell she has experience. Writer needs to have a solid draft of manuscript to use the workbook.	She debunks 38 reasons why faculty say they don't have time to write. Large format. Workbook pages can be duplicated.
3	Goodson, P.	*Becoming an Academic Writer: 50 Exercises for Paced, Productive and Powerful Writing* (2nd edition)	2017, SAGE	251 to index	$35.40	Part I: Practice becoming a productive academic writer. Part II: Practice writing sections of journal articles, research reports, and grant applications.	Has detailed contents following the general contents of the chapters. Designed as a self-paced workbook. But, there is little attention to the "self" except at the beginning. Few reflective activities or prompts.	Uses a timer for all exercises. Focuses on sub-skills of writing. Less focus on integrating skills. Eleven tables and figures. Has electronic resources, notes to ESL learners, sidebars with "Research shows . . ." References at the end of the chapter for that chapter. Index of authors at the end of the book.

Book publishers also typically want you to submit a chapter or two, or a writing sample if you haven't yet drafted any chapters, with your proposal. Generally, they do not want the whole book. Publishers are also used to receiving proposals that are outlines for a project and are intended to start a conversation about the viability of the topic and its treatment. Publishers understand that things change somewhat as the ideas for the book mature and become refined through the writing process. Some chapters may be subsumed in others, for instance. New chapters and introductions may be added. In this process of developing your book, ideally you and the editor will be constantly in contact. After you sign the contract, the process of writing may take six months to three years, depending on such considerations as the importance of launching the book at a particular event or the author's particular circumstances.

To get a book contract, you will need to write a book proposal, typically a document of four to eight pages. Table 10.4 is a list of the headings found in the book proposal submission guidelines for three publishers. As you read down and across these headings for sections of the book proposal, you will see some similar words, such as "audience," "market," and "competition," that signal you will need to know more than just the content of the book to write the proposal.

I have reviewed several publisher guidelines and created a summary of the six key objectives you will need to accomplish when you submit any book proposal:

1. Demonstrate that you know the audience.
2. Present an overall scope, content, and purpose.
3. Indicate that you know the competition.
4. Communicate your vision for chapters and text features.
5. Establish your expertise.
6. Demonstrate your writing ability.

In the second column of Table 10.5, I have given you some ideas about how to accomplish the objective in column 1. For example, for objective 1, "Demonstrate that you know your audience," the ways that you can demonstrate this are as follows:

Tell the publisher that you have taught the topic and gathered feedback from students or peers; reflecting on what you have learned and incorporating it into your proposal.

Show how you have gathered and used reviewer and audience feedback from conference presentations and journal articles to revise your proposal to meet audience needs.

In the final column, I show you where you will communicate what you know about that objective in each of the publisher guidelines.

When submitting, I make a point of meeting all of the book proposal expectations for each specific publisher and put them in the order that the publisher expects. Even though the items are similar, I make sure I read all of the material they offer. In fact, if they have not numbered the sections of their proposal (e.g., Wiley), I will number the items because it makes it easier to cut and paste some sections across

TABLE 10.4

Book proposal submission guidelines: Key elements to be included in proposal from three publishers

Stylus Publishing: Section headings	Taylor & Francis: Section headings	Wiley: Professional development books Section headings
1. Title	1. Statement of aims	1. Proposed title and a description of the topic
2. Description, scope, content, purpose		2. An explanation of why the product is needed by the marketplace
3. Audience	2. A detailed synopsis, including chapter summaries	3. The intended primary market and secondary markets
4. Need		4. A profile of the typical reader
5. Competition	3. A description of target market	5. A description of why the topic is important
6. (Your) Qualifications and related activities		6. A review of competitive works
7. Table of contents	4. Review of three to five main competing texts	7. Table of contents
8. Format, length, special features		8. A partial or complete manuscript
9. E-books	5. Format and time line	9. Reviews of the author's previous works
10. Timetable		
Accompanying material: Writing sample CV	Accompanying material: CV Names of academic referees	Accompanying material: CV

TABLE 10.5
Objectives for writing a book proposal based on publisher guidelines

Key objective to meet in writing a book proposal	How can you accomplish this objective?	Where key objective is found in publisher guidelines. Refer to Table 10.4 for a numbered list of three publisher guidelines: Stylus Publishing, Taylor & Francis, and Wiley
1. Demonstrate that you know your audience.	Tell the publisher that you have taught the topic and gathered feedback from students or peers. Reflect on what you have learned and incorporate it into your proposal. Show how you have gathered and used reviewer and audience feedback from conference presentations and journal articles to revise your proposal to meet audience needs.	#3 in Stylus Publishing #3 in Taylor & Francis #3 and #4 in Wiley Include your CV
2. Present an overall scope, content, and purpose.	Use feedback from audiences and your experience to create basic description, scope, and purpose of the book. Clarify purpose. See Exercise 2.1 for a writing activity to clarify purpose.	#1, #2, and #4 in Stylus Publishing #1 and #2 in Taylor & Francis #1, #2, #4, and #5 in Wiley
3. Indicate that you know the competition.	Gather books written by competition. Make book chart (Table 10.3).	#5 in Stylus Publishing #1 and #4 in Taylor & Francis #6 in Wiley
4. Communicate your vision for chapters and text features.	Present the publisher with your analysis of the competition: table of contents, content, purpose, features, length, cost. Use these ideas to decide on your text features. Lay out specific plan for all sections and chapters, including table of contents. See Table 10.4 for a model.	#7, #8, and #10 in Stylus Publishing #5 in Taylor & Francis #7 in Wiley
5. Communicate your expertise.	Make sure your CV is up to date. Assert your knowledge of the niche for the book based on your expertise, analysis of competition, and data gathering from audiences.	#6 in Stylus Publishing #1 in Taylor & Francis #9 in Wiley (also send in CV) Include your CV
6. Demonstrate your writing ability.	Include a chapter (at least). See specific publisher expectations.	Accompanying materials in Stylus Publishing #8 in Wiley

these guidelines. I also think complying with publishers' expectations sends a message that I am aware of and responsive to their requirements and will, therefore, be easy to work with in the future.

Even though these submission guidelines look very similar, in some ways they are different. Stylus Publishing has links throughout its guidelines to websites and articles that can assist the writer in writing the proposal: "Even your academic peers appreciate straightforward, clear prose. In general, more accessibly written books gain wider readership. We recommend you read Gail Hornstein's article 'Prune That Prose' that appeared in the *Chronicle of Higher Education* on September 9, 2009."

The guidelines from Stylus indicate that this publisher was interested in helping me craft a persuasive book proposal. Taylor & Francis, with its many imprints and wide range of book genres, has specific guidelines for different kinds of books such as research monographs, textbooks, and professional books. Taylor & Francis uses a series of questions within each of its headings to guide the writer. In addition, Taylor & Francis has an infographic on the publication process. Wiley has the leanest submission guidelines, with only a phrase that the author needs to interpret to meet its expectations. Before you submit your proposal, pay attention to the different suggestions and resources on the publisher's website.

My publisher, Stylus, appreciates one feature of my submissions that gives an initial framing for the book, which is a tabular table of contents that presents an abstract of each chapter. Table 10.6 is an example of part of the chart that I included in my book proposal submission for this book. I have included only two of the chapters here. You can see I have given an overview of the book, named the section, given each chapter a title, and clearly stated the purpose of the chapter. In addition, you may notice the strike-out phrases. I included those to show you how a manuscript changed over time after submission. These were added after the proposal was accepted. While you do need to give an overview of the chapters, you need to know that this is still a work in progress. That is why you don't want to submit the entire manuscript with the proposal. Publishers generally want to work with you and help you to craft the manuscript. After all, writing changes and develops over time. With the counsel of the editor, I have changed some chapters around and added several chapters, as noted by the strike-outs.

As you submit, Stylus and Wiley ask that you come up with a working book title, understanding that determining a final title may be an evolutionary process and that a good title may emerge during the writing process. Most publishers will consult with you on the title; some may insist on their choice if they feel they have a better sense of what will appeal to the market. As Stylus notes, I value the exercise of selecting a working title because it often helps with clarifying the focus of the book. I like to explore a variety of titles and will submit them with the book proposal. If you want to explore a variety of ways to write a title, I suggest you consult Lyon (2000) for a strategy to generate titles. Lyon asserts that titles can have a "slant," a hidden appeal to the audience, so it is important to consider the hidden message behind an effective title. The title for this book, for instance, has the slant of promises. I seek to convey the slant of a "promise" to readers that when

TABLE 10.6
Example from Stylus Publishing book proposal: Chapter overviews with some edits

Write more! Publish more! **Outline of contents and chapter descriptions:**

The book is divided into three sections.

- The first section shows ~~graduate students and~~ faculty the basic strategies to change their writing habits to build a base for a lifetime writing practice. Creating a sustainable and even enjoyable writing practice requires attention and intentional practice. I introduce my five key writing ~~strategies.~~ principles.
- The second section includes the basic strategies from Section I applied to typical writing projects that faculty encounter, such as book reviews and journal articles.
- ~~In the third section I zoom in on ways to boost motivation through creative activities, analysis of research articles and web-based supports~~

Section I	*Improve Your Writing Practice: Five Powerful ~~strategies~~ Principles*	
Chapter 1	~~Strategy~~ Principle 1: Know yourself as a writer	The purpose of this chapter is to provide evidence that demonstrates not only what is the value of knowing yourself as a writer but also how to get to know the writer in you. What keeps you from writing? What has been your experience in your writing? What do you say to yourself about writing? What gets you to write? How are you set up for writing in your home or office? To root out the unconscious messages you send yourself, take writing block questionnaire and write through reflective activities; dialogue with self as a writer.

Key words: self-awareness, writing habit |
| ~~Chapter 2~~ Chapter 3 | ~~Strategy~~ Principle 2: Reflect on your academic writing practices | After you have identified some of your current writing beliefs and practices, the purpose of this chapter is to provide you with a variety of ways to further reflect on your writing practice with an eye toward improvement. Reflection includes examining what you are doing every day as well as trying out some new ideas and reflecting on these ideas. What are your habits? What does your writing space look like? What time of the day do you write? When are you most productive? This chapter moves more into an examination of the practices you use. In addition, keeping a journal of these reflections will assist you in organizing and managing your writing life. Placing academic writing as a centerpiece in your academic life by keeping a journal assists in perspective-taking, organization, and deeper reflection.

Key words: practice, creativity, organization, reflection, motivation, sustainable, journal keeping |

Note. Strikeouts indicate how a proposal can change with publisher input.

they follow the principles and strategies in this book they will write more, publish more, and stress less. Lyon gives you some clues about writing a persuasive title with a definite slant. Again, this is a marketing issue. Better title ideas may emerge as the manuscript develops. And, using Lyon's guidelines, you can come up with a variety of titles. Check your contract to see how much leeway you have in creating your own title.

Another expectation in the book production process is for the author to respond to a marketing questionnaire that is usually sent when the author delivers the manuscript. This form goes to the marketing department to help them figure out who might be interested in the book, give them guidance on what journals to send review copies, and offer them your insights about other leads to pursue. Once again, you are back to marketing and being an entrepreneur. The questions are designed to help you consider the full range of promotion possibilities, from your contacts, ideas, and resources, as well as your activities that can promote sales. You may have to suggest people who can write blurbs for the book jacket that extol the virtues of the text. Given that sales revenues and the profit (or "surplus" in nonprofit university press speak) for most monographs are modest, the publisher may not have the resources to pursue all your ideas. That's where the advantage of choosing a publisher who is active in your field is important. It will have the economies of scale of promoting your book with others to the relevant audience.

Another way to market the book yourself is to have your own website or use the publisher's website to write a blog. A blog is another commitment. Yet, after the book is written, a blog can convey some specific ideas that are elaborated in the book. Most people suggest that you have five or six entries ready for a blog post before you announce that you have a blog.

Finally, if you go back and review the six key objectives in writing the book proposal, you can see that part of your job in writing the proposal is to demonstrate that you know what you want to write about, that you know the market, and that you have the skills and confidence to complete the project. You will need to convey this tone throughout your proposal. Your CV shows that you have been doing work in the area. I go one step further. After describing the audience, for example, I write, "I know this audience," I provide specific evidence of teaching the topic for seven years, making conference presentations on it, writing articles about it, and doing workshops and conducting research on it.

Submit the Proposal

Your final book proposal submission will contain the proposal as outlined by the publisher's guidelines, a chapter or two, your CV, and a chart of competing texts. Because you have a relationship with the acquisitions editor, e-mail the proposal to him or her and attach it, your CV, and your writing sample(s) to your message. More than likely, and unlike journal articles, you should receive a reasonably prompt acknowledgment. A final decision will take longer as your project goes through the review process within the publisher's world. Your editor will keep you informed of progress.

Meeting Book-Writing Challenges

Writing a book is a big, bold commitment. The basic thing to remember about it is that it begins with a seed of an idea and develops over time. Take advantage of every opportunity you can find to try out your ideas in your classes, at conference presentations, and in conversations with peers and acquisitions editors. Each step you take strengthens your proposal because you are "testing" the viability, plausibility, and marketability of your idea. Challenges lie ahead, even once you have the proposal and then the contract.

Challenge 1: Moving Back and Forth From the Micro to the Macro Tasks During the Writing Process

The tasks that go into book writing fall into the micro and then the macro level. You will need to allocate time for both. Micro tasks include getting words on the page, day in and day out, to keep steadily producing text. Macro tasks are setting up to-do lists, including attending to the book features, keeping your references in order, checking the length of chapters, maintaining consistent headings for tables and figures, and monitoring the coherence of the text. I suggest you refer to the ideas in chapter 3 on strategies to devise some way to allocate time to write and set aside time for the macro tasks by setting goals. In the book proposal, the publisher will want a time line of when you will send the final manuscript. At this early stage it is almost entirely guesswork. Yet, do think about your obligations over the next two years and how book writing will fit into those. The publisher has to think about when it can get the book into production and when is a good time to have it done for important conferences.

Challenge 2: Working With Coauthors

Working with others on a book has its benefits and challenges. You may know this person from your own institution or from other professional relationships. Writing a book is a different relationship. The benefits can be that you share the workload. You have someone you can consult, and you can review each other's work. The challenges come when your relationship with that person turns sour; yet, you have a contract to write this book together. This is very stressful. In the beginning, it is a good idea to establish some ground rules about your collaboration. I suggest clarification about who is first author; often that is the person with the idea in the first place. In addition, ask about what kind of feedback the coauthor wants and what response time seems appropriate. Try to think of things that have frustrated you in the past in working with others and seek to clarify as many of those frustrations as possible before you commit to work together. Remember, working with others to produce a book requires collaboration over several years, so maintaining a good working relationship is very important.

Challenge 3: Responding to Reviews

As your book proposal goes through the review process, you may receive feedback from the reviewers that the editor has solicited. Chapter 11 has some specific suggestions about how to handle those reviews and not be enervated by them. I remember our first reviews for the rubrics book were substantial and very critical; yet, the publisher still wanted to work with us. We took the reviews seriously and reorganized the book to address the comments. After the initial shock, we were grateful and thankful for the close attention that the reviewer had paid to our work.

Unforeseen challenges unrelated to your academic life may also appear, partly because of the length of time. In the end, it is your commitment to overcoming these challenges that can lead to your completion of the project.

Conclusion

Writing a book is a long and difficult process. Yet, there are rewards. When my first book was published, I recall setting it on my kitchen counter, stepping back, and taking a deep breath. Wow! My coauthors and I had created something that could help others who struggle with the tenure process, just as I had. This book has my name on it. You may find that other faculty members are struggling with similar ideas. You are making a difference for your colleagues or your students and you are contributing to the field, a worthy goal for a scholar.

CHAPTER 11

Handle a Revise-and-Resubmit Decision on Your Manuscript

Micki M. Caskey, Professor, Curriculum and Instruction, Portland State University; and Dannelle D. Stevens, Professor Emerita, Curriculum and Instruction, Portland State University

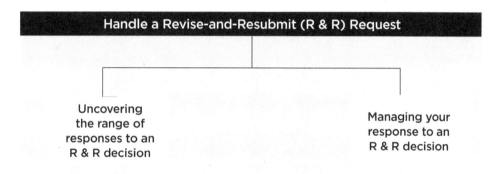

Ah, I find an e-mail from the editor of the journal. It has been four months since I felt that sense of relief of sending off the manuscript. It was a long, long time ago. Since then, to maintain the flow of my work, I started a new writing project. As I read the e-mail, I wonder, "Where is the decision?" I quickly scan down the e-mail. Great! The editor did not reject my manuscript. "We have reviewed your manuscript and have included the responses from three reviewers. We would like to have you make the suggested revisions and resubmit your work. We hope to get them back in 30 days." Okay. Now what? Do I drop everything and get it done, or . . .

An R & R decision is a positive response from a journal editor. Most journal editors do not outright accept an article without some revision. In fact, Algase (2014) asserted that the R & R decision is "[t]he most commonly occurring positive response to a manuscript submitted for publication" (p. 195).

Although an R & R decision does not guarantee that the editor will ultimately accept your manuscript for publication in the journal, the editors and reviewers have given you the opportunity to strengthen your work.

Most agree that the heart of academic work is the "peer review of materials." As academics, we serve as the monitors of the quality, the rigor, the originality, and the readability of each other's work. Peer review is a "blind" process; that is, the reviewers do not know your identity as the author, and, likewise, you do not know the identity of the reviewers. The intent of this blind process is a fair, unbiased, and impartial evaluation of the submitted manuscript. For this reason, the ideal orientation toward the review process is to respect its intention, embrace the freely given feedback, and leverage the information to make your writing more appealing to broader audiences (Textbook & Academic Authors Association, n.d.). In their roles, the editor and reviewers are often the first formal audience for your manuscript—peers who offer candid appraisal of your work.

The significance of the R & R process cannot be overstated. In fact, Ireland (2008), an experienced editor of a peer-reviewed journal, asserted: "Without doubt, the 'revise-and-resubmit' (R & R) part of the review process—revising a paper and preparing a response document for the action editor and the reviewers who have invited these actions—has great importance" (p. 1049).

We agree that the R & R process is important. The R & R process guides authors to develop a stronger and, typically, a more clearly written manuscript—making it more accessible and appealing to a larger audience. In addition, when successfully completed, the process helps ensure that the authors' findings and ideas become part of the disciplinary knowledge base. As authors of this chapter and recipients of R & R decisions, our experience confirms the incredible value of receiving specific feedback about our written work and compels us to respond thoughtfully to the reviewers' suggestions.

The purpose of this chapter is to show you ways to handle an R & R decision. Completing the revisions may feel like an "emotional roller coaster." Yet, when you apply your considerable intellectual, organizational, and analytical skills to the revision task, you will have more control over your emotions, which in turn will lead to a potentially more positive outcome. In this chapter, we first consider the range of responses to the R & R feedback: emotional and intellectual. Next, we delve into the actions you can take to organize and manage your response to the editor by doing the detective, reflective, and expressive work that undergirds a successful submission. Our action approach is strategic and analytical so that you can name and prioritize both the small and large tasks associated with completing a revision. Our purpose is to encourage you to act on the R & R feedback and then resubmit your work.

Uncovering the Range of Responses to an R & R Decision

Despite the importance of R & R work, we know that responding to an R & R takes time and effort. As we look across the landscape of responses, we identify two basic types of responding: emotional and intellectual.

Emotional Response

For most authors, including ourselves, receiving an R & R decision elicits an emotional response. Many acknowledge that these emotions may be quite mixed. For example, Kamler (2010) noted, "Revise and resubmit. These words can be simultaneously elating and terrifying for early career researchers" (p. 64).

You may experience a similar range of emotional responses to the R & R decision letter. Are you delighted that the editor or reviewers did not reject your manuscript? Evidently, they found many good qualities in your written work. Are you disheartened because you did not receive an "accept" or even an "accept with revision" decision? Plainly, the editor and/or reviewers did not deem your work worthy of publication without revision. Kamler (2010) also reported, "Everywhere I go I find confusion and despair about articles rejected or returned for further work. In the face of negative commentary, too many inexperienced writers crumble and never resubmit. Some take the critique so personally that they are incapacitated" (p. 65).

Whatever your initial feelings, we suggest that it is time to consider adopting a positive emotional response. Why? Because your emotional response connects inextricably to your intellectual response and your ability to move forward. For this reason, editors and authors across disciplines suggest adjusting your attitude toward an R & R decision. Take a moment to read some of their advice:

- The editors of *Journal for Research in Mathematics Education* recommended a congratulatory stance. "Pat yourself on the back!" (Martin & Miller, 2014, p. 286).
- An author of a book chapter about the R & R decision advised, "If your work receives a revise and resubmit (also called an R & R), celebrate. Don't despair. This is (usually) a good thing. The journal is interested in your work, and the editor would like to publish it—after you work a bit more on the piece" (Gullion, 2016, p. 125).
- The editor of *Research and Theory for Nursing Practice* suggested viewing an R & R decision as an invitation. According to Algase (2014),

When journal editors send a revise and resubmit notification on the outcome of a manuscript review, they usually intend it as an invitation to the author. The invitation is to consider making suggested changes to the work to better align it with the journal's mission and/or standards so that the work is better suited for eventual publication in their journal. (p. 195)

Going through the review process often seems tedious. Reviews can range from seemingly excessive attention to detail to much larger foundational conceptual issues. Some feedback feels like the reviewer wants you to succeed and offers the kind of advice that seems supportive and informative. Others are so critical that you begin to wonder whether you chose the wrong profession. As Agarwal, Echambadi, Franco, and Sarkar (2006) also noted, "Undergoing the review process is both an emotional and intellectual endeavor. The emotional roller coaster begins when you open the decision letter. The intellectual process requires revisiting each thought articulated in your submitted manuscript" (p. 191).

In the next section, we explore the intellectual response to the R & R decision.

Intellectual Response

An excellent initial intellectual response to an R & R decision is to weigh the advantages and disadvantages of actually completing and resubmitting a revision of your manuscript. To be able to leverage the R & R process, it is helpful to know what is encouraging about it as well as what may be potential roadblocks. Reflecting on the advantages and disadvantages will help you approach the task more analytically, objectively, and less emotionally. In addition, by considering these two perspectives, you will be better prepared to respond in a timely manner to the editor and reviewers' feedback and move closer to a publication.

Advantages

With the R & R decision, the editor and reviewers have decided that the manuscript fits the journal's focus. You sent your article to the right journal. You find that all the detective work you did in identifying the right journal paid off in this first level of review (see chapter 9). Does the work fit this journal's overall scope and purpose? Yes, it does!

The R & R decision means that your manuscript has merit. Your manuscript not only is an acceptable match or good fit for the journal but also has merit. An R & R decision indicates that the editor and reviewers found areas of strength in your work. While your work needs improvement, the reviewers provide you with sufficient and specific feedback to improve the quality of your manuscript.

You are building a connection with an editor. Typically, the editor compiles the reviewers' feedback and communicates with you, the author. The editor bases the R & R decision on the reviewers' ratings and commentary. So, read the editor's e-mail communication carefully. Typically, you will find that along with your invitation to R & R the editor is available for questions. Essentially, you are building a relationship with the editor.

As the author of your manuscript, you are in charge of your own work. You get to make decisions regarding how you will respond to the reviewers' specific feedback. You determine how much time, effort, and energy you are willing to devote to the revision. In most cases, you will find value in the reviewer feedback, so you will be able to respond systematically to each suggestion, comment, or critique. Being in charge also means that you may use the feedback offered and choose to send your manuscript elsewhere.

By responding to an R & R, you are demonstrating that you are grateful for the feedback and the opportunity to disseminate higher quality scholarly work. The commitment to revise your work represents the same type of commitment you made to write the manuscript in the first place. You want to share your thinking—whether you are reporting the results of a research study, advancing a theoretical or conceptual stance, describing your own lived experiences, or promoting your own ideas about a topic or practice. You want to get your work out there, and you want it to be as accessible to as many readers as possible.

Disadvantages

Reviews can be harsh. Yes, reviews can be brutal. Reviews for stretch and within-reach journals are usually double-blind peer reviews. In other words, you do not know the reviewers' names and the reviewers do not know your name. They do not have the benefit of knowing you, your background, or your expertise. All reviewers see in front of them is your written work. Recognize that we all get negative and even seemingly brutal comments. We are not condoning this type of feedback as it is demotivating; however, we feel you should be aware of the possibility.

The expectation with an R & R request is that you should R & R. This expectation can put uncalled for pressure on you to respond. If you decide not to respond to this editor, you will gain a reputation of not responding. The chance you take is that this response may color the editor's response to your next manuscript because the reviewers took time to give you feedback and you seem to have ignored it.

It is difficult to navigate contradictory feedback. You may feel confused by contradictory feedback where one reviewer said, "You need to get data from students when they entered the program." Then another said, "The data you collected fully describes the students' experience in the program." To handle contradictory feedback, think about it and decide whether you agree with the feedback. Develop a rationale for your choice. You may choose to contact the editor with your ideas about responding to the contradictions.

Just because you respond to an R & R request does not mean the journal will publish your manuscript. There is a risk that the journal will not publish your manuscript even if you make the revisions. Despite your diligent work to respond to the reviewer feedback and your belief that you have addressed all the reviewers' concerns, there are no guarantees that the editor will accept and publish your manuscript. It can happen that the original reviewer is no longer available, so the journal editor may have to send your revision to a new reviewer, who may have additional suggestions. Being aware of this possibility can help you decide whether to pursue the revision and resubmission of your work.

Because of the length of time from submission to receipt of the R & R, you may be involved in a new project that is more appealing. Rekindling the energy to tackle the manuscript again can be challenging. Just remember—you are closer to a publication with this manuscript than with the new, perhaps more appealing, "shiny object." Having a set of strategies to respond to reviewer feedback can ease your approach to handling the R & R.

Given that you are now aware of the advantages and disadvantages of completing and submitting a revised manuscript, let us get practical. Just what is the best way to respond to the R & R decision? How do I handle conflicting statements from the reviewers? What do I say to the editor? In the next section, we will lay out several strategies for organizing and managing your response to the R & R decision.

Managing Your Response to an R & R Decision

Once again, as in the other chapters, we have divided the work of responding to an R & R request into three approaches: detective work, scanning the external environment; reflective work; and expressive work, resubmitting the work to the journal editor.

Detective Work

Doing the detective work involves attending to and analyzing the reviews the editor sent to you. In the humanities, these reviews are "reader responses" rather than just "reviews." Whatever your discipline, we think it is best to be systematic about addressing these responses so that you do not miss any comments. As Algase (2014) recommended, "I create an organization that (a) supports my ability to address the feedback fully and systematically and (b) provides a basis for clearly communicating the resulting changes to the editor" (p. 197).

To manage your responses to reviewer feedback, we suggest choosing an approach that works well for you. In this section, we describe two common methods of managing your response—or even a third method that combines these two methods. Both methods involve reading the reviewer comments very closely and then sorting and rearranging them so that you can respond efficiently. For some of us, using a spreadsheet or a table is the easiest way to handle the reviews. For others, making lists and categorizing the feedback serves the same purpose.

Method 1: Create a Matrix for Managing the Reviewers' Comments

To create a matrix with rows and columns, you can use the table feature in Microsoft Word, an Excel spreadsheet, or Google Sheets. For each horizontal row, you will add a reviewer comment. Your job is to copy and paste the actual reviewer comments into rows of the table or spreadsheet. Make a new row for each comment that addresses a different issue. If there are two issues in the comment, then separate the ideas into different rows. After you have entered the comments into the matrix, number each one. For example, reviewer 1, comment number one would be numbered 1.1. This step is particularly helpful if you are collaborating on the manuscript and trying to communicate with a coauthor about the comments each of you will address. Be sure to copy the actual wording from the reviewers. This method helps you separate comments by individual reviewer.

The R & R matrix also has three vertical columns. The first column, "Reviewer feedback," consists of the list of reviewers' comments. The second column, "To-do tasks," is your to-do list—it contains your responses to each of the reviewers' comments. In other words, as you consider each comment, you will add a note about what you plan to do to address the comment. The third column, "My response," is what you actually did in response to each reviewer comment and where the response is located in the manuscript (i.e., page #). Table 11.1 includes the R & R matrix and step-by-step process for completing the matrix. The R & R matrix was made as a Microsoft Word table.

TABLE 11.1
R & R matrix for reviewer feedback with process

Reviewer feedback*	To-do tasks	My response with page #
Reviewer 1		
1.1		
1.2		
Reviewer 2		
2.1		
2.2		
Reviewer 3		
3.1		
3.2		

*Add rows as needed to accommodate all the reviewers' comments.

Purpose

Use the R & R matrix to guide your exploration and response to reviewers' feedback.

How to Use the Feedback Matrix: Detective Work

Steps:

1. Read reviewer 1's comments.
2. As you read each comment, copy it into the reviewer feedback column. Be sure to place each comment in a separate row of the matrix. Use a separate row for each comment.
3. Once you have copied all of reviewer 1's comments into the matrix, scan the text to identify the page number(s) associated with the comment. Add the page number to the page number column of the matrix.
4. Note your ideas about how to respond to the comment in the to-do task column. Use this column to list references suggested by the reviewers or others that you identify.
5. Repeat steps 1 through 4 for the feedback from reviewer 2 and reviewer 3.
6. Read all of the reviewers' comments. Look for similarities or overlap across the comments. Make note of these in the to-do task column of the matrix. (You could highlight or star the similar comments.) Also, look for contradictory or

(*Continues*)

TABLE 11.1 (*Continued*)

confusing comments. Add notes or questions to pose to the editor in the to-do task column.
7. Gather and read additional references (as needed).
8. Communicate with editor about confusing or contradictory feedback.

How to Use the Feedback Matrix: Reflective Work

Steps:

1. Review the feedback matrix. Reflect on the commentary offered by the reviewers and the tasks you have associated with the comments.
2. As you reflect, make decisions about the revisions you will make. For example, "I will add a reference to support an assertion." Also, make decisions about revisions you will not make. For example, "I will not add a new section about a related topic."
3. As you revise your manuscript, make note of your responses in the "my response" column. Using the matrix is a thoughtful process and one you can share with the editor when you resubmit your manuscript. It displays your systematic and reflective approach to reviewer feedback. It also communicates your commitment to improving your manuscript based on reviewer feedback.

When responding to the editor, plan to include a copy of the R & R matrix with your cover letter. First, delete the second column, "To-do tasks," as the editor does not need this information. Second, attach the modified R & R matrix to the letter to the editor. The modified R & R matrix allows the editor and reviewers to see how you dealt with every comment. In Table 11.2, we provide a sample of responses using the modified R & R matrix format. It includes a selection of reviewers' comments and authors' responses to those comments.

Method 2: Clustering the Reviewers' Comments by Type
For those of you who are less inclined to use matrices, tables, or spreadsheets to analyze your reviewer comments, then method 2 may be for you. This method still involves a careful analysis of the reviewers' comments; however, you do not place each reviewer comment in a matrix. Instead, you cluster the reviewer comments into categories or types of comments. We suggest clustering comments by the following types: (a) grammatical corrections, (b) formatting or style issues, and (c) requests for substantive change.

Common grammatical corrections include subject-verb agreement, verb tense, passive/active voice, relative pronouns, and misplaced modifiers. Typically, the grammatical corrections are often straightforward, relatively easy to remedy, and take authors the least amount of time to make.

TABLE 11.2
Actual example of reviewer comments and author responses

Reviewer comment	Response
1.1. Doesn't this sentence contradict what you said earlier about focusing on the results of student learning?	On p. 2, we changed the sentence to clarify our meaning: "Notably, the focus of Lesson Study remains on the collaborative intellectual process rather than the output of isolated products such as a collection of model lessons" (Chokshi & Fernandez, 2004).
1.2. What does Yinger (citation) mean in regard to education? Who specifically in education??? Lesson planning specialists? Curriculum experts? This seems awkward.	On p. 4, we added a direct quote to clarify Yinger's meaning: According to Yinger (1980), "Education for the most part adopted a rational model of planning based on models from economics and from national and city planning" (p. 108).
1.3. What are examples of the ways you teach candidates to plan? Please incorporate examples into your sentence: "We taught our candidates a variety of ways to plan including Lesson Study."	On p. 11, we added the following words to clarify the types of lesson planning: We taught our candidates a variety of ways to plan (e.g., differentiated lesson plan, inquiry-based lesson plan, PowerPoint lesson plan) including Lesson Study.
1.4. I would like to see some practical advice offered to teachers and administrators in this conclusion. What lessons can teachers and administrators learn from the body of research and your research? What should teachers do to get started? What should administrators do to support and facilitate this happening?	On p. 12, we added the reviewer's recommended section on practical advice. We placed this section before the conclusions.

Excerpts from response to comments for Lenski, S. J., & Caskey, M. M. (2009). Using the lesson study approach to plan for student learning. *Middle School Journal, 40*(3), 50–57.

Formatting or style issues arise when authors do not follow the particular style requirements of the journal or book publisher. Publishers typically specify a particular style (e.g., APA, MLA, Chicago, or Turabian) or have their own specific style. Common formatting and style issues include citation of sources, headings, numeration, seriation, capitalization, tables, and figures. To address formatting or style issues, you can refer to the style guide and then apply the specific style to your manuscript.

Requests for substantive changes occur when reviewers suggest that the author make significant changes to the manuscript. Substantive changes range from the addition of more sources to support the author's position to the inclusion of more description for a specific section (e.g., context, concept, method, analysis, results, or conclusion). Addressing the reviewers' requests for a substantive change requires you—as the author—to expend more time and thought. Remember, as the author, you get to make the decisions about what you are willing to change and how you will make changes to your manuscript.

Table 11.3 is a blank template that you can use to copy and paste the reviewer comments. Naturally, you can cluster reviewer comments in ways that best suit you and your particular manuscript. What is important is to develop and use a systematic clustering scheme. Clustering the reviewer comments will help you not only track and make the necessary changes to your manuscript but also communicate the changes to the editor when you submit your revised manuscript.

TABLE 11.3
Clustering reviewer comments by type of comment

Grammatical corrections	
Reviewer* comment	My response
Formatting or style issues	
Reviewer* comment	My response
Requests for substantive change	
Reviewer* comment	My response

*As you copy and paste the reviewer comments in these sections, be sure to put the reviewer number in parentheses (e.g., #1) after the comment so you can trace it easily.

After doing the detective work—your practical response—move on to the reflective work associated with the R & R process.

Reflective Work

Once your comments are in some order—in a matrix or clustered by type of reviewer comments—it is time for reflective work. What is it you will do about each comment? The next logical step is to analyze each reviewer's comments and figure out how you will respond. The following remarks from authors and journal editors exemplify some of the reasons for analyzing reviewer feedback:

- "I analyze the feedback to develop a clear understanding of the issues requiring a remedy" (Algase, 2014, p. 197).
- "Authors should evaluate how recommendations that require substantive revisions align with their theoretical foundations, philosophical frameworks, methodological procedures, and purpose for engaging in the study" (Hardré, 2013, p. 15).
- "Reviewers are guides who may point you in different directions. You need to be able to decide which way to go and follow through unerringly" (Agarwal et al., 2006, p. 196).

Yes, reviewers may give you disparate suggestions in regard to how to improve your manuscript. This is among the reasons that analyzing and reflecting on each reviewer comment is critical.

In method 1, you address the comments one by one. In method 2, the clustering method, you look across the comments and look for commonalities across the reviewers. Either way, a systematic approach allows you to make decisions about what actions you will take.

When you strongly disagree with a reviewer's feedback, you still need to respond. The reasons for your disagreement may be due to a difference of opinion, philosophical stance, theoretical position, or methodological approach. In fact, according to Gullion (2016), "There are admittedly a few occasions when you might choose to forego on the revise and resubmit. This decision should not be taken lightly, as there is a good chance that you are walking away from a publication" (p. 125).

Regardless of your decision, the good news is you get to decide what to retain and what to change. It is your work. That said, we encourage you to develop a response—a rebuttal if you will. Then, you can include and use your rationale and/ or documentation to strengthen your rebuttal.

Micki is an editor (Sidebar 11.1) who writes about the process of being a journal review editor. Sidebar 11.2 features Dannelle's experiences as a reviewer.

Sidebar 11.1 A Journal Editor: Micki

Viewpoints of an Editor

As an editor, I play a key role in the advancement of ideas and knowledge. It is [a] highly rewarding yet demanding role. The rewards include being among the first to become acquainted with the authors' reasons for writing, which include sharing ideas, advancing a position, critiquing a position, reporting research findings, and so on. Remember, editors are the first reviewer of the submitted manuscript. They read it carefully, noting the organization, flow, and completeness of the text. After this editorial review, the editor typically selects three reviewers for the peer review of your manuscript.

My tasks as the editor include: (a) reading the manuscript careful[ly], (b) matching the manuscript with reviewers, (c) sending the manuscript to the reviewers, (d) prompting reviewers to submit reviews, (e) compiling the reviewers' feedback (e.g., rating, comments, recommendation), and (f) communicating publication decision and reviewer feedback to the author.

Typical publication decisions are "accept," "accept with minor revisions," "revise and resubmit," and "reject." In the case of [an] R & R decision, as the editor, I will repeat my editor tasks (e.g., reading the manuscript carefully, sending the manuscript to reviewers, compiling the reviewers['] feedback, sharing the publication decision and reviewer feedback with the author) for the revised manuscript.

My role as an editor also has its challenges. Among these are the

- quality of reviewers, responsiveness of reviewers, and differences among reviewers; and
- content of the reviews may be contradictory, vague, and/or not very useful.

How do I address these challenges? As an editor, I work intentionally to build a strong pool of reviewers who have expertise across research topics and methodologies. I also develop and share guidelines for reviewers to use when conducting their reviews. Other ways that editors, like me, address challenges include offering workshops at conferences, pairing new reviewers with experienced reviewers, or providing other supports (e.g., model reviews) for reviewers.

Editors accept the responsibility of editorship for a number of reasons. Primarily, editors want to serve their profession. While they may receive some form of compensation (e.g., honorarium, graduate student support), editors want to contribute to their particular discipline through their service. They want to support both the current and the next generation of authors. Another reason to serve as an editor is to stay abreast of new ideas or learn about new research findings. Editors have a unique vantage point; they are the first to read the new and revised manuscripts. Additionally, editors may advance their knowledge of the discipline due to their role and affiliation with a journal or publisher.

Sidebar 11.2 A Journal Article Reviewer: Dannelle

Viewpoints of a Reviewer

As a reviewer, I conduct confidential reviews of submitted manuscripts. Drawing on my expertise and professional judgment, I know that I can play a critical role in the development of an author's writing. The role demands that I complete my review task within a reasonably short period. The thoroughness and promptness of my review makes a difference to the author and the publication's editor.

Remember, as a reviewer, I am among the first readers of your manuscript. You want to ensure that your text is accessible (friendly) to the reader. When you employ organizational structures (heading, tables, and figures) to guide the reader and you use transition sentences between ideas, the text is more reader friendly. It is just easier to grasp the ideas expressed.

As a reviewer, I look for the development and inclusion of an explicit purpose statement. Authors need to state the purpose of the article, chapter, or other publication early in the manuscript. "The purpose of this article is to . . ." I see the purpose statement as an anchor for the whole manuscript. No anchor . . . then, the text seems to drift.

Over time, I have read many manuscripts. Often reviewers develop "pet peeves" that distract them from the content. How do you avoid reviewers' "pet peeves"? Usually these fall into the category of grammatical errors and citation errors. As a writer, you can develop good proofreading habits such as reading your manuscript aloud so you can identify issues with prepositions, subject-verb agreement, long, incomplete, or awkward sentence[s]. You can also complete a reference scan, which entails checking that every in-text citation is in the reference list and that every citation in the reference list is in the text. Another tactic is to enlist a trusted colleague, friend, partner, or other person to give you feedback on your manuscript.

Reviewers have a variety of reasons to review manuscripts. We depend on each other to review our work. One of my most important reasons is to mentor the next generation of scholars. I see my work not so much as a gatekeeper but as a mentor whose job is to advise other scholars on how to improve their work. Some view this as a way to pay back and pay it forward.

Another less lofty but still important reason to be a reviewer is that reviewers get to see new ideas first. A more practical reason is that a scan of the reference list may introduce me to some references that I have missed in my own search of the topic.

Expressive Work

Expressive work is the actual revision of your manuscript that draws on your detective work—analyzing the reviewer feedback—and your reflective process—making decisions about the changes you will make in light of the feedback. Because you have already done the detective and reflective work, you have set the stage for revising your manuscript in a way that is professionally rewarding. Similarly, you have the information you need to write a coherent and informative letter to the editor—one that will accompany your revised manuscript.

The Process of Revising Your Manuscript

Whatever your particular discipline, editors (e.g., Algase, 2014; Ireland, 2008; Martin & Miller, 2014) and authors (e.g., Agarwal et al., 2006; Hardré, 2013; Kamler, 2010) offer suggestions for doing the revision work. Yet, the question remains, how will you begin the process of revising your manuscript?

Opinions vary about how to begin. Some suggest making the grammatical and most straightforward edits first (Hardré, 2013). Others recommend making planned changes "in the order of greatest to least difficulty or complexity" (Algase, 2014, p. 197). We think that you may find the most success with making the most expeditious changes first. Making these changes will allow you to see immediate progress in the revision of your manuscript. Then, you will be able to reserve time for delving into the substantive changes—ones, for example, that require the inclusion of additional sources of information. Regardless of your starting point, proceed through your revision process—the rewriting of your manuscript—in a logical manner.

Writing a Cover Letter to the Editor

After you complete the systematic and thoughtful revision of your manuscript, it is time to craft a letter to the editor—a cover letter to accompany your revised manuscript. Your cover letter is the best tool for communicating directly with the editor about the changes you have made to the manuscript and your resubmission. As the author, you can convey information that helps the editor to make decisions about your work. Be humble, be polite, and be appreciative in all correspondence. As Kamler (2010) noted, "The editor is the final arbiter of the review process. She both commissions and mediates the reviewer reports and uses these to make final judgements about the article's relevance and potential contribution" (pp. 72–73).

Given the volume of letters an editor may receive, we recommend that you write a succinct letter that documents the revisions to your manuscript. So, what exactly could or should this letter include?

Generally, you need to begin the letter with a statement about the revised manuscript and include identifying information such as the title and a manuscript number. Let the editor know that you appreciate the opportunity to R & R. Then, be sure to thank the reviewers for their time, expertise, and input. Acknowledge how the R & R process has improved your manuscript.

More specifically, we suggest that the letter to the editor include the following: (a) identifying information about the manuscript, (b) an acknowledgement of the opportunity to R & R, (c) a summary of the major changes, (d) reference to attachments (e.g., revised manuscript, R & R matrix), and (e) a closing statement. To help you get started on your letter to the letter, review Table 11.4.

TABLE 11.4
Template: Cover letter to the editor for author responses to reviewers' comments

Content	Format
Identifying information	Name Mailing address Phone number E-mail address Date Editor Journal title Mailing address RE: Manuscript title Manuscript number
Add section that acknowledges the opportunity to R & R*	Thank the editor and reviewers for the opportunity to respond to R & R. Note that the revised manuscript is attached (attachment 1).
Add section that describes major changes to manuscript	Summary of the major changes to the manuscript. Reference the attached matrix of changes as an attachment (attachment 2).
Add closing paragraph	Closing paragraph. Encourage the editor to let you know if he or she or the reviewers have any questions. A helpful phrase might be, "Look forward to hearing . . ." Include appreciation, once again, for the hard work of editors and reviewers to improve your manuscript.

*See Figure 11.1 for helpful phrases in writing your response in your letter to the editor.

We also think that it is essential to respond in a respectful and thoughtful way. We offer in Figure 11.1 a set of phrases as starting points for your letter to the editor.

In addition to a summary of major changes, include details about the specific changes you made to the revised manuscript. Ireland (2008) asserted:

> Moreover, we believe that providing point-by-point responses allows you to precisely explain each action you have taken to deal with issues the reviewers and action editor brought to your attention. However, *concisely* explaining the actions you have taken is desirable in that such explanations save reviewers' time while ensuring that your responses highlight the actions you have taken to deal with their concerns. (p. 1050)

Importantly, your letter to the editor allows you to describe and document the changes you have made to your revised manuscript.

Figure 11.1 Helpful phrases for the letter to the editor

Overall comments for introduction in letter to the editor:
  I appreciate your response and invitation to resubmit. . . .
  I appreciate reviewers' time and expertise. . . .
  As you may recall from the original submission, the topic of my manuscript is . . .
  The reviewers' comments helped me to improve the quality of . . .
  I have completed the revision of . . .
  I included a matrix (or table) to show . . .
Specific comments about feedback:
  I appreciate the feedback and opportunity to revise. . . .
  I value the detailed feedback from each reviewer. . . .
  The feedback made me think more deeply about . . .
  I agree with a number of the reviewers' suggestions. . . .
  I have systematically addressed the reviewers' feedback. . . .
  I responded thoughtfully to the reviewers' feedback. . . .
Specific way for author to say that he or she did not act on some feedback:
  I find that some suggestions are beyond the scope of . . .
  To make the recommended change is not in keeping with . . .
Final statements to thank reviewers and editors for the opportunity to improve the manuscript:
  Thank you for reviewing this revised manuscript for possible publication in . . .
  Thank you in advance for considering my revised manuscript. . . .
  Thank you for your time and consideration of my revised manuscript. . . .

If you decide not to R & R, be sure to write and send a letter to the editor. Use a neutral tone in your letter to the editor and communicate your decision not to revise. Remember to use the letter to withdraw your manuscript from consideration for publication in the journal. It is important that you formally withdraw your manuscript from this journal so that you can submit it to another journal.

Conclusion

Once you have decided to accept the invitation to R & R your manuscript, you can begin to address the challenges associated with this work. Revision, like drafting your manuscript, is work. Fortunately, revision can be rewarding—especially because it can lead you to consider other perspectives and help you to refine your own thinking.

As noted previously, revising your work can be an emotional experience. As Hardré (2013) suggested, the process of revision requires writers to set aside their egos—whether overdeveloped or underdeveloped—to move forward with revising the manuscript. Letting the reviewers' feedback rest a bit and completing the R & R matrix can help you explore the emotional side of receiving the R & R decision.

For this reason, we recommend that you adopt a growth mind-set (Dweck, 2006). As you may know, Dweck (2006) advanced a theory of mind-sets—a fixed mind-set or a growth mind-set. When you have a fixed mind-set, you believe that your basic qualities are "carved in stone" (p. 4)—fixed. In contrast, when you have a growth mind-set, you believe that your basic qualities improve through your own efforts, collaboration with others, or the use of specific strategies. In other words, you can find ways to change and develop your own qualities and abilities. Dweck added:

> The passion for stretching yourself and sticking to it, even (or especially) when it's not going well, is the hallmark of the growth mindset. This is the mindset that allows people to thrive during some of the most challenging times in their lives. (p. 7)

In the case of the R & R, possessing a growth mind-set will allow you to view the revision as an opportunity to grow as an academic writer and scholar. You can view revision as a challenge—one that you will accept with tenacity. This can feel somewhat like accepting a dare.

In this chapter, we described perspectives to consider when receiving an R & R decision. Then, we offered ways for managing your response to the R & R decision as well as for addressing the associated challenges. Certainly, we hope that our ideas will help you to advance your manuscript from an R & R to a publication.

CHAPTER 12

Create a Campus-Wide Faculty Writing Program

Dannelle D. Stevens, Faculty in Residence for Academic Writing, Portland State University; and Janelle Voegele, Director of Assessment, Teaching and Learning, Office of Academic Innovation, Portland State University

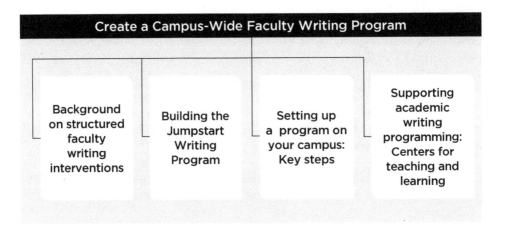

Yesterday I was talking with a colleague at another institution and he lamented about not being able to write during the academic year and feeling unproductive for large chunks of time. I realized that I don't share his anxiety around writing productivity at all. There's an important reason for that—PSU's Jumpstart program! Over the last couple of years, I've developed tools that keep me writing every day (or most every day!), helped me make reasonable goals, and allowed me to actually accomplish quite a bit, even when I'm busy with teaching, service, and all the other tasks I do. I just was really struck with the absence of anxiety and wanted to thank you both [Janelle and Dannelle] for making it possible.

Katy Barber, Portland State University Jumpstart Writing Program participant over four years, associate professor of history

Katy has been a participant in PSU's Jumpstart Writing Program for five years. Besides attending workshops and writing retreats, every year she participates in a weekly writing group with new faculty. As a tenured associate history professor, she asked her department chair what she needed to be promoted to the rank of full professor. "You need to have a book" was the chair's response. Her book will be published in spring 2018 (*In Defense of Wyam: Native-White Alliances and the Struggle for Celilo Village*) and she thanks the strategies and the new writing practice she has learned in the program for giving her the motivation and confidence to complete that project.

We realize that Katy is an "n" of one. In quantitative research, data from an "n" of one does not give us enough evidence to make a determination if the intervention, in this case, the Jumpstart writing program, has made any significant difference. Yet, our research and day-to-day experience in presenting and facilitating the program assures Janelle, the director of PSU's Office of Academic Innovation, and Dannelle, the faculty in residence for academic writing, that Katy is not alone (Voegele & Stevens, 2017). In fact, because of its success, the PSU administration has never wavered in its support for the program.

The purpose of this chapter is to describe the institutional context of faculty writing interventions in general, as well as lay out the objectives and activities of the Jumpstart Writing Program in particular so that you will be familiar with steps it could take to initiate such a program on your campus.

We open this chapter by offering you a palette of possibilities derived from the current research on "structured faculty writing interventions." We will address such questions as, "What is a structured faculty writing intervention?" and "What is the evidence that such initiatives actually impact faculty writing practices?" Next, we turn to the PSU Jumpstart Writing Program itself. The questions we will address are, "What were the program's objectives?" "How did the literature inform the program's structure?" and "What are the specific program features?" Finally, while acknowledging that campuses differ in very significant ways, we offer you some advice on several ways to set up your own program.

Background on Structured Faculty Writing Interventions

> We recommend that universities support the development of structured interventions for their staff in order to increase their writing for publication. A regular, ongoing arrangement seems to be most beneficial, with a format that can be adapted to meet the needs of the attendees. (McGrail et al., p. 34)

Call for Structured Faculty Writing Interventions

McGrail and colleagues (2006) call for universities to develop ways to help their staff increase their publication output. Their call is based on a systematic literature review of 17 studies of university writing interventions. They concluded that all interventions had some impact on writers' productivity. One effect they noted was the positive effect on publication rates. "There was consistency in the reported studies, with publication rates increasing after all interventions, regardless of whether they [the interventions] were a writing support group, writing course or writing coach" (p. 25).

In addition to the effect on publication productivity, McGrail and colleagues (2006) found a positive impact of these writing interventions on psychosocial outcomes, such as a decrease in anxiety and a concomitant increase in confidence. As their writing skills developed, faculty involved in the programs acknowledged that they had learned more about writing in general, and especially academic writing, and this knowledge affected their motivation to write as well. "Support, encouragement and motivation are key benefits of writing interventions, apart from an increase in knowledge and skills gained that help to achieve an increase in published writing" (p. 30).

Following McGrail and colleagues' work in 2006, studies continue to demonstrate the positive outcomes with systematic writing interventions. Here is a sampling of the results:

> [Faculty] reported many changes in their approaches to writing and in their sense of themselves as writers and some of these changes were sustained on return to campus. This paper argues that (a) structured retreat [live-in, two-day writing retreat] increases learning through participation and helps academics to mainstream writing in their lives and careers. (Murray & Newton, 2009, p. 541)

> [T]he most valued aspect of the programme [12-week program using Belcher's (2009b) book with weekly meetings] by far was having a writing group to work with. The discipline of regular writing and targets was the next most valuable aspect, followed by the facilitator and the structure of the programme. Participants were asked how confident they felt about completing a peer-reviewed publication in the future . . . with almost half indicating that they were very confident. (Devlin & Radloff, 2014, p. 240)

> Engaging in NRP (narrative reflective process) [monthly meetings over a year using NRP in a research and writing group] permitted the group [of nurses] to creatively enter into critical dialogue, address both individual and collective needs, and establish a supportive environment that nurtures the creative process—all of which ultimately enhances scholarship and academic productivity. (Schwind et al., 2014, p. 164)

> The majority of faculty indicated that . . . the workshop (two days with individual tutorials), in effect, reduced the level of anxiety associated with academic writing. (Dankowski et al., 2012, p. 53)

These studies indicate the power of structured faculty writing interventions in a variety of writing venues. Yet, one question is, Do these interventions achieve a sustained impact, not just over a year, but on how faculty view themselves as writers and, do faculty fundamentally change their writing practice? Weaver and colleagues (2014) returned to participants in their program (nine participants in a 12-week program using Belcher's book) one year later, and noted, "[A]lthough five papers were published, a 12-month follow-up revealed that original writing intentions were not sustained" (p. 212). By contrast, three years after the writing retreats described in Murray and Newton (2009), MacLeod and colleagues (2012) interviewed faculty who had participated in one to six writing retreats and found that

[t]hey identified [that the] benefits of this [two-day live-in writing retreat] were twofold: first, increased confidence from seeing more experienced writers struggling—like them—but also modeling working through those struggles; and, second, working through their thoughts and difficulties with other writers in a way that reduced anxiety. (p. 648)

Given these two different outcomes from writing interventions, the question is, What interventions really help faculty be more productive and confident in their writing? Further, what fosters such a foundational change in writing practice that faculty can sustain the gains over the years, as Katy stated in her unsolicited e-mail at the beginning of this chapter? Before we delve further into the question of how to foster sustainable change, let us provide some background from the literature on "structured faculty writing interventions," such as those described.

What Is a Structured Faculty Writing Intervention?

A structured faculty writing intervention is a set of professional development activities designed to assist faculty in writing and publishing. The goal for these professional development activities is to provide the resources, space, and dedicated time to develop the behaviors, dispositions, knowledge, and skills that undergird a successful writing practice.

A few institutions rely on their centers for teaching and learning to develop a variety of activities focused on writing and publishing. In their work on service-learning activities in centers for teaching and learning, Gravett and Borscheid (2018) describe a classification system for professional development activities. The categories they developed—information resources, short-term programs, and extended and immersive programs—are useful for classifying structured faculty writing interventions as well. Table 12.1 shows a variety of structured writing interventions within these classifications, noting their respective advantages and disadvantages. We elaborate on these three classifications next.

Information Resources

These are the online and people resources that faculty can use to get more information about academic writing. These could include websites, blogs, and libraries. Because of the need for faculty to know the current research literature on their topics, one obvious partner and resource for academic writing programs is the university library. Some universities are large enough that they have librarians assigned to different disciplines who can assist with discipline-specific research and writing resources. Some university libraries have developed materials that assist with various aspects of the research process, such as writing a literature review using the University of Minnesota at Duluth library (Mongan-Rallis, 2018). The university library often supports workshops on CMS that faculty can use to organize, classify, and access the massive numbers of online references available today. Staff at the centers for teaching and learning often support faculty as they write about their teaching and learning practices. In addition, centers for teaching and learning often have information

TABLE 12.1

Descriptions of structured faculty writing programs with duration and advantages and disadvantages of each

Writing program options	Characteristics	Duration	Advantages	Disadvantages
Information resources				
Resource library	Library in center for teaching and learning solely devoted to teaching, learning, and academic writing	Available when center is open	Offers opportunity for faculty to survey books and resources to buy or use to improve their writing practice.	Offers limited hours of access.
Online resources	E-mail, websites, blogs, social media	Open all the time	Remind faculty of key practices as well as events on campus.	May add to e-mail fatigue to capture faculty attention.
Short-term programs				
Writing retreats: short-term; on campus or off campus	Brings diverse faculty together to work on individual projects or get minimal feedback from peers Provides basic needs such as breakfast, lunch, and coffee Can offer coaching or mini-workshops	One day	Present a dedicated time to a writing project. Build a community of practice around writing. Encourage faculty to get some writing done. Reduce stress of not meeting writing expectations.	May reinforce binge writing rather than a steady, consistent, and sustainable writing practice.
Workshops with outside experts	Guest presenter shares expertise on academic writing	One day	Include opportunity for active learning and sharing among faculty. Develop discrete knowledge and skills. May bring in new faculty who have not thought about academic writing resources. Contribute to community of practice around writing.	Require a large chunk of time for faculty on one day.
Institutes	Organized by campus teaching and learning centers for faculty group to focus on one topic in an active learning environment	Two to five days	Develop skills of one group to apply practices to teaching, research, or writing. Build community capacity in one topic area.	Require a large chunk of time for faculty.

Consultations	Writing coach available to meet individual faculty writing needs and challenges	One hour	Assist individuals in working through writing challenges.	Focus on only one faculty member at a time.
Extended or immersive programs				
Writing groups: accountability	Small writing groups (three to four people) focused on sharing writing goals each week and being accountable to peers	Weekly One hour Over the year	Work to foster accountability for writing goals. Encourage and supports group members.	Commitment can waver. Scheduling time can be challenging.
Writing groups: feedback	Small writing groups (three to four people) focused on sharing goals as well as sharing bits of writing for feedback	Weekly One hour Over the year	Work to foster accountability for writing goals. Encourage and supports group members. Peer feedback can be invaluable in shaping writing for the reader. Create a safe, trusting environment to share writing drafts.	Need to take time to establish trust. Need to establish feedback rules.
Writing workshops	Monthly writing workshops focused on program objectives such as behavioral change, techniques, or resources	Monthly One hour	Present a wide range of topics related to academic writing. Deemphasize potential isolation among faculty. Identify like-minded peers.	Need for marketing to include faculty. May be difficult for faculty to prioritize this one hour.
Writing retreats: weeklong	Writing retreat (immersive)	One full week Five hours a day	Build writing community Accommodate basic needs to focus; meals, coffee provided. Include different formats, including "live-in" retreats, mini-workshops about writing, and writing buddies. Faculty get a good-sized chunk of their writing done.	Can reinforce binge-writing practice.

resources for faculty in terms of their own specialized, satellite library devoted to teaching, learning, and sometimes writing. The advantage of a satellite library is its convenient gathering of relevant resources in one place as these kinds of specific resources devoted to teaching, learning, and writing might be scattered throughout the larger university library. The disadvantage is that the centers often do not have as many open hours as the university library.

Short-Term Programs

Short-term programs include one-day writing retreats, workshops with outside experts, institutes, and consultations. These are considered short-term not only because of their limited duration but also because there is generally no follow-up to measure the gains that faculty have received from attendance. The advantage of short-term programs is that faculty can be focused and actively engaged in writing for a limited period of time, either doing it at a retreat, learning more about managing it in a workshop, or learning more about their own practice through a one-hour consultation. These opportunities can boost immediate momentum and commitment with a set of fresh ideas and approaches. Faculty can also experience the advantage of focusing on writing and nothing else. However, the disadvantage is that it is a one-time event. What we know about a successful writing practice is that, just like any other practice, it has to be threaded through the day-to-day activities of a busy faculty member. These short-term programs may provide a booster shot. Some universities recognize the limitations of short-term gain from short-term programs so they follow up with longer-term programming to support faculty writing development.

Extended or Immersive Programs

Extended and immersive programs are offered over a longer period of time. These programs are characterized by weekly extensive meetings over a term or through immersive weeklong retreats. The advantage of extended programs that last over a term is that faculty can begin to tackle the challenge of integrating writing into the rhythm of their daily lives. Characterized by accountability through community, extended programs help faculty get support and learn from others how to weave writing into everything else they do during the week. Meeting with other peers every week in a small writing group also reminds faculty that they are indeed writers and that they are not alone in their struggles. Immersive programs, such as weeklong writing retreats, show faculty how much they can accomplish when they just write for a week. In addition, working along with other faculty from other disciplines in the same quiet room seems to build a sense of community. The disadvantage is that if the program has only a few participants faculty depend on each other to show up and be accountable. If one faculty member doesn't show up, the group may dissolve and faculty may become discouraged. One other disadvantage of immersive programs is that faculty may depend too much on these programs to write and not do writing at other times. Hence, immersive programs can suffer from short-term gain not accompanied by long-term change in writing practice at other times.

Given these three classifications and referring to Table 12.1, you can see that there are many choices that campuses can make if they wish to develop a faculty writing program. At PSU, we gradually built our Jumpstart Writing Program over five years, offering a variety of programs including all the variants described in the table.

Building the Jumpstart Writing Program

As we developed the faculty academic writing program at PSU, we continually referred to the literature. One theme came though over and over again: Writing as an academic craft is rarely explicitly taught (Antoniou & Moriarty, 2008; Blaxter, Hughes, & Tight 1998; DeLyser, 2003). Others note, "Few faculty, particularly in the health professions and sciences, receive formal training on the craft of writing" (Dankoski, et al, 2012, p. 47) and "Some writers have a limited understanding of the writing and publication processes, as well as emotional barriers like a fear of rejection, fear of competition and an uncertainty of what ideas are worthy of publication" (Dies, 1993 in McGrail et al., 2006, p. 20).

As faculty members ourselves at an urban comprehensive university, we knew from our own experience how difficult it is to fit writing into a busy schedule of teaching, service, and research. We observed how easy it is to put writing, the least urgent activity, at the bottom of our to-do list. We felt stress as a result of not attending to meeting the expectations of writing and publishing. The burgeoning literature on faculty writing assured us that the challenges for faculty do not lie so much in disciplinary knowledge. The challenges lie in the context in which writing is done: the behavioral change, emotional, technical (knowledge of academic writing as a craft), and social context. Using these components as a framework, the following literature guided our program development:

Behavioral change components

- Prioritizing writing through strategies that include behavioral change (Belcher, 2009b; Boice, 1990; Goodson, 2017; Silvia, 2007)
- Fostering creative responses that increase productivity and reduce stress (Cameron et al., 2009; Stevens & Cooper, 2009) (e.g., focused free-writes and dialogues with key ideas and components of the research; see chapter 5)

Emotional components

- Building a new identity as a writer through reflective activities (Cameron et al. 2009; Grant & Knowles, 2000; O'Connell & Dyment, 2011; Stevens & Cooper, 2009)
- Acknowledging the emotional aspects of writing through discussions and building a community of practice (Antonio & Moriarty, 2008; Dirkx, 2008; Turner, Brown, & Edward-Jones, 2014)

Technical components

- Increasing knowledge of the craft of academic writing (Belcher, 2009b; Boice, 1990; Cameron et al., 2009; Graff & Birkenstein, 2010; Morss & Murray, 2001; Sword, 2012)

Social context components

- Supporting the development of a community of practice as writers to challenge notions of writing as a solitary activity (Aitchison & Lee, 2006; Grant & Knowles, 2000; Wenger, 1998)
- Responding to the call for institutional support of faculty writing by providing consistent and responsive support through a program based on faculty needs (Aitchison & Lee, 2006; McGrail et al., 2006)

Our next job was to use these four components as a foundation on which to develop a comprehensive faculty writing program. Interestingly, when the program was launched, a group of five faculty from the English department became concerned that the faculty in residence for academic writing, Dannelle, was not from their department, where students are taught to write. The director, Janelle, countered by explaining that the program differed from the English department's mission because of its focus on the larger context in which writing occurs—the emotional, the social, the technical (rhetorical structures), and the psychological (behavioral change) aspects of writing. The Jumpstart Writing Program is more of a strategic approach to the whole context in which writing occurs that includes time management, writing groups, reflective writing, and other activities not normally the purview of the English department. We will elaborate on the key features of the program next.

What Are the Key Features of the Jumpstart Writing Program?

To offer food for thought about what you might consider when developing the structure for your own program, we will illuminate the objectives, duration, participants, and campus partners, that is, the key features of our program. We are less concerned with what faculty write, but more concerned with offering strategies and activities that support the context in which they write.

Objectives

An essential step in developing any program is to begin with the end in mind, as Fink (2013) urges. The rationale is that this "backward-design" approach leads to stronger and more coherent programs. Once the objectives are in place, the educational developers can more easily create activities to meet those objectives. Given this framework, we divided the objectives into behavioral, emotional, technical, and social.

Behavioral objectives

- Faculty will know more about allocating time to writing and writing good goals.
- Faculty will become more aware of writing roadblocks and the strategies to overcome them.
- Faculty will increase their writing productivity.
- Faculty will become more skilled as writers.
- Faculty will have a repertoire of research-based strategies to choose from to generate text, maintain momentum, and support the development of their ideas.

Emotional objectives

- Faculty will become more confident as writers.
- Faculty will be less stressed about writing.

Technical objectives

- Faculty will learn more about the underlying rhetorical structures in the genre of academic writing itself.

Social objectives

- Faculty will feel that they are not alone as writers. They belong to a writing community. The community will be cross-disciplinary and cross-rank.
- Faculty will be acknowledged for their writing accomplishments through public celebrations.
- Toward the goal of supporting a community of writers, the campus center for teaching and learning, along with the university administration, will provide logistical and financial support for the program.

Duration. The Jumpstart Writing Program began in 2012 with two key program features: monthly meetings and small writing groups. During the monthly meetings, the faculty in residence for academic writing presented strategies designed to address some of the key needs that faculty identified, such as how to allocate time for writing, how to choose the best journal, how to select a journal for publication, and how to work in a writing group. We set up cross-disciplinary writing groups with three to four faculty who were to meet weekly and set goals for the following week. We kept the size of the groups small because we found it was easier to find a common meeting time, especially because these groups were cross-disciplinary, and each department had different meeting schedules.

Jumpstart 1.0 was and continues to be a three-term program: fall, winter, and spring with monthly meetings and small writing groups. Box 12.1 illustrates the content of a typical announcement that we e-mail to all faculty who have participated in any activity in the center for teaching and learning. The monthly workshop schedule is included as well as the invitation to participate in the small writing groups. The following is the outline of the topics for the monthly meetings of Jumpstart 1.0.

BOX 12.1
Jumpstart 1.0 program 2017–2018: Faculty academic writing program

Office of Academic Innovation, Portland State University
Facilitated by Dannelle D. Stevens, PhD, Professor Emerita, Faculty in Residence for Academic Writing. Contact: stevensd@pdx.edu, 503-705-9828 (cell)

Program features:

Monthly large group meetings for all participants
Monday 12:00 p.m. and Thursday 8:30 a.m. (repeat of Monday session)
    Office of Academic Innovation, Smith Center, 2nd floor
    Learn strategies, share insights, boost motivation
Weekly small writing group meetings
    Cross-disciplinary groups, two to four people
    Meet weekly, set writing goals
    Increase accountability, build community
Mid-month, "booster shots" via e-mail
    Articles, references, websites

Dates	Topics
FALL	
Oct. 2; Oct. 5	Orientation: Program features, form writing groups
Nov. 6; Nov. 9	Know yourself as a writer, set doable goals
Nov. 27; Nov. 30	Allocating time to writing: Strategies for success
WINTER	
Jan. 22; Jan. 25	Fine tuning your journal submission: Text structure analysis
Feb. 19; Feb. 22	Main reason journal articles are rejected, "no argument": Template
SPRING	
April 9; April 12 May 7; May 10 June 4; June 7	We will survey faculty to see what you might want to focus on this spring, such as the following: • Studying your own teaching (scholarship of teaching and learning) • Writing a book review • Writing a book proposal • Giving and receiving feedback from peers • Using Jumpstart strategies with students • Using technological tools: Wikis, citation management system • Writing a narrative for promotion and tenure

- Fall: Focus on learning about yourself as a writer and setting doable yearly and daily writing goals.
- Winter: Focus on the research literature: making an argument, selecting a journal, and responding to an R & R request.
- Spring (topics vary because they are voted on by faculty): Focus on writing a book proposal, writing the narrative for promotion, learning about how to do research on your own, teaching, writing a compelling title and abstract for a paper, using a CMS, making plans to write in the summer.

We added Jumpstart 2.0 a few years after we started the program with Jumpstart 1.0. Typically, our writing groups were not peer feedback groups where faculty brought their writing to the group for critique. Over time, several faculty indicated that they wanted to get feedback on their writing. We surveyed faculty to find out who was interested and created Jumpstart 2.0 with eight small writing groups. We gave the groups some materials on how to provide constructive feedback as well as some ideas on how they could structure their weekly meetings. Some of the faculty found the groups to be quite helpful in furthering a stalled writing project. Several groups mentioned that it was vital that the group spend a couple of weeks establishing rapport and trust before they gave each other feedback on their writing.

The Jumpstart Writing Program is now in its fifth year. Over time we have added several new features. Table 12.2 describes the array of programming that we offer over the year.

Participants. The Jumpstart Writing Program is open to all faculty and staff on campus. It is voluntary and includes faculty at all ranks, from adjunct faculty to full professors to administrators and staff. After faculty indicate an interest in being in a small cross-disciplinary writing group, we set up the groups and identify one member who is responsible for convening the first meeting. We also e-mail the "decision tree for writing groups" (Figures 4.1a and 4.1b) and suggest that the group discuss how it will function: day, time, location, and agenda. This begins to help faculty get acquainted with one another and to create a set of shared norms and expectations.

Features. As you can see from Table 12.2, the program offers many opportunities for faculty to increase their knowledge and skills about academic writing and to celebrate their accomplishments with other faculty. We have information resources, short-term programs, and extended and immersive programs.

Campus partners. We believe that part of the strength and longevity of the program is that we have invaluable campus partners. The library offers information resources, such as workshops on CMS, at our summer writing retreats as well as at monthly meetings. In addition, after a call from our nonnative writers of English faculty for help with writing in English, we worked with the applied linguistics department to set up editing sessions for their particular needs. Another partner, the Office of Academic Affairs (OAA), where the university president and provost reside, supports the program with a modest financial contribution for the faculty in residence

TABLE 12.2
Components of PSU Jumpstart Writing Program: 2012–2018

Type	Goal	Duration	Characteristics
Information resources			
Resource library	Provides faculty with set of focused resources on teaching, learning, and writing.	Opens during workday (8:00 a.m. to 5:00 p.m.)	Allows faculty to check out books for a term.
Librarians	Set up workshops on CMS.	Offer workshops all year long, several each term	Support faculty at retreats and workshops.
Monthly "writing booster shots"	Provide faculty with access to online resources to support their writing.	E-mails once a month between monthly writing workshops	Links to references and websites that support academic writing.
TAA	Delivers a print quarterly newsletter full of short articles on academic writing and webinars Presents annual conference	Offers annual membership Gives free membership when university is a TAA chapter; PSU is a TAA chapter	Presents free webinars on academic and textbook writing (www.taaonline.net).
Short-term programs			
Writing retreat (one day)	Works in a very quiet space on campus for one day.	One day 9:00 a.m. to 4:00 p.m. Two days each term	Offers quiet space for medium-sized faculty groups. Meets basic needs (meals and coffee).
Workshops (outside experts)	Expose faculty to new perspectives on writing.	One time a year Example topics: How to write a textbook; publish and flourish	Meet for one day. Include active learning practices.
Institute	Focuses on one topic.	Two to three days Between terms Active learning In-depth focus	Focuses on one topic for a concentrated time—one day.

Consultations	Offer support/advice for individual faculty writing.	One hour, when requested	Set appointments for faculty with writing concerns.
Extended or immersive programs			
Workshops (monthly): Jumpstart 1.0	Deliver content about academic writing as a genre. Focus on the context of writing not the text itself. Build community. Provide resources.	Monthly One hour Offered Monday and Thursday	Facilitated by faculty in residence. Topics set for the year (Box 12.1).
Workshops (special topic)	Develop an ongoing writing project to submission. Build community. Share resources.	12 weeks One hour a week Use Belcher's (2009b) book One term a year	Facilitated by faculty in residence. Focus on manuscript development.
Writing groups: Jumpstart 1.0	Foster accountability for writing to a small group of peers. Set goals. Include write on site.	One hour a week Fall, winter, spring	Include cross-disciplinary groups. Use decision tree (Figures 4.1a and 4.1b) to establish norms.
Writing groups: Jumpstart 2.0	Set goals. Share writing and get feedback from peers.	One hour a week Winter term only	Include cross-disciplinary groups. Use decision tree (Figures 4.1a and 4.1b) to establish norms.
Writing retreat (five days)	Fosters individual work in quiet space in remote spot on campus.	Five days Summer 9:00 a.m. to 4:00 p.m. each day	Meets basic needs (meals and coffee). Encourages writing buddies to set daily goals. Offers voluntary hourlong mini workshops.

for academic writing. We provide regular reports to them about the program and faculty productivity, and we encourage faculty to pass on their experiences in the program to OAA as well.

When you read this, you may think, "Oh, my, that is a lot. Monthly meetings, writing groups, retreats, workshops. . . . I don't think we can do that on our campus." When we started the program, we had not planned on such extensive programming. It developed over time. Faculty "vote with their feet" by attending the workshops and writing groups and encouraging us to continue and expand our offerings. The writing retreats always have waiting lists. Incidentally, one outcome is that faculty search committees and the administration have used the program as a recruiting tool and we give special workshops just for new faculty. In the next section, we offer some suggestions about how to include support for faculty writing in your professional development programming.

Setting Up a Program on Your Campus: Key Steps

As with most new ideas on campus, bringing together a committee of faculty to organize a campus-wide writing program is essential. If you decide you want a cross-disciplinary program, not a department program, then the committee should be cross-disciplinary, of course. Its task is to develop the objectives and consider the basic program components that will accomplish the objectives.

Start Small

Given the list of possible program options in Table 12.1 the faculty writing committee will have to weigh the advantages and disadvantages for each option to decide what makes sense for its campus. In general, we believe in starting small with one or two program features, such as writing groups and monthly meetings. Some universities have started with a workshop led by a nationally recognized expert on faculty writing. With the enthusiasm generated by the workshop, the committee can then plan yearlong programming.

Communicate Clearly and Consistently

The downloadable flyer for Jumpstart 1.0 provides faculty with the dates and topics of the monthly workshops for the whole year. Midmonth the faculty in residence for academic writing e-mails a "booster shot" about academic writing. The booster shot often includes links to useful articles on academic writing or a blog post. My most recent blog was entitled "Read Like a Writer." Workshops are announced via e-mail and on the center for teaching and learning website. Having consistent programming fosters faculty support.

Focus on Text and Context of Academic Writing

As you develop your objectives, remember there is more to building a sustainable and less stressful writing practice than disciplinary knowledge. We assume that faculty come into the program with a solid foundation in their disciplinary knowledge. Then, we divide the world of academic writing into text and context challenges. On one hand, the text is the writing, the words on the page, the manuscript produced. There are many challenges associated with producing the text, such as having credible references for your assertions and conclusions. The context, on the other hand, includes other challenges, such as knowing more about the typical structures of academic writing (the genre of academic writing), knowing more about yourself as a writer, learning how to set doable goals, allocating time to writing, finding ways to maintain momentum, and being held accountable for self-imposed goals in writing groups.

The traditional approach to improving academic writing ignores the context in which text is produced, and focuses only on the text. This practice has consequences. By ignoring the context—the behavioral, emotional, technical, and social contexts of writing—faculty continue to perceive academic writing as a solitary endeavor. When giving feedback to students, faculty pay attention only to the words in front of them on the page. Writing centers tend to focus solely on the text produced as well. This is a narrow view of what writers need to know to write well and consistently.

Our experience in Jumpstart, as well as the research on writing (Antoniou & Moriarty, 2008; Boice, 1990; Grant & Knowles, 2000; Murray & Newton, 2009; Voegele & Stevens, 2017), supports the idea that attention to the behavioral, emotional, technical, and social context of writing leads to a more sustainable and less stressful writing practice. Precisely because we know that improvement in academic writing and publication outcomes depend on many factors, the Jumpstart Writing Program views the development of a sustainable writing practice in a community of writers as a holistic process that involves the development of and attention to many aspects of a faculty member's life.

Find Campus Partners

In the early stages of a faculty writing program, finding campus partners is key to establishing support for the program, connecting the program with established institutional structures, and communicating the value and need for writing professional development. Potential partners can include campus writing programs, human resources, the library, offices that support diversity and inclusion, academic affairs, department chairs, deans and associate deans, and programs that support new faculty. The director of our teaching and learning center is on the committee that plans the campus-wide orientation program for new faculty. We work with the applied linguistics department to support faculty who are nonnative speakers of English and are struggling to write in English. As noted previously, we work closely with our librarians as well. The director regularly meets with the campus administrators about the program to apprise them of faculty participation.

Supporting Academic Writing Programming: Centers for Teaching and Learning

Although scholars often recommend institutional support for writing programming (Gopee & Deane, 2013; McGrail et al., 2006), there has been very little discussion on the structure this support takes on college and university campuses. For this reason, we wanted to share that our faculty writing program is located in the CTL, and association with the center impacts the writing program itself. Our hope is that the lessons learned from the growth of our program may resonate with others who are considering how to integrate writing programming with other educational development resources on their campuses.

Why would a CTL be an effective partner for a faculty academic writing program? PSU's CTL, the Office of Academic Innovation, not only is a partner but also hosts the Jumpstart Writing Program and the faculty in residence for academic writing. At the outset, we wondered if the Jumpstart Writing Program would beneficially affect the core mission of our office in promoting good teaching and learning. Would supporting faculty as writers interact with our goals for furthering good teaching and learning? The answer was a resounding "yes," as the examples that follow will illustrate. In an era of budget reductions, however, we are aware that CTLs may legitimately be questioned about programming that does not initially appear congruent with the central mission of teaching and learning. We would argue there are several reasons for including academic writing programming within a CTL's portfolio.

A Structured Faculty Writing Program Is Faculty Professional Development

By including a faculty writing program in a CTL program portfolio, the CTL is demonstrating a more holistic approach to faculty professional development. When faculty are continually reporting (as they did to us) that writing responsibilities have a significant impact on the quality of and energy they have for teaching, then solely offering ideas for energizing teaching may have a limited effect. However strong an overall teaching program a CTL may offer, if it does not also focus on this other stressful part of faculty work, their writing and publishing, little may be gained in teaching improvement. By including academic writing programming in the portfolio of a CTL's work, faculty gain integrated opportunities to energize and destress both their teaching and writing.

Although college and university CTLs can (and should) continue to focus time and resources on fostering excellence in teaching and learning, the function of CTLs is also evolving. In an era of rapid postsecondary transition, transformation, and change, a growing number of scholars are documenting the increasingly central role that CTLs are playing in organizational and institutional development, in addition to educational development (Kelley, Cruz, & Fire, 2017; Schroeder, 2011). Seeing the CTL as a broader institutional change agent, not just limited to teaching and learning improvement, is a more holistic response to real issues in faculty professional life. Envisioning ways that CTL programming can interconnect the various aspects of faculty academic roles (teaching, writing, research, service, assessment, leading, etc.) may encourage greater faculty engagement and willingness to try new ways of teaching.

Writing Development Feeds Teaching Development, and Teaching Development Feeds Writing Development

Feedback and assessment data from Jumpstart faculty have demonstrated the impact of the program on their academic writing practice as well as on many aspects of their professional life, including teaching. Jumpstart faculty report that the more relaxed, self-aware, and productive writing practices have led to more energy for teaching and other responsibilities, as well as more time for other educational development activities. Given this finding, we weren't surprised to learn that most faculty who first got involved in our CTL through Jumpstart subsequently attended teaching-focused programming.

Another way that faculty reported the connection between Jumpstart and other professional work was the impact on their pedagogical approaches to writing. Faculty share their writing insights and tools with their classes to improve students' writing; apply their own growth as writers toward the creation of course assignments; and, in some cases, work with colleagues to revise their department's curriculum connected to writing. Several faculty have published articles showing how they have used some of the strategies developed in Jumpstart in their own classrooms (Santelmann et al., 2018)

CTLs Encourage Reframing of Teaching and Writing Improvement as Lifelong Endeavors

In our experience working with faculty across multiple campuses, very few of them see teaching as something they "already know all about." Most faculty indeed view teaching as something about which they could potentially continue to learn over their careers; however, academic writing seems to be a different story. Faculty often grapple with the idea that they should already know how to write and publish. Most have previously assumed that they should "just know" how to deal with their writing challenges. Due to their experiences in Jumpstart, however, many faculty have reported great relief in learning that they are not alone in their struggles to maintain momentum and be productive as well as find satisfaction in their writing. Just as they realize that teaching improvement is a lifelong endeavor, writing improvement is also. In Jumpstart, we suggest that faculty become students of academic writing, just as they are students of their teaching practice. By offering programming in both these areas, CTLs are conveying respect for both these important areas of faculty professional life.

CTLs Encourage an Integrated Approach to Writing and Teaching

Our CTL fosters an integrated approach to professional development that supports the range of faculty's professional responsibilities, including writing. We have also learned that there are three basic ways that our CTL can support the growth and sustainability of the Jumpstart Writing Program.

CTLs Can Recruit Academic Writing Faculty Leadership

Faculty leadership makes a difference in academic writing programs. Faculty who have experienced both the satisfactions and stressors of academic writing can bring insights into what other faculty might need for support and professional growth. Besides being an academic writer, however, there are additional qualifications that create effective leadership in this area:

- Familiarity with scholarship on academic writing (or willingness to learn)
- Experience with various professional stages (e.g., has been promoted at least once)
- Possession of insights into own writing challenges and what was done to address those
- Skilled at creating and supporting interdisciplinary communities of practice
- Ability to empathize with feelings of stress, fear, and uncertainty
- Strong listening, coaching, and facilitation skills; ability to share strategies with others
- Capacity to address both academic text *and* context

Faculty leadership in writing programming can take many forms. In our case, we have designated a faculty-in-residence position; applicants can be assessed on how they meet the qualifications, as described. Leadership might also come from partnerships with other offices, or it can be created in less formal ways.

CTLs Can Support Faculty Leadership in Educational Development

CTLs do so by establishing clear roles that can support writing community efforts. In our case, the role of the faculty in residence for academic writing is to provide strategic leadership, facilitation, and research on the program. The CTL's role is to offer meeting spaces away from participants' home departments, create campus communications that advertise writing events, and provide needed supplies and logistical support for writing events and celebrations. The CTL also fosters additional partnerships with campus administration, dean's offices, and department chairs to encourage participation in the program.

CTLs Can Facilitate the Development of Communities of Practice

CTLs often have a great deal of experience with bringing faculty together from multiple programs with the goals of collegiality, educational development, and professional growth. In the beginning of a writing program, focus not just on academic writing, but on how strong communities of practice can be created and connected to academic writing. Throughout this book there are numerous examples of how growth in academic writing practice is developed using social, collaborative activities. CTL staff can contribute ideas and strategies for fostering effective learning communities connected to academic writing.

Conclusion

In this chapter, we have spread out an array of ways to begin a structured faculty writing program using institutional resources. We recognize that each campus is unique and some of these options are not possible on some campuses. You may not have a CTL, or, if you do, the CTL may not envision faculty academic writing professional development as part of its mission. Yet, there are other options. With some guidance, a group of committed faculty could start a small program by themselves without administrative support using some of the ideas in this chapter and in the overall book. As Murray, Steckley, and MacLeod (2012) acknowledge,

> The question remains, however, about how this [academic writing program] leadership can be modeled in campus settings in order to continue to support academics in managing the complexity of their multiple roles as teachers, researchers and writers, beyond purely technical-rational approaches. (p. 765)

One of our goals in this chapter was to address that question about how to model academic writing program leadership. The Jumpstart Writing Program seeks to help faculty create a sustainable and satisfying writing practice that complements and supports their multiple roles. Embedded in the heart of the Jumpstart Writing Program are the five key principles of scholarly and creative writing around which this book is organized.

Table 12.3 lists the principles and identifies the program activity associated with each principle. The five principles start with ways to get to know yourself as a writer (principle one), and then move on to building a knowledge base about the craft of academic writing itself (principle two). Next, the focus changes to offering a variety of practical strategies to track and prioritize your writing (principle three). Focusing on the idea that academic writing is a conversation, principle four illustrates a number of ways to work with others around your writing. The fifth principle zeroes in on ways to tap the reflective and creative aspects of academic writing. We believe that these principles are fundamental in creating a sustainable and satisfying individual writing practice. Yet, as you can see, they can be fundamental in creating a more substantial program as well. As Antoniou and Moriarty (2008) remind us,

> Writing and publishing are crucial to the development of a successful academic career. However, lecturers typically receive little guidance on this strand of their job. Any support that does exist tends to focus on the technical and practical aspects of scholarly writing. Advice is rarely provided on managing creative and emotional factors that greatly contribute to writing quality and success. (p. 157)

TABLE 12.3
Map of the five key principles of creative and sustainable academic writing aligned with the key features of the Jumpstart Writing Program

Principle	Jumpstart Writing Program feature where principle is addressed with examples of strategies and exercises
One: Know yourself	Jumpstart 1.0: Monthly meetings (fall) Focused free-writes; writing experiences questionnaire Mini workshops at five-day writing retreats (summer) (e.g., how to structure an argument, text structure analysis) Individual consultations
Two: Know the craft of academic writing	Jumpstart 1.0: Monthly meetings (winter) Mini workshops at five-day writing retreats (summer) (e.g., responding to an R & R request) Workshops on special topics (e.g., doing research and writing in your own classroom; scholarship of teaching and learning [SOTL] workshops) Workshops with outside experts (spring)
Three: Be strategic	Jumpstart 1.0: Monthly meetings (fall) Mini workshops at five-day writing retreats (summer) Workshops with outside experts (spring) Individual consultations Library workshops on CMS
Four: Be social	Jumpstart 1.0: Writing groups—Accountability Set up groups for faculty Jumpstart 2.0: Writing groups—Feedback Set up groups for faculty Workshops, special topics, and outside experts (all year) Meet in small groups during workshops Five-day writing retreats (summer) Facilitate writing buddies at retreat
Five: Reflect and create	Jumpstart 1.0: Monthly meetings (fall, winter, spring) Mini workshops at five-day writing retreats (summer) Reflective writing activities

Our primary objective in the Jumpstart Writing Program is to offer advice on "managing the creative and emotional facets" of academic writing, provide guidance on the technical and practical aspects, as well as create a community of practice around academic writing (Wenger, 1998). We hope that this book and this chapter will encourage you to consider developing a community of practice around academic writing on your campus.

References

Agarwal, R., Echambadi, R., Franco, A. M., & Sarkar, M. B. (2006). Reap rewards: Maximizing benefits from reviewer comments. *The Academy of Management Journal*, *49*(2), 191–196.

Aitchison, C., & Lee, A. (2006). Research writing: Problems and pedagogies. *Teaching in Higher Education*, *11*(3), 265–278. doi:10.1080/13562510600680574

Aitchison, C., & Mowbray, S. (2013). Doctoral women: Managing emotions, managing doctoral studies. *Teaching in Higher Education*, *18*(8), 859–870. doi:10.1080/13562517.2013.827642

Algase, D. L. (2014). Revise and resubmit: Now what? *Research and Theory for Nursing Practice*, *28*(3), 195–198. doi:10.1891/1541-6577.28.3.195

Antoniou, M., & Moriarty, J. (2008). What can academic writers learn from creative writers? Developing guidance and support for lecturers in higher education. *Teaching in Higher Education*, *13*(2), 157–167.

Association of American Colleges and Universities (n.d.). Creative Thinking VALUE Rubric. Available from https://www.aacu.org/value/rubrics/creative-thinking

Belcher, W. L. (2009a). Reflections on ten years of teaching writing for publication to graduate students and junior faculty. *Journal of Scholarly Publishing*, *40*(2), 184–200. doi:10.3138/jsp.40.2.184

Belcher, W. L. (2009b). *Writing your journal article in twelve weeks: A guide to academic publishing success*. Thousand Oaks, CA: SAGE.

Blaxter, L., Hughes, C., & Tight, M. (1999). Writing on academic careers. *Studies in Higher Education*, *23*(3), 281–295. https://doi.org/10.1080/03075079812331380256

Boice, R. (1987). Is released time an effective component of faculty development programs? *Research in Higher Education*, *26*(3), 311–326.

Boice, R. (1990). *Professors as writers: A self-help guide to productive writing*. Stillwater, OK: New Forums Press.

Boice, R. (1992). *The new faculty member: Supporting and fostering professional development*. San Francisco, CA: Jossey-Bass. Available from http://www.barnesandnoble.com/w/advice-for-new-faculty-members-robert-boice/1100328728

Boice, R. (2000). *Advice for the new faculty members*. Needham Heights, MA: Allyn & Bacon.

Boon, S. (2016, January 7). *21st century science overload*. Canadian Science Publishing. Available from http://www.cdnsciencepub.com/21st-century-science-overload

Buehler, R., Griffin, D., & Ross, M. (1994). Exploring the "planning fallacy": Why people underestimate their task completion times. *Journal of Personality and Social Psychology*, *67*(3), 366–381.

Bullet Journal. (2015). *How to bullet journal* [video file]. Available from https://www.youtube.com/watch?v=fm15cmYU0IM

Business Dictionary. (n.d.). Task analysis [definition]. Available from http://www.business dictionary.com/definition/task-analysis.html

Cameron, J., Nairn, K., & Higgins, J. (2009). Demystifying academic writing: Reflections on emotions, know-how and academic identity. *Journal of Geography in Higher Education, 33*(2), 269–284. doi:10.1080/03098260902734943

Cho, K., Cho, M. H., & Hacker, D. J. (2010). Self-monitoring support for learning to write. *Interactive Learning Environments, 18*(2), 101–113. doi:10.1080/10494820802292386

Cirillo, F. (n.d.). The Pomodoro Technique [website]. Available from https://francescocirillo .com/pages/pomodoro-technique

Cohen, E. G. (1986). *Designing groupwork: Strategies for the heterogeneous classroom.* New York, NY: Teachers College Press.

Cooper, J. E., & Stevens, D. D. (2002). *Tenure in the sacred grove: Issues and strategies for women and minority faculty.* Albany, NY: SUNY. Available from https://books.google.com/ books?hl=en&lr=&id=XFHypeXRxg4C&oi=fnd&pg=PR7&dq=dannelle+d+stevens&ot s=pm7y7j9aQj&sig=Pg-mgRD7XqS7HBe4OEiJcV4ssIY

Dadkhah, M., Borchardt, G., & Maliszewski, T. (2017). Fraud in academic publishing: Researchers under cyber-attacks. *The American Journal of Medicine, 130*(1), 27–30. doi:10.1016/j.amjmed.2016.08.030

Dankoski, M. E., Palmer, M. M., Banks, J., Brutkiewicz, R. R., Walvoord, E., Bogdewic, S. P., & Gopen, G. E. (2012). Academic writing: Supporting faculty in a critical competency for success. *Journal of Faculty Development, 26*(2), 47–55.

Delyser, D. (2003). Teaching graduate students to write: A seminar for thesis and dissertation writers. *Journal of Geography in Higher Education, 27*(2), 169–181.

Devlin, M., & Radloff, A. (2014). A structured writing programme for staff: Facilitating knowledge, skills, confidence and publishing outcomes. *Journal of Further and Higher Education, 38*(2), 230–248. doi:10.1080/0309877X.2012.722194

Dickson-Swift, V., James, E. L., Kippen, S., Talbot, L., Verrinder, G., & Ward, B. (2009). A non-residential alternative to off campus writers' retreats for academics. *Journal of Further and Higher Education, 33*(3), 229–239. doi:10.1080/03098770903026156

Dirkx, J. M. (2008). The meaning and role of emotions in adult learning. *New Directions for Adult & Continuing Education, 2008*(120), 7–18.

Dweck, C. (2006). *Mindset: The new psychology of success.* New York, NY: Random House.

Edmundson, M. (2002). *Teacher: The one who made the difference.* New York, NY: Random House.

Elbow, P. (1973). *Writing without teachers.* New York, NY: Oxford University Press.

Englert, C. S., Raphael, T. E., Anderson, L. M., Anthony, H. M., & Stevens, D. D. (1991). Making strategies and self-talk visible: Writing instruction in regular and special education classrooms. *American Educational Research Journal, 28*(2), 337–372. doi:10.3102/00028312028002337

Ettienne-Gittens, R., Lisako, E., McKyer, J., Goodson, P., Guidry, J., & Outley, C. (2012). What about health educators? Nutrition education for allied health professionals: A review of the literature. *American Journal of Health Education, 43*(5), 288–309. doi:10.1080/193 25037.2012.10599247

Faulconer, J., Atkinson, T., Griffith, R., Matusevich, M., & Swaggerty, E. (2010). The power of living the writerly life: A group model for women writers. *NASPA Journal About Women in Higher Education, 3*(1), 210–238. doi:10.2202/1940-7890.1047

Fernandez, S. C., Chelliah, K. K., & Halim, L. (2015). A peek into oneself: Reflective writing amongst undergraduate medical imaging students. *Reflective Practice*, *16*(1), 109–122. doi:10.1080/14623943.2014.982524

Fink, L. D. (2013). *Creating Significant Learning Experiences, Revised and Updated: An integrated approach to designing college courses*. San Francisco, CA: Jossey-Bass.

Forsyth, D. K., & Burt, C. D. B. (2008). Allocating time to future tasks: The effect of task segmentation on planning fallacy bias. *Memory & Cognition*, *36*(4), 791–798. https://doi.org/10.3758/MC.36.4.791

Garcia-Laborda, J. (2009). Book review of *High stakes testing: New challenges and opportunities for school psychology*, edited by L. J. Kruger and D.Shriberg]. *European Journal of Teacher Education*, *32*(3), 337–340.

Germano, W. (2013). *From dissertation to book* (2nd ed.). Chicago, IL: University of Chicago Press.

Goodson, P. (2017). *Becoming an academic writer: 50 exercises for paced, productive, and powerful writing* (2nd ed.). Thousand Oaks, CA: SAGE.

Gopee, N., & Deane, M. (2013). Strategies for successful academic writing—Institutional and non-institutional support for students. *Nurse Education Today*, *33*(12), 1624–1631. doi:10.1016/j.nedt.2013.02.004

Graff, G., & Birkenstein, C. (2010). *They say/I say: The moves that matter in academic writing* (2nd ed.). New York, NY: W. W. Norton.

Grant, B. (2006). Writing in the company of other women: Exceeding the boundaries. *Studies in Higher Education*, *31*(4), 483–495.

Grant, B., & Knowles, S. (2000). Flights of imagination: Academic women be(com)ing writers. *International Journal for Academic Development*, *5*(1), 6–19. doi:10.1080/136014400410060

Gravett, E. O., & Broscheid, A. (2018). Models and genres of faculty development. In B. Berkey, C. Meixner, P. M. Green, & E. A. Eddins (Eds.), *Reconceptualizing Faculty Development in Service-Learning/Community Engagement: Exploring Intersections, Frameworks, and Models of Practice* (pp. 85–106). Sterling, VA: Stylus Publishing.

Gullion, J. S. (2016). *Writing ethnography*. Rotterdam, The Netherlands: Sense Publishers.

Haas, S. (2014). Pick-n-Mix: A typology for writers' groups. In C. Aitchison & C. Guerin (Eds.), *Writing groups for doctoral education and beyond: Innovations in practice and theory* (pp. 30–47). London, UK: Routledge.

Hanson, R. (2009). *Buddha's brain: The practical neuroscience of happiness, love, and wisdom*. Oakland, CA: Harbinger.

Hardré, P. (2013). The power and strategic art of revise-and-resubmit: Maintaining balance in academic publishing. *Journal of Faculty Development*, *27*(1), 13–19.

Harks, B., Rakoczy, K., Hattie, J., Besser, M., & Klieme, E. (2014). The effects of feedback on achievement, interest and self-evaluation: The role of feedback's perceived usefulness. *Educational Psychology*, *34*(3), 269–290. doi:10.1080/01443410.2013.785384

Harman, G. (2005). Australian social scientists and transition to a more commercial university environment. *Higher Education Research & Development*, *24*(1), 79–94. doi:10.1080/0729436052000318587

Harris, G. L., & Stevens, D. D. (2013, Summer). The value of midterm student feedback in cross-disciplinary graduate programs. *Journal of Public Administration Education*, *19*(3), 537–565.

Hattie, J., & Timperley, H. (2007). The power of feedback. *Review of Educational Research*, *77*(1), 81–112. doi:10.3102/003465430298487

Hayes, N., & Sternberg, R. (2017, September–October). *How should textbook authorship count in evaluating scholarly merit, or should it count at all?* American Association of University Professors. Available from https://www.aaup.org/article/how-should-textbook-authorship-count-evaluating-scholarly-merit-or-should-it-count-all#.WbLEALJ 94dU?link_id=12&can_id=bc5e509f3d4336a512737152cde2b280&source=email-in-the-crosshairs&email_referrer=email_231119&email_subject=in-the-crosshairs

Heinrichs, J. (2013). *Thank you for arguing: What Aristotle, Lincoln, and Homer Simpson can teach us about the art of persuasion* (2nd ed.). New York, NY: Three Rivers Press.

Hess, M. E. (2010). Review: Journal keeping Review of the book. *How to use reflective writing for learning, teaching, professional insight and positive change*, by Dannelle D. Stevens and Joanne E. Cooper. *Teaching Theology & Religion, 13*(4), 384–385. https://doi.org/10.1111/j.1467-9647.2010.00656.x

Holligan, C., Wilson, M., & Humes, W. (2011). Research cultures in English and Scottish university education departments: an exploratory study of academic staff perceptions. *British Educational Research Journal, 37*(4), 713–734. https://doi.org/10.1080/0141192 6.2010.489146

Huff, A. S. (1999). *Writing for scholarly publication*. Thousand Oaks, CA: SAGE.

Humphrey, R., & Simpson, B. (2012). Writes of passage: Writing up qualitative data as a threshold concept in doctoral research. *Teaching in Higher Education, 17*(6), 735–746. https://doi.org/10.1080/13562517.2012.678328

Ireland, R. D. (2008). Revisiting AMJ'S revise-and-resubmit process. *Academy of Management Journal, 51*(6), 1049–1050.

Johnston, M. (2002). *In the deep heart's core*. New York, NY: Grove Press. *Journal of Teacher Education, 58*(5), 412–421. doi:10.1177/0022487107307951

Kabat-Zinn, J. (2012). *Mindfulness for beginners: Reclaiming the present moment—and your life*. Boulder, CO: Sounds True.

Kagan, S. (1989). *Cooperative learning resources for teachers*. Riverside, CA: University of California, Riverside.

Kamler, B. (2010). Revise and resubmit: The role of publication brokers. In C. Aitchison, B. Kamler, & A. Lee (Eds.), *Publishing pedagogies for the doctorate and beyond* (pp. 64–82). London, UK: Routledge.

Kelley, B., Cruz, L., & Fire, N. (2017). Moving toward the center: The integration of educational development in an era of historic change in higher education. *To Improve the Academy, 36*(1), 1–8. doi:10.1002/tia2.20052

Kennesaw State University. (n.d.a). Teaching and Learning Conference. Available from https://cetl.kennesaw.edu/conferences

Kennesaw State Unviersity. (n.d.b). Center for Excellence in Teaching and Learning. Available from https://cetl.kennesaw.edu/teaching-journals-directory

King, K. P. (2013). Successful writing: Five roadblocks to overcome. *New Horizons in Adult Education & Human Resource Development, 25*(2), 95–98. doi:10.1002/nha.20019

Korzybski, A. (1933). *Science and sanity: An introduction to the non-Aristotelian systems and general semantics*. Brooklyn, NY: Institute of General Semantics.

Lee, A., & Boud, D. (2003). Writing groups, change and academic identity: Research development as local practice. *Studies in Higher Education, 28*(2), 187–200. doi:10.1080/0307507032000058109

Lenski, S. J., & Caskey, M. M. (2009). Using the lesson study approach to plan for student learning. *Middle School Journal, 40*(3), 50–57.

Lyon, E. (2000). *Non-fiction book proposals anybody can write: How to get a contract and advance before you write the book.* New York, NY: Berkley Publishing.

MacLeod, I., Steckley, L., & Murray, R. (2012). Time is not enough: Promoting strategic engagement with writing for publication. *Studies in Higher Education, 37*(6), 641–654. doi:10.1080/03075079.2010.527934

Magritte, R. (1952). *Les valeurs personnelles (Personal values)* [painting]. Available from https://www.sfmoma.org/artwork/98.562

Martin, T. S., & Miller, A. L. (2014). I received a "revise and resubmit" decision: Now what? *Journal for Research in Mathematics Education, 45*(3), 286–287.

McGrail, M. R., Rickard, C. M., & Jones, R. (2006). Publish or perish: A systematic review of interventions to increase academic publication rates. *Higher Education Research & Development, 25*(1), 19–35. doi:10.1080/07294360500453053

Monaghan, C. H. (2010). Communities of practice: A learning strategy for management education. *Journal of Management Education, 35*(3), 428–453.

Mongan-Rallis, H. (2018, April 19). *Guidelines for writing a literature review.* Available from http://www.duluth.umn.edu/~hrallis/guides/researching/litreview.html

Moore, S. (2003). Writers' retreats for academics: Exploring and increasing the motivation to write. *Journal of Further and Higher Education, 27*(3), 333–342. doi:10.1080/0309877032000098734

Morley, J. (2014). *Academic phrasebank: A compendium of commonly used phrasal elements in academic English in PDF format.* The University of Manchester. Available from http://www.kfs.edu.eg/com/pdf/2082015294739.pdf

Morss, K., & Murray, R. (2001). Researching academic writing within a structured programme: Insights and outcomes. *Studies in Higher Education, 26*(1), 35–52.

Murray, R. (2012). Developing a community of research practice. *British Educational Research Journal, 38*(5), 783–800. doi:10.1080/01411926.2011.583635

Murray, R. (2014). Practical strategies for writing for publication: It's not just about time. *International Journal of Therapy & Rehabilitation, 21*(2), 58–59.

Murray, R., & Newton, M. (2009). Writing retreat as structured intervention: Margin or mainstream? *Higher Education Research & Development, 28*(5), 541–553. doi:10.1080/07294360903154126

Murray, R., Steckley, L., & MacLeod, I. (2012). Research leadership in writing for publication: A theoretical framework. *British Educational Research Journal, 38*(5), 765–781. doi:10.1080/01411926.2011.580049

Murray, R., Thow, M., Moore, S., & Murphy, M. (2008). The writing consultation: Developing academic writing practices. *Journal of Further and Higher Education, 32*(2), 119–128. https://doi.org/10.1080/03098770701851854

Neck, C. P., & Manz, C. C. (1996). Thought self-leadership: The impact of mental strategies training on employee cognition, behavior, and affect. *Journal of Organizational Behavior, 17*(5), 445–467.

O'Connell, T. S., & Dyment, J. E. (2011). The case of reflective journals: Is the jury still out? *Reflective Practice, 12*(1), 47–59. doi:10.1080/14623943.2011.541093

Palumbo, D. (2016, February 19). Breaking news: Writing is hard! *Psychology Today.* Available from https://www.psychologytoday.com/blog/hollywood-the-couch/201602/breaking-news-writing-is-hard

Parsons, S. A., Vaughn, M., Scales, R. Q., Gallagher, M. A., Parsons, A. W., Davis, S. G., . . . & Allen, M. (2018). Teachers' instructional adaptations: A research synthesis. *Review of Educational Research, 88*(2), 205–242. doi:10.3102/0034654317743198

Paulus, P. B., Kohn, N. W., & Arditti, L. E. (2011). Effects of Quantity and Quality Instructions on Brainstorming. *Journal of Creative Behavior, 45*(1), 38–46.

Peat, B. (2006). Integrating writing and research skills: Development and testing of a rubric to measure student outcomes. *Journal of Public Affairs Education, 12*(3), 295–311.

Pennebaker, J. W. (2000). Telling stories: The health benefits of narrative. *Literature and Medicine, 19*(1), 3–18. doi:10.1353/lm.2000.0011

Perry, J. (2012). *The art of procrastination: A guide to effective dawdling, lollygagging and postponing.* New York, NY: Workman.

Pololi, L., Knight, S., & Dunn, K. (2004). Facilitating scholarly writing in academic medicine. *Journal of General Internal Medicine, 19*(1), 64–68.

Reynolds, C., Stevens, D. D., & West, E. (2013). "I'm in a professional school! Why are you making me do this?" A cross-disciplinary study of the use of creative classroom projects on student learning. *College Teaching, 61*(2), 51–59. doi:10.1080/87567555.2012.731660

Richert, A. E. (2007). Book reviews: Deliberating over dispositions—Campano, G. (2007). *Immigrant students and literacy: Reading, writing and remembering.* New York, NY: Teachers College Press.

Rickard, C. M., McGrail, M. R., Jones, R., O'Meara, P., Robinson, A., Burley, M., & Ray-Barruel, G. (2009). Supporting academic publication: Evaluation of a writing course combined with writers' support group. *Nurse Education Today, 29*(5), 516–521. https://doi.org/10.1016/j.nedt.2008.11.005

Roberts, A., & Weston, K. (2014). Releasing the hidden academic? Learning from teacher-educators' responses to a writing support programme. *Professional Development in Education, 40*(5), 698–716. doi:10.1080/19415257.2013.835277

Rose, M. (1981). *Questionnaire for identifying writer's block (QIWB).* Available from http://eric.ed.gov/?id=ED236652

Rose, M. A. (2004). *The mind at work: Valuing the intelligence of the American worker.* New York, NY: Viking.

Santelmann, L., Stevens, D. D., & Martin, S. B. (2018). Fostering master's students' metacognition and self-regulation practices for research writing. *College Teaching, 46*(1), 1–13. doi:10.1080/87567555.2018.1446898

Sarino, J. (2014, January). *How many universities are there in the world?* Available from http://www.answers.com/Q/How_many_universities_are_there_in_the_world?#slide=2-

Schneider, P. (2003). *Writing alone and with others.* Oxford; New York: Oxford University Press.

Schroeder, C. M. (2011). *Coming in from the margins: Faculty development's emerging organizational development role in institutional change.* Sterling, VA: Stylus.

Schwind, J. K., McCay, E., Lapum, J., Fredericks, S., Beanlands, H., Romaniuk, D., . . . & Edwards, S. (2014). The experience of developing a faculty research cluster using the creativity of the narrative reflective process. *Creative Nursing, 20*(3), 164–170. doi:10.1891/1078-4535.20.3.164

Seuss, D. (1990). *Oh the places you'll go.* New York, NY: Random House

Shepherd, M. (2006). Using a learning journal to improve professional practice: A journey of personal and professional self-discovery. *Reflective Practice, 7*(3), 333–348.

Silvia, P. J. (2007). *How to write a lot: A practical guide to productive academic writing.* Washington, DC: American Psychological Association.

Sinclair, J., Barnacle, R., & Cuthbert, D. (2014). How the doctorate contributes to the formation of active researchers: What the research tells us. *Studies in Higher Education, 39*(10), 1972–1986. doi:10.1080/03075079.2013.806460

Slavin, R. E. (1996). *Student team learning: An overview and practical guide.* Washington, DC: National Education Association.

Stevens, D. D. (1999). The ideal, real and surreal in school–university partnerships: Reflections of a boundary spanner. *Teaching and Teacher Education, 15*(3), 287–299.

Stevens, D. D., & Cooper, J. E. (2009). *Journal keeping: How to use reflective writing for learning, teaching, professional insight and positive change.* Sterling, VA: Stylus.

Stevens, D. D., & Levi, A. J. (2013). *Introduction to rubrics: An assessment tool to save grading time, convey effective feedback, and promote student learning.* Sterling, VA: Stylus. Available from https://books.google.com/books?hl=en&lr=&id=bDKFAwAAQBAJ&oi=fnd&pg=PT10&dq=dannelle+d+stevens&ots=STNYJayjtM&sig=KF58WnzAIePXLtMIiZZJwALNOdE

Sweller, J. (1988). Cognitive load during problem solving: Effects on learning. *Cognitive Science, 12*(2), 257–285. doi:10.1207/s15516709cog1202_4

Sword, H. (2012). *Stylish academic writing.* Cambridge, MA: Harvard University Press.

Sword, H. (2016). `Write every day!': A mantra dismantled. *International Journal for Academic Development, 21*(4), 312–322. https://doi.org/10.1080/1360144X.2016.1210153

Textbook & Academic Authors Association. (n.d.). Webinars [website]. http://www.taaonline.net/about-taa

Tuckman, B. W. (1965). Developmental sequence in small groups. *Psychological Bulletin, 63*(6), 384–399. doi:10.1037/h0022100

Turner, R., Brown, T., & Edwards-Jones, A. (2014). "Writing my first academic article feels like dancing around naked": Research development for higher education lecturers working in further education colleges. *International Journal for Academic Development, 19*(2), 87–98. doi:10.1080/1360144X.2013.792729

Voegele, J., & Stevens, D. D. (2017). Communities of practice in higher education: Transformative dialogues toward a productive academic writing practice. *Transformative Dialogues: Teaching & Learning Journal, 10*(1). Available from http://www.kpu.ca/sites/default/files/Transformative%20Dialogues/TD.10.1.5_Voegele%26Stevens_Academic_Writing_Practice.pdf

Walsh, E., Anders, K., Hancock, S., & Elvidge, L. (2013). Reclaiming creativity in the era of impact: exploring ideas about creative research in science and engineering. *Studies in Higher Education, 38*(9), 1259–1273. https://doi.org/10.1080/03075079.2011.620091

Weaver, D., Robbie, D., & Radloff, A. (2014). Demystifying the publication process—A structured writing program to facilitate dissemination of teaching and learning scholarship. *International Journal for Academic Development, 19*(3), 212–225. doi:10.1080/1360144X.2013.805692

Wellington, J. (2010). More than a matter of cognition: An exploration of affective writing problems of post-graduate students and their possible solutions. *Teaching in Higher Education, 15*(2), 135–150. doi:10.1080/13562511003619961

Wenger, E. (1998). *Communities of practice: Learning, meaning, and identity.* Cambridge, UK: Cambridge University Press.

Text Structure Analysis (TSA)

Journal Article

Compare three journal articles for the following text structures.

Goal: Look for patterns in three articles across one journal to inform the text structure of your submission.

Title of journal: _____

Date of review: _____

Text structure and possible descriptors: author, year	Article #1	Article #2	Article #3	Patterns across articles
1. Brief 10-word gist of article, not sentences. Big ideas, participants, themes, content				
2. Title: Friendly, formal, long, colon, tone, inviting, academic? Number of words:				
3. Abstract-length, content				
4. Purpose of research: Where is it stated? What is it?				
5. Research questions, evident, clear				
6. Number of headings in article, their levels, use of subheadings				
7. Paragraphs devoted to introduction, literature review and background, method, results, discussion	Intro/Literature/ Background: Methods: Results: Discussion: Conclusion:			

8. Number of figures/tables Content of figures/tables		
9. Research methods: Type (survey, etc.), participants		
10. Overall tone of article: first person (I, we), third person		
11. References: Number, age, type (journals [J], book [B], book chapters [BC], report [R], conference presentation [CP], other [O]. Articles from this journal? Total = J = B = BC = R = CP = O = Articles from this journal?		
12. Other noteworthy items: International focus, audience, different research methods		

©Dannelle D. Stevens, 2017

Description and Purpose of Common Text Features for Journal Articles in a Text Structure Analysis (TSA)*

Text feature to be noted in TSA	Description of text feature	Purpose of identifying this text structure feature
1. Author, year, title	Who is the author and what is the year of publication?	Note the author and the year so that you find the work later and know how current it is.
2. Title	Is the title formal and academic sounding, or informal and inviting? Is it designed to attract attention or just share the basic facts of the content? Does it have a colon?	Titles vary and signal the reader about the content. Some seek to go beyond the simple facts and engage the reader. Looking for patterns across your three selected publications can show you any consistent patterns that you might want to use in writing your own title.
3. "Gist" of academic work: Ten words	What are the basic topics covered in the work? Write a series of short phrases that include basic themes, such as audience for the work, topics covered, and time frame. Look at key words in the title and abstract.	By writing key phrases that summarize three works, you can compare the typical audience included or the topics addressed across the three works.
4. Overall tone	What is the tone of the publication? Is it written in first person and familiar, using "I" and "we"? Or, is it written in third person and distant such as "Data were collected" or "The researcher found …"?	Identifying the tone helps you craft your submission to an acceptable tone for a particular journal or publisher.
5. Abstract/ summary	Find the short statement at the beginning of the work that summarizes the text that follows. Most journal articles have an abstract. For books, overall book summaries similar to abstracts are found in the introduction or on the book jacket.	By analyzing the abstract or introduction, you can see some models for writing your abstract answer such questions as "How long is the abstract?" and "What do these abstracts generally include?"
6. Purpose statement	What and where is the one sentence that succinctly describes the purpose of the publication? At the end of the introduction before methods (for journal articles)? On the book jacket? In the abstract?	The purpose statement summarizes the focus of the work. By reading other purpose statements, you can see where they occur in the text and then identify different ways that others have written purpose statements.

7. Headings	All works will have headings, even if just chapter headings, and sometimes subheadings. The headings divide the work into logical sections. Headings are often labeled with subheads under headings.	By noting the headings in the work, you are seeing how it is organized and adding to your repertoire of heading formats for your work.
8. Tables/figures	What is in the tables? Figures? How does the author use tables/figures in relation to the text?	Tables and figures reinforce the content. Again, how the author uses tables and headings can offer you choices of what you might put in a table or figure to supplement your work.
9. References	How many references are there? What kind of references are they? Label by type: J = journal article; B = book; BC = book chapter; R = report; CP = conference proceeding; O = other (web, blog, personal communication).	Some editors and publishers expect exhaustive reference lists. Others want a shorter list that does not include, for example, book chapters or reports. Others want you to cite their work in the list.
10. Other noteworthy items	This section is for features that jump out at you as unusual, interesting, or even distracting. For example, does the text have an international focus? Sidebars? Cartoons? Glossary? Annotated bibliography?	If you note some special features that seem unique or interesting, you may want to add these to your submission.

*A TSA is a method for analyzing and comparing the features found in three different works. See appendix A for a blank TSA for journal articles. Others can be found on the Stylus website (https://styluspub2.presswarehouse.com/landing/WM-PM-SL)

Methods Structure Analysis

Methods structure analysis (MSA): What text structures are used when writing about this method?

Name of journal: _____

Method used in articles: _____

Date of analysis: _____

Criteria: Author:_____ Year:_____ Publisher:	Journal article #1	Journal article #2	Patterns, comparisons, notes, observations
1. Title: Write out. Underline key words.			
2. Purpose (aim): Write out. Key words? Where in the manuscript is the purpose in relation to introduction of methods section?			
3. Research questions?			
4. Overall number of paragraphs in paper			
5. Theoretical frame: Yes/no? Number of paragraphs			
6. Method: Qualitative, quantitative, or mixed methods			
7. Intervention: Yes/no? What was it? Brief description			
8. Data sources: Survey, semistructured interview, focus groups; number of participants			

9. In methods section, how many paragraphs devoted to descriptions?	Description of participants: ___ Procedures (data collection): ___ Data analysis: ___ Overall number of paragraphs: ___ Methods: ___	Description of participants: ___ Procedures (data collection): ___ Data analysis: ___ Overall number of paragraphs: ___ Methods: ___			
10. In results section, how many paragraphs devoted to results (quantitative, qualitative, mixed methods)?	Qualitative, number of paragraphs: ___ # of themes: ___ # of quotes: ___ Overall number of paragraphs in the paper: ___ Percentage devoted to results: ___ % Quantitative, number of paragraphs: ___	Qualitative, number of paragraphs: ___ # of themes: ___ # of quotes: ___ Overall number of paragraphs in the paper: ___ Percentage devoted to results: ___ % Quantitative number of paragraphs: ___			
11. Tables/figures	# of tables: ___ # of figures: ___	# of tables: ___ # of figures: ___			
12. References: Check reference list and text for methodological researchers used.	Total number: ___ Number from journal itself: ___ Number of methodological references: ___	Total number: ___ Number from journal itself: ___ Number of methodological references: ___			
13. Noteworthy and unique presentation of methods and results (e.g., unique collection of data, limitations)					

Functionalities of Zotero, a Citation Management System

Advantages of Zotero as a citation management system:

Sorting references by author, title, date, journal, and tags
Creating reference lists instantly in correct style such as APA or Chicago
Tagging not only references but also quotes within references in notes section
Collaborating and sharing references with others in group folders

THE BASICS

Level 1 Storage	*Storage place for PDFs and other references related to your scholarly practice.* After you load Zotero on your computer, you can add references from any source, whether from a library database by simply clicking on an icon on your tool bar, or from files stored on your computer by dragging them into Zotero. Zotero enables you to store URLs, documents, and entire journal articles that are in PDF form.
Level 2 Subfiles	*Use Zotero to make subfiles from the Zotero "library" of all your references.* Create subfiles for references for topics you care about and subfiles for all the references for one submitted paper or project. Note: Even when you move a citation from one file to the next, it does not get deleted in the first file in Zotero.
Level 3 Reference Lists	*By highlighting a group of references in Zotero, you can instantly make a correctly formatted reference list in your chosen format.* Create a subfile for all the references for a particular manuscript or for a certain topic. Export this as a correctly formatted reference list to your clipboard and then paste it into a Word document.
Level 4 Share	*Take advantage of Zotero as a place to share references with collaborators in the group library.* Create groups within Zotero to share common reference lists. Feel confident that references are automatically updated on your list and collaborators' lists as you add more references.

BEYOND THE BASICS

Level 5 Taking Notes	*Take notes and direct quotations from your references within Zotero.* Take and store notes in your own words to retrieve later in the notes section. Cut and paste direct quotations from your references. Make sure you add an in-text citation for the quotation with the page number.
Level 6 Tags	*Tag individual notes and direct quotations within article in the notes section.* After you have written a note or cut and pasted a direct quotation, Zotero enables you to tag that individual note or quotation with a label. This tagging feature allows you to retrieve the specific note by searching for it. Zotero is the only CMS that allows you to tag and then retrieve individual notes and quotations. You might use tags such as "participants," "methods," "results," or "programs." Tagging features of research articles allows you to search for particular aspects of research to compare across articles, such as tagging quotations that establish that there is a "lack of research in . . ." I tag articles for specific kinds of writing programs with "Program: Writing retreat." When I want to write an article about writing retreats, I can quickly search across all my references for only those that have researched writing retreats in the past.

Word Count Log

Year:		Words written								
Day	Date	100	200	300	400	500	600	700+	Total	I worked on . . .
1										
2										
3										
4										
5										
6										
7										
8										
9										
10										
11										
12										
13										
14										
15										
16										
17										
18										
19										
20										

What I completed over these _____ days was:
How does this word count log work for me?

Writing Time Log

Year: _____

Day	Date	Hours worked										I worked on . . .
		0.5	1.0	1.5	2.0	2.5	3.0	3.5	4.0	4.5	5	6+	
1													
2													
3													
4													
5													
6													
7													
8													
9													
10													
11													
12													
13													
14													
15													
16													
17													
18													
19													
20													

What I completed over these _____ days was:
How does this time log work for me?

Daily Writing Goals Log

Year:_____

Day	Date	Goal	Met	Not met	Reflections
1					
2					
3					
4					
5					
6					
7					
8					
9					
10					
11					
12					
13					
14					
15					
16					
17					
18					
19					
20					

What I accomplished in these 20 days of writing was:

Writing Group Weekly Goals Log

Year: _____

Week	Day	Date	Name	Goal(s)	Met	Not met	Reflections
1							
2							
3							
4							
5							
6							
7							
8							
9							
10							
11							
12							
13							
14							
15							
16							
17							
18							
19							
20							

INDEX

but offers a great deal of advice about good teaching, good collaboration, and good assessment. In short, this book is a great tool."— **Barbara E. Walvoord,** *Professor Emerita, University of Notre Dame, and author of* Effective Grading *and* Assessment Clear and Simple

Sty/us

22883 Quicksilver Drive

Sterling, VA 20166-2019   Subscribe to our e-mail alerts: www.Styluspub.com

Also available from Stylus

Journal Keeping

How to Use Reflective Writing for Learning, Teaching, Professional Insight and Positive Change

Dannelle D. Stevens and Joanne E. Cooper

"Dannelle Stevens and Joanne Cooper bring years of personal and professional experience with journal writing to inform the content of their book. This fact creates a level of credibility to their writing, and their approach to the material makes reading the text feel like a conversation with trusted friends. The intent of their volume is to explain the use of journaling in teaching and how to keep a journal to help organize professional lives. Therefore, this book should appeal to a variety of academic readers including faculty members, students, staff, and administrators. In addition, both the novice and seasoned journal writer should find several takeaways. . . . Among the several strengths of the book is the potential for immediate application of journal writing strategies to support active learning. . . . *Journal Keeping* should be on everyone's short list. The writing is approachable, the book well organized and the material easy to implement in practice. Rarely have I found a book that I have been so enthusiastic about and that I highly recommend to others"—***Community College Review***.

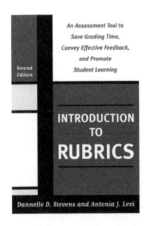

Introduction to Rubrics

An Assessment Tool to Save Grading Time, Convey Effective Feedback, and Promote Student Learning

Second Edition

Dannelle D. Stevens and Antonia J. Levi

Foreword by Barbara E. Walvoord

"A rubric, the authors emphasize, is a tool. And their book itself is a wonderful tool for exploring how to use rubrics as tools. For a long time, I have been recommending the first edition to faculty in workshops I lead. I can recommend this second edition with even greater enthusiasm, because it does so much more, and does it so intelligently. The authors offer advice about all the surrounding situations and problems that may accompany rubrics: how to get students involved in rubrics, how to use rubrics with TA's, how to collaborate with other faculty in constructing common rubrics, and how to use rubrics that someone else has constructed. The book focuses on rubrics

(Continues on preceding page)